BUDDHA NATURE

SUNY Series in Buddhist Studies
Kenneth K. Inada, editor

BUDDHA NATURE

Sallie B. King

STATE UNIVERSITY OF NEW YORK PRESS

Published by
State University of New York Press, Albany

Printed in the United States of America

For information, address State University of New York Press, State University Plaza, Albany, N.Y., 12246

Production by Marilyn P. Semerad
Marketing by Fran Keneston

Library of Congress Cataloging-in-Publication Data

King, Sallie B.
Buddha nature / Sallie B. King.
p. cm. — (SUNY series in Buddhist studies)
ISBN 0-7914-0427-7 (alk. paper). — ISBN 0-7914-0428-5 (pbk. : alk. paper)
1. Buddha (The concept) I. Title. II. Series.
BQ4180.K56 1991
294.3′422—dc20 89-77740
CIP

10 9 8 7 6 5 4 3 2 1

For my parents,
James Forrest King, Sr.
and
Carolyn Prout King

CONTENTS

Preface

It is a pleasure to express my gratitude for the help of the many persons and institutions who supported my work. The National Endowment for the Humanities funded this project in 1985 with a Summer Stipend that supported the early stages of the book. Portions of this book appeared in journal articles as Sallie B. King, "Buddha Nature and the Concept of Person," *Philosophy East and West* 39, no. 2 (1989), published by the University of Hawaii Press; and Sallie Behn King, "The Buddha Nature: True Self as Action," *Religious Studies* 20 (1984), published by Cambridge University Press. My appreciation goes to these journals and presses for their permission to publish this material.

I especially thank Professor Leon Hurvitz for checking many of my Chinese translations against the original. Thanks also to Professor Minoru Kiyota for introducing me to Buddha nature thought and raising the issue of monism for me, to Professor Thomas Dean for thinking through philosophical issues with me, and to Professor John Keenan for reading the manuscript and making helpful suggestions, especially on Yogācāra matters (this despite the fact that he disagrees with my major thesis). My thanks to the Series Editor, Kenneth Inada, for recommending additions to the book that have considerably strengthened it. Whatever shortcomings remain in this work are clearly my responsibility alone. Finally, thanks to my husband for his constant practical and moral support.

The romanization system used in this work is the Pinyin system. For the convenience of those more familiar with the Wade-Giles system, I have added Wade-Giles romanizations in parentheses after the Pinyin romanization the first time I introduce a familiar term or name. A glossary of Chinese characters can be found at the back of the book.

I have conceived of this book not only as a discussion of Buddha nature thought, but also as an introduction to some important themes in Chinese Buddhist thought. Though I require most of the book to develop these themes, I have listed them at the end of the Introduction so that the reader who is especially interested in this facet of the book may bear these themes in mind as she or he reads. In the final chapter I focus on these themes directly.

Abbreviations

BNT	*Buddha Nature Treatise* (*Fo Xing Lun*)
IBK	*Indogaku Bukkyōgaku Kenkyū*
Ratnagotra	*Ratnagotravibhāga*
Taishō	*Taishō Shinshū Daizōkyō*

CHAPTER ONE

Introduction

A. The Role of the Buddha Nature Concept

The concept of Buddha nature, though little discussed in Western surveys of Buddhism, is one of the most important ideas in East Asian Buddhism. In its simplest form, the Buddha nature concept provides the answer to a question with which the ancient Chinese were very much concerned: Are all beings capable of attaining Buddhahood, or are there some who will never be free of the sufferings of *saṃsāra?* Buddha nature theory answers without equivocation: "All sentient beings possess the Buddha nature" and thus are guaranteed the realization of Buddhahood. Not only human beings, but all beings born and reborn in the six destinies—hell beings, hungry ghosts, animals, fighting demons, human beings, and gods—are promised that Buddhahood awaits them. The belief in the *icchantika,* the one forever incapable of attaining Buddhahood, is expressly rejected. At its basis, then, the Buddha nature concept is an optimistic and encouraging doctrine.

When we look further into this notion, its optimism increases, as do the philosophical problems attached to it. When one asks how the promise of future Buddhahood is realized, what the present mechanism for this future achievement is, the answer is that insofar as we "possess" the Buddha nature, we already are Buddhalike, we already possess the attributes of a Buddha—wisdom and compassion. This introduces the second level of the Buddha nature concept: Not only will we be Buddhas in the future, we already are Buddhas now. Buddha nature, then, is both the potential to realize Buddhahood that is possessed by all and the already complete Buddhahood that is ours in the present.

Obviously, we do not experience ourselves as Buddhas—perfectly wise and compassionate beings—in our present condition of delusion. Insofar as our Buddha nature is not experientially realized—insofar, that is, as we experience ourselves as deluded beings—we *are* deluded beings and not, experientially, Buddhas. In such a case, our Buddha nature is covered up or concealed from us by "adventitious defilements," such as ignorance, hatred, fear, desire—all the Buddhist vices. These defilements constitute our "ordinary" experience in *saṃsāra.* Buddha nature theory holds that these defilements are adventitious or accidental; in other words, they are not necessary, not essential to the human condition, but simply the products of past karma.

It is possible, however, to free oneself of that past karma and thus of the power that the defilements have to construct our reality. Once we are free of the defilements, our Buddha nature will become experientially available to us. It, unlike the defilements, is essential to the human condition; it is there for us always, whether or not we are experientially in touch with it. The defilements are able to conceal the Buddha nature from us only to the extent that we allow our past karma to determine our lives. With meditation and meritorious deeds we can free ourselves of our karma and realize our Buddhahood. Our Buddha nature, then, is our true and essential nature and identity. Buddha nature theory affirms that each of us is fully capable of realizing—making experientially present to ourselves—this enlightened nature that is our birthright as sentient beings.

This optimistic view of both human nature and of our ultimate spiritual destiny was attractive to the Chinese. Indeed, the acceptance of Buddha nature became normative for Chinese Buddhism as a whole. The Fa-xiang school (Fa-hsiang; Chinese Yogācāra) of Xuan-zang (Hsüan-tsang) was relegated to a relatively low status in the hierarchical rankings of Buddhist doctrine constructed by leading Chinese thinkers due to its affirmation of the *icchantika* doctrine and rejection of universal Buddhahood.

This acceptance of Buddha nature entered into the foundations of the indigenous Chinese Buddhist schools, especially Tian-tai (T'ien-t'ai), Hua-yan (Hua-yen) and Chan (Ch'an), in all of which it played a major role. The influence of Buddha nature thought on the Pure Land school, with its emphasis on faith in Amida, is somewhat less straightforward. Several texts of the *tathāgatagarbha*–Buddha nature tradition,[1] such as the *Śrīmālādevī Siṃhanāda Sūtra* and the *Wu Shang Yi Jing,* make much of the fact that Buddha nature, as such, is inconceivable, and on this basis they recommend faith in the Buddha who teaches this doctrine as the appropriate religious practice. Moreover, the *tathāgatagarbha*-Buddha nature doctrine of the four "perfections" possessed by the Buddha's *dharmakāya* and the very positive language with which the Buddha, *dharmakāya, nirvāṇa,* and the like are lauded in texts of this tradition open the door to devotional practices in Buddhism. Takasaki Jikidō goes so far as to say that "the core of the *tathāgatagarbha* theory is in . . . the 'pure' faith in the Buddha" and asserts that there is an "essential interrelation" among *tathāgatagarbha* theory, laudation of the Buddha, and *stūpa* worship.[2] This claim of an essential interrelationship, however, applies only to one part of the *tathāgatagarbha*–Buddha nature textual corpus, not, in fact, to the text that is the subject of this study. It is true, though, that texts of the devotional *tathāgatagarbha*–Buddha nature tradition probably contributed in a general way to the development of the devotional Pure Land tradition. A direct link can be seen in Japan, where Shinran stated that the actualization of faith (the faith upon which all else hinges in his Jōdo Shinshū sect) is accomplished in the individual by the action of the Buddha nature.[3]

As appropriated and developed by the four major indigenous schools of Chinese Buddhism, the Buddha nature concept traveled to the other East Asian Buddhist countries, where it played a vital role. In short, the Buddha nature concept is pivotal for all of East Asian Buddhism. It stands at the foundation of East Asian Buddhist concepts of human being and spirituality and informs their understanding of the possibilities and ends of human life. It is an essential piece to the puzzle of East Asian Buddhist thought and practice.

B. Terms

Any discussion of the term *Buddha nature* must begin with consideration of the term *tathāgatagarbha,* to which it is closely linked. The Sanskrit work *tathāgatagarbha* is a compound of two terms, *tathāgata* and *garbha. Tathāgata* is itself understood as a compound word that can be interpreted in two ways: as *tathā* + *āgata,* "thus come"; or *tathā* + *gata,* "thus gone." It is an epithet for a Buddha, who is "thus gone" in realization from *saṃsāra* to *nirvāṇa,* and "thus come" from *nirvāṇa* to *saṃsāra* to work for the salvation of all. The term *garbha* also has two meanings, embryo and womb. Thus, the term *tathāgatagarbha* may mean either "embryonic Tathāgata" (i.e., the incipient Buddha) or "womb of the Tathāgata," understood as that which possesses the essential attributes of the Tathāgata in their fully developed form. The first meaning often is discussed as the "cause" of the Tathāgata, and the latter meaning as the "fruit" of Tathāgata. As "fruit," it represents the fulfillment of the Buddha Path and is linked with such terms as *dharmakāya, nirvāṇa,* perfect wisdom, and realization.

The Chinese decided generally to translate the term *tathāgatagarbha* in the latter sense as womb of the Tathāgata. In Chinese, the term is rendered *ru-lai-zang* (Japanese *nyoraizō*). The term *ru-lai* exactly renders *tathāgata* as "thus come," and a *zang* is a storehouse. Thus the Chinese translation shows a preference for conceiving the *tathāgatagarbha* as the container of the Tathāgata (i.e., the womb) rather than that which is contained (the embryo).

The *Buddha Nature Treatise* (hereafter *BNT*),[4] the focal text of this study, uses a distinctive device to maintain the double meaning of the Sanskrit *tathāgatagarbha* in Chinese. The author of our text glosses *ru-lai-zang* as (1) the contained, that which is held within the storehouse, and (2) the storehouse as the container (*BNT* 795c–796a). The first meaning represents the understanding of *garbha* as embryo; the *BNT* specifies that that which is contained in the storehouse, the embryo, is ordinary sentient beings. The second meaning represents *garbha* understood as womb qua the fruit of the Buddhist path. This text likens the *tathāgatagarbha* in this respect to jewels, which represent the Buddha's merits. These two readings thus retain the bivalent sense of the Sanskrit *garbha.*

The term *Buddha nature* (Chinese *fo xing,* Japanese *busshō*) is closely related in meaning to *tathāgatagarbha.* However, it is not the Chinese translation of the latter; in fact, *fo xing* is a Chinese term for which the Sanskrit equivalent is not readily apparent. This missing Sanskrit equivalent has been the topic of considerable discussion among

Buddhist scholars.[5] Scholars now generally agree that the Sanskrit equivalent is *buddhadhātu*. Takasaki Jikidō explains *buddhadhātu* as signifying: (1) the nature (*dhātu* = *dharmatā*) of the Buddha, thus equivalent to the term *dharmakāya*, and (2) the cause (*dhātu* = *hetu*) of the Buddha. Moreover, he says, "the link between the cause and the result is the nature (*dhātu*) common to both, which is nothing but the *dharmadhātu*."[6] It should be noted that this understanding claims for the Sanskrit *buddhadhātu* the bivalence of the Chinese *fo xing*, embracing as it does the sense of *buddhadhātu* as cause of Buddhahood and as Buddhahood in fruition.

In passing we may also mention Whalen Lai's observation that the Chinese had a predilection for the use of the term *xing*, due to the use of the term *xing* (nature, or human nature) in the Confucian tradition, where it represented the essence or core of human personhood.[7] The Confucian tradition assumed that the essence of a human being was a moral nature and debated the loftiness or depravity of that moral nature. The Buddhist use of the term *xing* in *fo xing*, unlike the Confucian use, is not concerned primarily with the moral nature of the human being, although ethical implications are imbedded in the notion. Like the Confucian use, however, the term *fo xing* refers to what, in the Buddhist view, is essential in the human being. Given the history of the term *xing* in China, it was a natural choice for the translators of Buddhist texts. As the indigenous Chinese Buddhist tradition developed, the term *ru-lai-zang* rapidly faded in prominence, whereas the term *fo xing* grew to become central for the entire tradition.

C. History

Buddha nature thought is rooted in the Indian Mahāyāna doctrinal tradition. It will be helpful for a proper understanding of the *Buddha Nature Treatise* to place it historically in the context of the history of Yogācāra, *prajñāpāramitā,* Mādhyamika, and *tathāgatagarbha* thought.

The Yogācāra School

An intellectual history of the Yogācāra school cannot be given with any confidence at present. Not only are the authorship and dates of a number of the major Yogācāra works subject to debate and the lineage of ideas within the school undetermined, the very ideas themselves are subject to a great breadth of interpretation. For this reason, our understanding of even the most basic history and principles of this school is constantly subject to revision.

The Yogācāra school is based upon the works of two brothers, Asaṅga and Vasubandhu, fourth-century C.E., and a third figure, Maitreya (or Maitreya-nātha), the historical status of whom is subject to debate but who is regarded as the teacher of Asaṅga.[8] Tibetan tradition ascribes to Maitreya the authorship of five books: the *Mahāyānasūtrālaṅkāra, Madhyāntavibhāga, Dharmadharmatāvibhāga, Abhisamayālaṅkāra,* and *Ratnogotravibhāga* (*Uttaratantra*). The first three of these are foundational to Yogācāra thought and represent pre-Asaṅgan Yogācāra thought. The *Abhisamayālaṅkāra,* on the other hand, is concerned with *prajñāpāramitā* ideas; and the *Ratnagotravibhāga* belongs to the *tathāgatagarbha* line.

Asaṅga wrote a number of important Yogācāra works, including the *Abhidharmasamuccaya, Mahāyānasaṃgraha,* and *Vajracchedikāprajñāpāramitā-sūtra-śāstra-kārikā.* In addition to his literary works, Asaṅga is famous for converting his younger brother, Vasubandhu, to Mahāyāna and Yogācāra. Following his conversion, Vasubandhu is said to have pored over the Mahāyāna literature, especially the *prajñāpāramitā sūtra* literature and to have counted *sūtras* in this category among his favorites.[9] Thereafter, the brothers Asaṅga and Vasubandhu, together with the historical or nonhistorical Maitreya, were regarded as the founders of the Yogācāra school.

Vasubandhu's intellectual career had two major chapters. He early composed a commentary on Sarvāstivāda teachings, his famous *Abhidharmakośa-bhāṣya.* After his conversion to Mahāyāna, Vasubandhu wrote voluminously, including *Viṃśatikā-kārikā, Triṃśikā-kārikā, Madhyānta-vibhāga-bhāṣya, Mahāyānasūtrālaṅkāra-bhāṣya,* and *Trisvabhāva-nirdeśa,* as well as commentaries on many Mahāyāna *sūtras,* including the *Lotus* (*Saddharma-puṇḍarīka*), *Mahāparinirvāṇa* and *Daśabhūmika.*[10]

Until recently, modern scholars have thought of the two great Indian Mahāyāna schools, Mādhyamika and Yogācāra, as inherently opposed to each other. Mādhyamika has been conceived as the *śūnya* school, the school characterized by the relentless critical dialectic of Nāgārjuna that demolishes all metaphysical views. Without substituting a "view" of his own, Nāgārjuna demonstrates that due to the interdependence and hence mutual relativity of all things (as taught in the early Buddhist *pratītyasamutpāda*), all entities are empty (*śūnya*) of own-being (*svabhāva*)—the ability to "own" their own being, the ability to be themselves by themselves—and hence are lacking in all *independent* identity and characteristics.

As part of his avoidance of establishing any constructive view of his own, Nāgārjuna emphasized that *śūnyatā* (emptiness) is not to be regarded as the Truth, but merely as a tool (*upāya*) to be used for soteriological purposes; that is, the purposes of the Buddhist practitioner striving for liberation. *Śūnyatā* itself is empty and surely not any kind of ultimate. The teaching of emptiness, however, is not nihilistic, because as a teaching it promotes liberation and, moreover, is identical with the principle of *pratītyasamutpāda* or the dependent coarising of all things. Nevertheless, these balancing points did not prevent the Mādhyamika school's standpoint from being viewed as negative. Given the school's emphasis on destructive criticism, its refusal to advocate any "view," and its espousal of the term *śūnyatā,* this response was inevitable.

In contrast, the Yogācāra school, until recently, has been viewed by modern scholars as espousing a metaphysical view; namely, Idealism. Yogācāra was regarded as teaching that external objects are not real as such, that the category of "objects" is empty, and that what we take to be objects simply are constructions of the mind. In this understanding of Yogācāra, the Mind itself is real; in fact, the only reality. The apparent fact that the advocacy of this view by the Yogācārins could follow on the heels of Nāgārjuna's destruction of the very possibility of holding metaphysical views at all has puzzled and dismayed many a Buddhist scholar. Recently the scholarly community, however, has determined that this picture of two antithetical Mahāyāna schools has been overstated, that Mādhyamika and Yogācāra, at least in their classical forms, are not in fact mutually incompatible in a philosophical sense.

First, as we have seen, Mādhyamika is not nihilistic and is negative only in the form of its language and dialectic; strictly speaking, its philosophical standpoint is not negative, because negativity is dualistic and *śūnyatā* is the emptying of all dualisms. Thus, regardless of the philosophical status of Yogācāra, Mādhyamika itself cannot occupy a negative pole in any typology of philosophical positions.

Second, most scholars now believe that Yogācāra and Mādhyamika should be seen as differing in emphasis, though not disagreeing on major points. Nagao Gadjin, for example, has long held that classical Mādhyamika and Yogācāra should be seen as complementary rather than antagonistic: the former stressing logic and the dialectic of *śūnyatā,* the latter stressing meditation and the understanding of consciousness. Of course, later Yogācāra and Mādhyamika thinkers did come to argue as adversaries, but such was not the attitude of the founders of the schools. Nagao summarizes the situation in the East Asian context as follows:

> In the Sino-Japanese Buddhist tradition, the Mādhyamika and Yogācāra-Vijñānavāda tenets have been understood to be both parallel and opposite to each other. The San-lun-tsun, the Chinese version of the Mādhyamika, was regarded as nihilistic or an Emptiness School, and the Fa-hsiang-tsun, the Vijñānavāda, was regarded as realistic or an Existence School. . . . These traditional but erroneous views have now been revised by most modern scholars. Presently, the Mādhyamika philosophy . . . is believed to be wholly inherited by Maitreya-nātha, Asaṅga, and other Yogācāras. The *Prajñāpāramitā sūtras* are equally revered as authentic by both schools, and further, the doctrine of emptiness occupies an important position even in the Yogācāra school.[11]

Third, as Nagao mentions, it is important to bear in mind that the Yogācāra school, in its classical form, does not reject the emptiness teaching of the Mādhyamika school, but on the contrary integrates it in an essential way into its own philosophy. As Nagao stated, the works of Maitreya, Asaṅga, and Vasubandhu, in their original form, have "wholly inherited" the emptiness teachings of the Mādhyamika. Thus the founders of Yogācāra are not the opponents of Mādhyamika, but their successors. We have seen that both Asaṅga and Vasubandhu commented upon *prajñā* texts and that Vasubandhu was so taken by the *prajñāpāramitā* literature that coming to terms with it formed one of the pillars of his Mahāyāna conversion. Their work, and the works attributed to Maitreya, reflect an acceptance of *śūnyatā* as foundational, but with an interpretation and extension of that thought in a fresh direction.

With *śūnyatā* at its roots, what are we to make of the view that Yogācāra teaches an Idealism that regards objects as false and the mind as real? In brief, we must recognize the existence of more than one view within Yogācāra. Minimally, we must distinguish between three chapters of Yogācāra thought: (1) the original teachings of Maitreya, Asaṅga, and Vasubandhu; and the interpretations of the original teachings made by (2) Dharmapāla and Xuan-zang and (3) Paramārtha.

Dharmapāla and Xuan-zang's work may properly be called *Idealism.* The importance of Xuan-zang in the East Asian tradition is one reason why the label of *Idealism* has been attached to the Yogācāra school as a whole. However, the idea that the Yogācāra school as a whole may simply be labeled *Idealist* is mistaken or misleading in two senses. First, it is a moot point whether Idealism is present in the texts of Maitreya, Asaṅga, and Vasubandhu in their original form. Contemporary scholars line up on both sides of this issue. Second, it is definitely not the case that the Yogācāra of Paramārtha (Zhen-di, the translator of the present *Buddha Nature Treatise*) is Idealism.

Those scholars who argue that Vasubandhu's views are not Idealist generally agree on an alternative view as to what is his philosophy of mind. Ueda summarizes his understanding as follows:

> *Vikalpa* or *vijñānapariṇāma* refers to the consciousness of an ordinary man, i.e., a man who is not yet enlightened. The object which is known through this *vijñānapariṇāma* is not a thing as it really is, but rather a conceptualized thing. In other words, this mind does not grasp the object as it really is, but rather as a concept or name. In truth, he does not take real existence itself as the object, but instead takes the concept as the object and thinks that he is taking real existence as the object, not realizing what he has done. . . . In contrast to this, the mind of the Yogacara philosopher is called *prajñā* or *nirvikalpa jñāna* (wisdom "apart" or different in its nature from *vikalpa* or *vijñāna*). This mind does not know an object through conception, but rather it knows directly the object as it really exists (*yathābhūtārtha*).[12]

Janice Willis agrees with this assessment as applying to both Vasubandhu and Asaṅga:

> [T]he *Viṃśatikā* [of Vasubandhu] illuminates the ordinary being's chief delusion, namely, his mistaking the commonly perceived universe of appearance to exist *as perceived* rather than as a universe distorted by conceptualization of all sorts. Indeed, this overlay of constructive imaginations (*kalpanā, vijñapti, vikalpa*) is all that we commonly contact

> and cognize. We do not see the thing as it really is; we see only a conceptualized thing. And this is precisely Vasubandhu's point (as it had been Asaṅga's also). All that we commonly perceive is *vijñaptimātra*. It is only "representation" or "just conceptualization." And because of this, it is not ultimate reality.[13]

Whether this assessment fairly represents Vasubandhu's corpus as a whole will continue to be debated by the scholarly community. I am confident, however, that this summary does represent the Vasubandhu that Paramārtha understands himself to be transmitting to China. In other words, what "consciousness-only" means in Vasubandhu, as understood by Paramārtha, is a strong version of something we realize in a weak way in contemporary Western psychology and philosophy: Ordinary human consciousness does not have access to a purely "objective" reality. Our experiential world, the world we perceive and in which we live, is shaped in all moments of ordinary consciousness by what we project—our expectations, fears, memories, confusions, suspicions, beliefs, and so forth—onto what is given to us. We do not experience reality; we experience our personally shaped (and consequently distorted) perceptions of reality.

Unlike Western thought, however, the raison-d'être of the Yogācāra school is the belief that it is possible, and ultimately necessary, by means of meditation to effect a revolution in the manner of one's being conscious such that one no longer lives in a distorted perception of reality but can actually perceive reality As It Is. This is the aim of Yogācāra practice; it is toward this that Vasubandhu's writings, as understood by Paramārtha, point. This also is a prominent theme of the *BNT*.

The main points here, moreover, are in harmony with the emptiness teachings of Mādhyamika. As part of the realization of reality As It Is, this understanding of Yogācāra includes a realization of the falseness of the dualistic split between subject and object that ordinary consciousness believes is real. We have seen earlier that "subjectivity" participates in what we ordinarily take to be the "objective" and from this follows the emptiness of the "objective"; that is, the deep dependence of the "objective" upon the "subjective." The same applies, in reverse, to the status of the "subjective." When one realizes the emptiness of the "objective," realization of the emptiness of the "subjective" follows in its wake. If there is no "object" to perceive, there can be no "subject" perceiving. Hence the categories subject and object are mutually dependent and as such demonstrate each other's emptiness. Again, Janice Willis summarizes: "far from advocating the superiority of thought over objects, Asaṅga's explication of śūnyatā and the Middle Path involves the cessation of both subject and object, both apprehender and thing apprehended."[14] We shall meet this idea again in the *BNT*. The dualistic distinction between "subject" and "object" itself is false; freedom from experience in the form of this distinction constitutes access to experience of reality As It Is. This is subject-object nondualism.

So far I have emphasized the common ground shared by Mādhyamika and Yogācāra, their shared foundation in *śūnya* thought, but it is obvious that the two schools also differ on this very subject. This difference can be summarized in two points. First, for pedagogical reasons, Yogācāra authors did not like the negative form of Mādhyamika. In their experience this negativity frightened or demoralized people. Since all Buddhist forms are *upāya* anyway, it made no sense to espouse a form that drove people from the Dharma when a more appealing form easily could be used. This sentiment is abundantly clear in many Yogācāra texts. Second, and more substantively, Yogācāra authors believed that the Mādhyamika version of Mahāyāna did not say everything it could say; it was incomplete. Even today one can read Nāgārjuna's *Mūlamadhyamaka-kārikā* and debate forever about whether, for Nāgārjuna, Buddhist practice gives access to reality As It Is. The *Kārikā* themselves give us no basis for deciding yes or no. This is a mark of the perfection of the *Kārikā.* A literary or logical perfection, however, is not sufficient for most religious practitioners. Yogācāra authors felt it important to affirm the existential and spiritual benefits that resulted from the practice of their disciplines. For these reasons, they took up the language of Thusness (*tathatā*) and reality As It Is (*yathābhūta*), being careful to note that these pointed in the direction of the experiential fulfillment of emptiness, not its negation.

Tathāgatagarbha *Literary History*

The *tathāgatagarbha* literature, like the *prajñāpāramitā* literature, is not the property of any identifiable school in Indian Buddhism. In the former we have a body of texts introducing and expanding upon a similar theme, the idea that "all sentient beings posses the *tathāgatagarbha.*" Although this theme and the set of concerns associated with it are readily identifiable in the texts, we cannot identify the authors of the texts nor even, with any specificity, the group among whom the texts circulated at the time of their composition. The four most important early *tathāgatagarbha sūtras* are the *Tathāgatagarbha sūtra, Śrīmālādevī–siṃhanāda-sūtra, Anūnatvāpūrṇatva-nirdeśa,* and *Mahāparinirvāṇa-sūtra.*[15] These texts were composed in India between approximately 200 and 350 C.E.[16] That puts them before the time of Asaṅga and Vasubandhu.

The *Tathāgatagarbha-sūtra* may have been the first of the *tathāgatagarbha* texts; it introduces the idea that "all sentient beings possess the *tathāgatagarbha*" in a metaphorical and philosophically unsophisticated manner. The text consists of nine examples that represent the relationship between the *tathāgatagarbha* and the adventitious defilements that conceal it. Thus the *tathāgatagarbha* is compared to grain covered by the husk, a treasure buried under the ground, a Buddha statue wrapped in a rag, and so on; where the defilements are the husk, the ground, the rag—whatever covers or conceals that which is precious. Although these images are not philosophically developed, as images they are appealing to the imagination and convey the basic idea of the universal immanence of Buddhahood that nonetheless is experientially unavailable to ordinary persons.

Other texts built on this basic idea, and sometimes on the images themselves, in a much more sophisticated manner. The *Śrīmālādevī–siṃhanāda-sūtra,* in which Queen Śrīmālā instructs the assembly, speaks in both a devotional and a philosophically astute manner of a *tathāgatagarbha* conceived in terms of positive attributes. It is critical of a purely negative understanding of *śūnyatā* and teaches that the *tathāgatagarbha* is both *śūnya* (with respect to all defilements) and *aśūnya,* "not-empty" (with respect to the perfection of the *buddhadharmas*). The *garbha* possesses the four *guṇapāramitā,* or perfections, of permanence, bliss, self, and purity. It is the intrinsically pure mind that is concealed by defilement. This relationship between the intrinsically pure mind and the defilement that conceals it is incomprehensible, understood only by a Buddha. Ultimately, the *garbha* is identified with the *dharmakāya* of the Tathāgata; thus only a Buddha attains *nirvāṇa.* This kind of elevation and laudation of the Buddha and his attributes is a popular theme in much of the *tathāgatagarbha* literature and often is seen as an important foundation of Mahāyāna devotionalism.

The *Anūnatvāpūrṇatva-nirdeśa* is a short text with a simply stated but paradoxical theme: the absolute identification of *tathāgatagarbha, sattvadhātu* (the totality of all sentient beings in their essential nature), and *dharmakāya* or *dharmadhātu.* The text emphasizes that in order to become free of wrong views, one thing must be known; namely, the single *dharmadhātu.* The latter is identified with the *tathāgatagarbha* and the *dharmakāya.* This *dharmakāya,* when bound by defilements, "drifting on the waves of *saṃsāra,*" is called *sentient beings.* This same *dharmakāya,* when filled with repugnance for the suffering of *saṃsāra,* in putting aside all desires, practicing the ten *pāramitā,* embracing the 84,000 Dharma gates, and cultivating *bodhisattva* practices, is called *bodhisattvas.* Again, this same *dharmakāya,* when free from all defilements and utterly pure, is called *Tathāgata.* Thus the *dharmakāya* is the realm of sentient beings, and the realm of sentient beings is the *dharmakāya.* These are two names with one meaning.[17] Hence, whereas the *Śrīmālā-sūtra* emphasizes the transcendence of the *tathāgatagarbha* in the Buddha, this text emphasizes the immanence of *tathāgatagarbha* in ordinary sentient beings. These, of course, are not contradictory positions but complementary emphases, given the basic *tathāgatagarbha* doctrine of concealed immanence; that is, ontological immanence joined with existential transcendence.

The *Mahāparinirvāṇa-sūtra* is a Mahāyāna alternative to the *Mahāparinibbāna-suttanta* of early Buddhism.[18] The former text's teachings on the Buddha nature exerted enormous influence on the history of Buddha nature thought in China, especially the question of the universality of future Buddhahood. The Chinese debate on the question was framed by the fifth century translations of the *Mahāparinirvāṇa-sūtra* by Dharmakṣema and Fa-xian (Fa-hsien). The first translation, that of Fa-xian, indicated that the *icchantika* would not attain Buddhahood. Despite the authority of this scripture, the great monk Dao-sheng (Tao-sheng) doggedly insisted upon universal Buddhahood and consequently was ostracized from the Sangha. He later was vindicated and elevated to prominence when the much longer translation by Dharmakṣema was seen to include passages supporting universal Buddhahood, even for the *icchantika.*[19] With this resolved,

Chinese scholars settled into careful and extensive study of the text's teachings about what Buddha nature is.

Despite this important historical role, the *Mahāparinirvāṇa-sūtra* does not present any important innovation in *tathāgatagarbha* theory comparable to the three texts already discussed. As we have seen, it tends to be rather unsystematic and seems to speak with many voices. This very imprecision, however, made the text a fruitful one for later students and commentators, who were obliged to create their own order and bring it to the text. Substantively, the text emphasizes the eternity of the Buddha, implicitly criticizing the idea that *nirvāṇa* means extinction, and linking this belief with the idea of the *tathāgatagarbha.*[20] Within this framework, however, the text speaks of Buddha nature in so many different ways that Chinese scholars created a variety of lists of types of Buddha nature that they discerned in the course of their studies of the text.[21]

The most important innovation of the text in the context of the development of *tathāgatagarbha*–Buddha nature thought is its linking of the term *buddhadhātu* or *tathāgatadhātu,* which appears to be used for the first time in this text, with the *tathāgatagarbha.*[22] We saw earlier that the Chinese term *fo xing* best translates the Sanskrit *buddhadhātu* or *tathāgatadhātu,* so this is a crucial point for Chinese Buddha nature thought.

These are the four most important *tathāgatagarbha sūtras* of the early period. This early tradition is summarized by an important *śāstra,* the *Ratnagotravibhāga,* also know as the *Mahāyānôttaratantraśās tra* or simply *Uttaratantra.* In the West this text is perhaps the best known of the early *tathāgatagarbha* texts (with the arguable exception of the *Śrīmālādevī-sūtra,* which has received recent attention), having been translated into English and studied by both Obermiller and Takasaki.[23] Modern scholarship has revised our beliefs about the text of the *Ratnagotra.* As we have seen, Tibetan tradition attributes the *Ratnagotra* to Maitreya, as one of the Five Books of the latter. On the basis of his studies, Takasaki leaves the attribution of the *Ratnagotra*'s verses to Maitreya intact (though unsure) but names Sāramati as the author of the prose commentary of the text.[24] He dates the text as we have it to the early fifth-century C.E. and places the verses sometime between Nāgārjuna and Asaṅga.[25] Sanskrit, Tibetan, and Chinese versions of the text all exist, though the Sanskrit text was discovered only recently, with the edited version published in 1950.[26]

Although the basic verses are from Maitreya, the *Ratnagotra* lacks characteristic Yogācāra teachings and is a text of the *tathāgatagarbha* group. The *Ratnagotra* quotes extensively from the first three *tathāgatagarbha sūtras* listed earlier and less extensively from the *Mahāparinirvāṇa-sūtra.* It does quote two Yogācāra texts, *Mahāyānābhidharma-sūtra* and *Mahāyānasūtrālaṅkāra,* but without referring to their specifically Yogācāra teachings.[27] In general it is a summary and systematization of then-extant *tathāgatagarbha* thought.

The *Ratnagotra* is noted for its discussion of the Three Jewels—Buddha, Dharma, and Sangha—and clear elevation of the Buddha as the Supreme Refuge as compared to the Dharma and Sangha. Like the *Śrīmālādevī-sūtra* this manifests the tendency of some *tathāgatagarbha* literature to provide a foundation for Mahāyāna devotionalism. There is a glorification of the Buddha followed by a discussion of the importance of faith at the end of the text.

The *Ratnagotra* also is important for its systematization of *tathāgatagarbha* discourse around ten characteristics in terms of which the *tathāgatagarbha* is discussed. These ten characteristics reappear in the *BNT* together with considerable additions.[28] As found in the *Ratnagotra,* they are: own-nature (essential nature of the *tathāgatagarbha*); *tathāgatagarbha* as cause (of purification, i.e., realization); *tathāgatagarbha* as result (of purification, i.e., the four *guṇapāramitā*); function of *tathāgatagarbha* (i.e., the urge towards realization); yoga or union (with the Buddha's qualities of purity, wisdom, and compassion); manifestation (of the *tathāgatagarbha* in various classes of beings); states of manifestation (of the *tathāgatagarbha* among ordinary persons, *bodhisattvas,* and the Tathāgata); all-pervadingness (of the *tathāgatagarbha* in these three states); unchangeability (of the *tathāgatagarbha* in these three states); and nondifferentiation (of the *tathāgatagarbha* and *dharmakāya,* Tathāgata, *nirvāṇa*).[29]

These are the early, important texts of *tathāgatagarbha* thought. We need now to consider the relationship of these ideas to the idea of emptiness as found in the *prajñāpāramitā* literature, as we did with the Yogācāra tradition. As with the Yogācāra, we will see that *tathāgatagarbha* thought, at least as it is found in the *Ratnagotra* and closely related texts, is a successor to *śūnya* thought, a development from within this tradition, rather than an antagonistic opponent standing without.

In his *Hannya Shisōshi* (*History of Prajñā Thought*), Yamaguchi Susumu traces the development of Buddhist thought from *pratītya-samutpāda* and *śūnyatā* to the *tathāgatagarbha* thought of the *Ratnagotra.*[30] He argues for a single tradition in which the Buddha speaks of *pratītya-samutpāda;* Nāgārjuna extends this idea to *śūnyatā;* and the *Ratnagotra* extends the same idea to *tathāgatagarbha.* The *Ratnagotra* itself invites us to see this continuity. The text first quotes the *Śrīmālā-sūtra* to the effect that *tathāgatagarbha* is not accessible to those outside of *śūnya* realization and then proceeds to claim its *tathāgatagarbha* teachings to be a corrective to the errors of those fledgling *bodhisattvas* who have misunderstood *śūnya* teachings in a nihilistic or absolutistic manner.[31] This means that realization of emptiness is a necessary precondition to realization of *tathāgatagarbha.* However, a one-sidedly negative perspective betrays an incorrect apprehension of emptiness that can be corrected by realization of *tathāgatagarbha.* The role assigned *śūnyatā* here is much like that assigned it in the Yogācāra evaluation: *Śūnyatā* is essential, but must not be understood in a negative sense (and we may safely conclude on the basis of all this concern that it frequently was so understood).

Like the Yogācāra authors, the author of the *Ratnagotra* feels even this is not enough; there is something positive to be realized when one's vision has been cleared by *śūnyatā;* namely, the *tathāgatagarbha-dharmakāya,* resplendent with the four *guṇapāramitā* of eternity, bliss, self, and purity, identical to *nirvāṇa* and realization of the Supreme Truth. Thus the *śūnya* teachings as they stand in the *prajñāpāramitā* teachings are true but incomplete. They require further elucidation, which the *Ratnagotra* provides. This is reflected in the alternative name of the *Ratnagotra,* namely *Uttaratantra.* The *Ratnagotra* assumes the *prajñāpāramitā* teachings as the *pūrva* or prior teachings; it itself is *uttara,* in the sense of both subsequent and superior.[32] Thus the *Ratnagotra*'s *tathāgatagarbha* teaching does not negate but extends *prajñā* teachings. It both corrects the misunderstanding of *śūnya* as nihilistic and completes the message that *śūnyatā* merely begins by naming the superlatives that *śūnyatā* prepares the mind to perceive.

Yamaguchi's analysis of the relationship between *prajñā* thought and the *tathāgatagarbha* thought of the *Ratnagotra* is persuasive to me for one reason: my reading of the *Buddha Nature Treatise.* This text, which closely follows the *Ratnagotra* in many respects, states in unmistakable terms: "Buddha nature is the Thusness revealed by the dual emptiness of person and things. . . . If one does not speak of Buddha nature, then one does not understand emptiness" (787b). One may argue whether the authors of the *Ratnagotra* and the *BNT* succeed in their portrayal of *tathāgatagarbha*–Buddha nature thought as the extension and fulfillment of *prajñā* thought, fully compatible with the latter. But that this is the intention of these authors is beyond dispute. I hope to show in the present study that the author of the *BNT* succeeds.

Yogācāra-Tathāgatagarbha *Thought*

The historical relationship between Yogācāra and *tathāgatagarbha* lines of thought has not yet been settled. It is clear that the border between the two sets of ideas was not absolute, and that there was a definite overlap between them. On the other hand, it is also clear that the two sets of ideas cannot simply be regarded as the property of a single school, as quite distinctive, sometimes incompatible ideas may be found in some of the texts of the two groups.

One view has it that what would come to be known separately as Yogācāra and *tathāgatagarbha* ideas first developed together in a single community. Evidence for this view can be seen in the *Mahāyānasūtrālaṅkāra,* an early Yogācāra text attributed to Maitreya, in which reference to the *tathāgatagarbha* can be found. This view holds that classical Yogācāra thought (in Asaṅga and Vasubandhu) developed out of this line, emphasizing the formulation of a critical philosophy of consciousness. Later still, Yogācāra commentators and translators tended to fall into two categories, representing the divergent emphases within Yogācāra history. Thus Paramārtha emphasized the affinity of Yogācāra and *tathāgatagarbha* ideas that always had been part of the tradition, whereas Dharmapāla and Xuan-zang emphasized the critical philosophy of consciousness, which had been part of the tradition from the time of Asaṅga and Vasubandhu.[33]

Another view sees Yogācāra-*tathāgatagarbha* thought as a syncretism of two originally distinct lines. In this view, though the identities of the authors and earliest enthusiasts for *tathāgatagarbha* thought are unknown, it was a portion of the Yogācāra community who subsequently took up the *tathāgatagarbha* texts, studied them, and ultimately combined *tathāgatagarbha* ideas with their own Yogācāra philosophy. Thus, some time after the composition of the exclusively *tathāgatagarbha* texts discussed earlier, a number of syncretic Yogācāra-*tathāgatagarbha* texts were written.[34] Prominent examples of such texts include the *Laṅkāvatāra-sūtra,*[35] the *Awakening of Faith in Mahāyāna* (*Da Sheng Qi Xin Lun*), and the present *Buddha Nature Treatise.*

This is not to say that all later Yogācārins embraced *tathāgatagarbha* thought. The school of Dharmapāla and Xuan-zang tended to keep its distance from *tathāgatagarbha* ideas. This school maintained the *gotra* theory, according to which different beings had differing potentials for spiritual attainment, depending upon the nature of the "seeds" or *bīja* stored in the *ālaya-vijñāna* and responsible for shaping the nature of their subsequent births. In this view each being belonged to one of the five *gotra,* fixing his or her spiritual destination as Tathāgata, *pratyekabuddha, arhat,* worldly rebirth (*icchantika* or *atyantika*), or indeterminate. The latter *gotra,* "was undoubtedly created to fit the *ekayāna* [One Vehicle] teaching of the *buddhadhātu* [Buddha nature] into the *triyāna* [Three Vehicles] model, for it was maintained that the teaching of the Buddha that all beings possess the *buddhadhātu* was intended for the edification of those who belonged to this indeterminate *gotra.*"[36] Thus, though this teaching incorporates *tathāgatagarbha* doctrine in a minor way, it is an obvious patchwork of inherently contradictory ideas. Another area of incompatibility can be found in this school's emphasis upon the idea of an impure mind infected with unwholesome seeds that must be uprooted one by one through an indefinitely long period of yoga practice. This view is entirely alien to the *tathāgatagarbha*–Buddha nature emphasis upon an innately pure mind that needs only to manifest itself.[37]

Outside of this stream represented by Dharmapāla were other Yogācārins whose views put them in a position to welcome consideration of *tathāgatagarbha* thought. Who were the authors of the most important Yogācāra-*tathāgatagarbha* texts is difficult to say, but we do know the identities of a number of individuals who translated into Chinese some combination of Yogācāra, *tathāgatagarbha,* or Yogācāra-*tathāgatagarbha* texts. These men, Ratnamati (fifth–sixth-centuries), Guṇabhadra (394–468), Bodhiruci (sixth-century), and Paramārtha (499–569), demonstrated in their life's work that they highly valued this double stream.[38]

Grosnick isolates three factors in non-Dharmapāla Yogācāra that were sufficiently compatible with *tathāgatagarbha* ideas to pave the way for syncretism.[39] All three are central features of Yogācāra thought, and all are prominent in the *BNT*. The first is the belief that *śūnya* teachings leave themselves open to a nihilistic misunderstanding and are incomplete as found in *prajñā* and Mādhyamika texts. As discussed earlier, Yogācāra and *tathāgatagarbha* thinking on this point is remarkably close: They agree that it is vital to convey that Buddhist practice not only frees one from delusion but also frees one to realize Truth, Truth that is not nihilistic but affirmative of that which one will discover.

The second feature of Yogācāra that Grosnick cites as opening it to *tathāgatagarbha* thought is subject-object nondualism. In Yogācāra, subject-object nondualism is a feature of Thusness (*tathatā*), and Thusness is an expression for what one realizes at the end of the Path. It is in this affirmative function that both subject-object nondualism and Thusness are identified with Buddha nature in the *BNT*.

Finally, the Yogācāra doctrine of *trisvabhāva,* the three natures, also appears prominently in a number of syncretic texts, including the *BNT*. This doctrine in its Yogācāra context explains the relationship between delusion and enlightenment. *Parikalpita-svabhāva* is delusion experience, *pariniṣpanna-svabhāva* is enlightenment experience, or seeing things as they are. *Paratantra-svabhāva,* the dependent nature, is the given: When seen through delusion, it is *parikalpita;* when seen without delusion, it is *pariniṣpanna.* Because the relationship between delusion and enlightenment is a weak point of *tathāgatagarbha* thought (the *Śrīmālā-sūtra* is typical of *tathāgatagarbha* literature in avoiding this issue by stating "only a Buddha understands this"), the *trisvabhāva* doctrine strengthened *tathāgatagarbha* thought by supplementing its account of delusion and enlightenment. Moreover, used in this way, the *trisvabhāva* doctrine integrates perfectly with the dual Yogācāra-*tathāgatagarbha* insistence upon confirming the positive nature of what one attains through Buddhist practice: One attains Thusness (*tathatā*), or in other words, *parinispanna-svabhāva.*

These three points are prominent in the *BNT*. However, the most familiar syncretic texts, the *Laṅkāvatāra-sūtra* and the *Awakening of Faith,* are better known for amalgamating the Yogācāra concept of *ālaya-vijñāna,* the "storehouse consciousness," and the *tathāgatagarbha.* This association, however, is not a straightforward matter. In the *Awakening,* the *tathāgatagarbha* is given at least two roles. First, *ālaya-vijñāna* and the *tathāgatagarbha* are spoken of side by side in connection with the production of *saṃsāra:* "On the basis of the *tathāgatagarbha* there is the mind of production and destruction. *Ālaya-vijñāna* is the name for the harmonious joining of 'nonproduction-and-nondestruction' with 'production-and-destruction' such that they are neither one nor different."[40] Later in the text, after listing the superlative attributes of Thusness (*tathatā*), we are told that, because the latter possesses these attributes, it is identified with both *tathāgatagarbha* and *dharmakāya.*[41] It seems, then, that in this text when *tathāgatagarbha* is identified with *tathatā* its innately pure nature that is full of superlative attributes is connoted, whereas when it is identified with *ālaya-vijñāna* its immanence and participation in the world of *saṃsāra* and delusion is indicated. The *Awakening* is so terse, however, as to leave the exact relationship among *ālaya-vijñāna, tathatā,* and *tathāgatagarbha* in need of further interpretation by the commentators.

Although the *Laṅkāvatāra-sūtra* is encyclopedic rather than terse, its account of the relationship between *tathāgatagarbha* and *ālaya-vijñāna* also is ambivalent. In some passages it teaches a straightforward identification of *tathāgatagarbha* and *ālaya-vijñāna,* as follows:

> Mahāmati, the Tathāgata-garbha holds within it the cause for both good and evil, and by it all the forms of existence are produced. . . . [W]hen a revulsion [or turning-back] has not taken place in the Ālayavijñāna known under the name of Tathāgata-garbha, there is no cessation of the seven evolving Vijñānas. . . . For this reason, Mahāmati, let those Bodhisattva-Mahāsattvas who are seeking after the exalted truth effect the purification of the Tathāgata-garbha which is known as Ālayavijñāna.[42]

Such a passage as this, in which *tathāgatagarbha* and *ālaya-vijñāna* are identified, seems to effect this identification by canceling out the *tathāgatagarbha*'s own qualities of innate purity, wisdom, and so on as discussed in the *tathāgatagarbha* texts.[43] Here, the name *tathāgatagarbha* merely is appended to the *ālaya*'s attributes.

Elsewhere in the text, however, the *tathāgatagarbha* is spoken of with no connection to *ālaya-vijñāna*, and here it retains its expected character: "By tranquillity is meant oneness (*ekāgra*), and oneness gives birth to the highest Samādhi, which is gained by entering into the womb of Tathāgatahood [*tathāgatagarbha*], which is the realm of noble wisdom realized in one's inmost self."[44] We may conclude that while the *Laṅkāvatāra* embraces both *tathāgatagarbha* and *ālaya-vijñāna,* it has not given us a completely worked through philosophy in which all the terms of its system are clearly understood in their mutual relations.

Though the *ālaya-vijñāna* is mentioned in a minor way in the *BNT,* this is an insignificant feature of out text. The *BNT* does, though, manifest profound influence from Yogācāra thought, especially from the *Yogācārabhūmi* (attributed to Asaṅga) and, to a lesser degree, from the *Mahāyānasaṃgraha,* the *Mahāyānasūtrālaṅkāra,* and other texts. In addition to the three points discussed earlier (a positive interpretation of emptiness, subject-object nondualism, and *trisvabhāva*), the *BNT* very heavily emphasizes the Yogācāra ideas of Thusness (*tathatā*) and of *āśrayaparāvṛtti* (transformation of the basis), though the latter is interpreted in a way different from the standard Yogācāra understanding.

Paramārtha

Of the many translators of Buddhist scriptures that China saw, Paramārtha (Zhen-di) (499–569) is considered to have been the greatest of his time and ranks with Kumārajīva and Xuan-zang as one of the greatest ever.[45] He was born into a Brahman family in Ujjain (Ujjayinī) in western India. After becoming a Buddhist monk and completing his studies, he traveled to Funan. There he was invited by emissaries of Emperor Wu of Liang to come to China to transmit the Dharma. This he did, arriving in China in 546. Soon after his arrival, a rebellion displaced Paramārtha's patron, Emperor Wu, leaving Paramārtha in a perilous and rootless position. Paramārtha was forced to seek out a more peaceful place where he could proceed with his translations. Unfortunately, in neither the Liang nor the succeeding Chen (Ch'en) dynasty did political conditions stabilize in South China, and Paramārtha was frequently obliged to interrupt his work to move to a safe location. As a result, he "spent a wretched life translating sūtras [and śāstras] while wandering from place to place, accompanied by a small band of disciples."[46] He twice tried to leave China but the first time was dissuaded by his disciples, and the second time, though he set sail, was returned by strong winds and his "fate."[47] Toward the end of his life he attempted suicide but was restrained by the combined efforts of monks and government officials. Though he acquired fame for his work and monks traveled great distances to learn from him, he faced the opposition of powerful monks at court and was blocked from moving to the capital. He died at the age of 70, with his disciples determined to transmit his work.

When one considers the kind of life Paramārtha lived, it is difficult to imagine how he managed to produce the number and quality of works that he did, works whose message and intellectual power were to influence the development of Chinese Buddhism for centuries to come. Clearly, Paramārtha was not only a brilliant scholar but, despite periodic struggles with depression, dedicated with a religious devotion to his lifework. It also is remarkable that he cared to transmit such an optimistic line of thought as that of the Yogācāra and Yogācāra-*tathāgatagarbha* line, given the conditions in South China and the human behavior to which he was witness, which made the practical circumstances of his own life so difficult. He had precious little reinforcement from the "real" world of the pure mind or the innate and universal Buddhahood extolled in the works he transmitted.

Paramārtha is one of the major translators who rendered into Chinese both Yogācāra texts and Yogācāra-*tathāgatagarbha* texts. There is no doubt that a major component of his missionary's zeal was his commitment to the transmission of these lines of Buddhist thought. His syncretic translations include, in addition to the *Buddha Nature Treatise: Wu Shang Yi Jing,* a text not extant in any form other than the "translation" of which he may have been the author, and the *Awakening of Faith in Mahāyāna* (*Da Sheng Qi Xin Lun*) of which, again, he may have been the author. His Yogācāra translations include *Madhyāntavibhāga-bhāsya* by Vasubandhu; the *Mahāyānasaṃgraha* of Asaṅga, and *Mahāyānasaṃgraha-bhāṣya,* Vasubandhu's commentary on Asaṅga's work; *Jue Ding Zang Lun,* part of Asaṅga's *Yogācārabhūmi;* and Vasubandhu's *Viṃśatikā* and *Triṃśikā.* As part of his evident devotion to Vasubandhu, he translated the latter's non-Yogācāran *Abhidharmakośa-bhāṣya* and wrote a highly esteemed biography of Vasubandhu. He also translated *prajñā* and Mādhyamika works, including the *Diamond Sūtra* (*Vajracchedikā-prajñāpāramitā-sūtra*) and the *Ratnāvalī* of Nāgārjuna, works that, as we have seen, he probably would not have regarded as competing with the Yogācāra and Yogācāra-*tathāgatagarbha* texts. Paramārtha translated many other works—we have over thirty translations from his turbulent twenty-three years in China, and many others of his works were lost—but his greatness and importance lies for the most part in his transmission of Yogācāra and Yogācāra-*tathāgatagarbha* texts.[48]

Paramārtha's translations constituted crucial contributions to the Chinese Buddhist intellectual world. Paramārtha's translation of Vasubandhu's *Mahāyānasaṃgraha-bhāṣya* stimulated the establishment of the She-lun school, an important sixth-century school that, together with the Di-lun (Ti-lun) school, focused the discussion of Yogācāra and Yogācāra-*tathāgatagarbha* ideas. This discussion contributed heavily to the development of the indigenous Chinese Buddhist schools that developed during the Sui and Tang dynasties. Chih-yi and Fa-zang, for example, were very familiar with Paramārtha's work; Fa-zang's commentary on the *Awakening of Faith* is regarded as the most authoritative of the many commentaries on that important text. Without Paramārtha's work, the evolution of Chinese Buddhist thought would have been significantly altered.

D. The Text of the *Buddha Nature Treatise*

The authorship of the *Buddha Nature Treatise*[49] is attributed to Vasubandhu, and the Chinese translation is attributed to Paramārtha. Only the Chinese translation is extant; neither a Tibetan translation nor a Sanskrit original survives. There is no reason to suspect that the text might be a purely Chinese original, as it contains an extensive refutation of several non-Buddhist Indian philosophical schools, which would not be expected in a Chinese original. There is a considerable degree of doubt, however, as to whether Vasubandhu actually wrote the text. Takasaki and Hattori, for example, are convinced that the text was not translated but actually written by

Paramārtha, on the basis of his knowledge of the *Ratnagotravibhāga*.[50] It is true that there is an unmistakable overlap between the *BNT* and the *Ratnagotravibhāga*. The two texts have a good deal of material in common, and it is quite evident that the former was partially based on the latter. Takemura, though, finds insufficient reason to overturn the authority of the statement recorded on the text that the authorship is Vasubandhu's and the translation Paramārtha's.[51] It is difficult not to be suspicious of Paramārtha, however, inasmuch as he is given as the translator of both the *BNT* and the *Wu Shang Yi Jing*, neither of which is extant in other than its Chinese (Paramārtha) version and both of which contain extensive similarities with the *Ratnagotravibhāga*.

This is not the only difficulty with the text of the *BNT*. The circumstances of the text's composition, translation (if it was translated), and transmission are all very little known. There is no record of the date or place of translation on the manuscript. Ui puts the translation of the text between 557 and 569;[52] Takemura puts it at approximately 558.[53]

One particularly troublesome aspect of the text is the existence of several passages preceded by the term *comment*. It is uncertain what person or persons may have added these comments. Takasaki believes that fragments of a lost commentary on the *BNT* by Paramārtha have been preserved here.[54] Takemura makes a considered attempt to determine whether Vasubandhu, Paramārtha, or someone else may have added these commentary like passages. He believes each case has to be treated individually and that it is very difficult to be sure in one's judgment.

It is not my intention to further research the problem of the authorship of the *BNT*. The scholars mentioned here who argue for the authorship of Paramārtha are persuasive, as is the connection between Paramārtha, the *BNT*, the *Ratnagotravibhāga*, and the *Wu Shang Yi Jing*. It does seem likely that Paramārtha was the author of the *BNT*, though this cannot be regarded as conclusively settled. Although it is impossible to identify the author of the text with absolute confidence, there is no doubt that the work was in some way in the hands of Paramārtha, either as author of the text as a whole, as author of the inserted comments, as translator, or in a combination of these roles. In this limited sense, we can identify the text as belonging to Paramārtha. As such, it bears his stamp and is representative of the views that he bequeathed to later generations of East Asian Buddhists.

The *BNT* is just one of many cases demonstrating the great difficulty of determining to what extent Paramārtha was the transmitter of the ideas of others, such as Vasubandhu, and to what extent he was the originator of some of these ideas. Paramārtha is known to have interpolated passages dealing with *tathāgatagarbha* into Yogācāra texts he was translating into Chinese without even alerting the reader that he had done so. For example, a comparison of Paramārtha's translation of Vasubandhu's *Mahāyānasaṃgraha-bhāṣya,* with the Tibetan and Xuan-zang versions of the text, reveals insertions of *tathāgatagarbha* ideas in Paramārtha's translation that are entirely lacking in the Tibetan and the Xuan-zang versions.[55]

The same kind of thing may be at work in the *Buddha Nature Treatise.* Chapter Four of the *BNT,* "Analysis of the Characteristics," which analyzes Buddha nature in terms of ten characteristics, is very close to that part of Chapter One of the *Ratnagotra,* which analyzes the *tathāgatagarbha* in terms of virtually the same ten characteristics. The author of the *BNT,* however, has greatly expanded the text by adding Yogācāra concepts, discussed at considerable length, to the *tathāgatagarbha* discourse of the *Ratnagotra.* Assuming that Paramārtha is the author of the *BNT,* we can see that he was responsible not only for transmitting Yogācāra-*tathāgatagarbha* texts, but also for effecting some of the synthesis himself—and in both directions (adding *tathāgatagarbha* passages to Yogācāra texts and Yogācāra passages to *tathāgatagarbha* texts).

The *Awakening of Faith in the Mahāyāna* is another text "translated" by Paramārtha, attributed to another (Aśvaghoṣa), in which the attribution is widely doubted, if not discredited outright. Many scholars believe this text was a Chinese original. William Grosnick, however, argues that Paramārtha is the likely author of this text.[56] *If,* as is quite possible but unproven, Paramārtha was the author of the *BNT* as well as the *Wu Shang Yi Jing* and the *Awakening of Faith in the Mahāyāna,* he would deserve a large share of the credit for the articulation of the Yogācāra-*tathāgatagarbha* ideas that so heavily influenced the development of Chinese Buddhist thought. But even though we cannot be sure whether he authored these texts, we do know that he chose to transmit them, that Yogācāra and Yogācāra-*tathāgatagarbha* teachings were focal concerns of his, that his choice of words as a translator determined in large measure the language in which these ideas were subsequently considered (until the time of Xuan-zang), and that he had a tendency to "supplement" the texts he translated with his own thoughts. To this extent at least his role in this history must be credited, and a significant role it is.

Within the corpus of Paramārtha's works, the *BNT* stands out for its importance for understanding Buddha nature thought. The *BNT* held a position of considerable influence in the body of *tathāgatagarbha*–Buddha nature texts transmitted to China. In Sino-Japanese Buddhism there was a significant and sustained controversy concerning the "existence" of Buddha nature; that is, the issue of whether all beings or only some possess the Buddha nature and thereby are assured the attainment of Buddhahood. In this context, the *BNT* was well known and seriously studied in China and Japan because of its thorough elucidation of the Buddha nature concept and its persuasive defense of the reality of Buddha nature. Ling-run (Ling-jun), for example, who was one of the early advocates of the universal Buddha nature theory, quoted the *BNT* in his attempt to refute the view that some do not possess the Buddha nature.[57] Many commentaries, both Chinese and Japanese, were written on the *BNT*, though only one Japanese commentary survives.[58]

As Takemura points out, however, the very existence of such a "Buddha nature controversy" is based on an understanding of the Buddha nature quite antithetical to that concept as presented in the *BNT*.[59] The controversy, that is, is formulated on an understanding of the Buddha nature as some kind of original principle or metaphysical entity that can either exist or not exist. The essential theme that we shall see in the *BNT*, however, is that the Buddha nature is not a metaphysical thing or entity of any kind. It is thus, strictly speaking, improper to say either that it exists or does not exist, though the author of the *BNT* does assert, for soteriological reasons, that the Buddha nature can be said to exist in a sense that he specifies. This clear affirmation of the Buddha nature, and the philosophically and doctrinally sophisticated manner in which it is expressed, enabled the *BNT* to play the important role it played in the Buddha nature controversy.

E. The *Buddha Nature Treatise* and Chinese Buddhist Thought

The importance of the *BNT* for Chinese Buddhist philosophy is not limited to its philosophy of Buddha nature, narrowly conceived. The text is remarkably useful today as an introduction to the Yogācāra-related foundations of Chinese Buddhist philosophy. Many of the views articulated in the text, and especially the overall standpoint from which the author speaks, are very much in harmony with widespread ideas in Chinese Buddhist thought as they are expressed in the various indigenous Chinese Buddhist schools. This is especially true of Chan, but it also is true to a lesser degree of Tian-tai and Hua-yan.

Some of the themes that will emerge in this book as the philosophy of the *BNT* and that are important components of the foundation of Chinese Buddhist thought are as follows:

1. An emphasis on the positive nature of realization; a view of enlightenment as an experiential reality that goes beyond emptiness.
2. An optimistic concept of human nature based on the idea of a universal, active Buddha nature.
3. An ontology based upon nondualism, as opposed to monism, and expressed in the language of Thusness.
4. Subject-object nondualism, the idea that mind and world arise together in mutual creation, whether in a deluded or an enlightened manner.
5. A positive view of phenomenal reality, based upon the views given in points 1 and 3.
6. The concept of a pivotal conversion experience from delusion to enlightenment or from impurity to purity.
7. The equation of Buddha nature and Buddhist practice (a view that ultimately becomes more representative of Japanese Buddhism, in Dōgen, than of Chinese).[60]

The clear and systematic expression of these themes in the *BNT* provides an accessible door into some of the most important, but often puzzling, tenets of Chinese Buddhist thought. In this sense, one can think of this book as an introduction to themes that subsequently would become core Chinese Buddhist ideas. We are introduced to them in the *BNT* at the point of their importation from India to China (via Paramārtha), prior to their appropriation by Chinese Buddhist thinkers. Because these ideas were established at the ground of the then-emerging indigenous Chinese Buddhist schools and were not the exclusive property of any one of these schools, the importance of these ideas for Chinese Buddhism is unusually broad. The elucidation of these themes is one purpose of this book.

A second purpose of this book is to grapple with the common charge that the notion of Buddha nature (or *tathāgatagarbha*) introduces into Buddhism the non-Buddhist, crypto-Hindu element of *ātmavāda* (a view of an entitative, metaphysical self or soul) or idealistic monism. I will explore the extent to which it is possible to defend the Buddha nature concept from a purely Buddhist perspective, in terms of purely Buddhist philosophical principles. I believe this reflects the author's own understanding of the Buddha nature.

I begin this project by discussing the Buddha nature concept in the jargon of the text itself. I hope to show in this way that the author simply does not think in either entitative or monistic terms, but bases his philosophy from the ground up on entirely other principles. As my "Buddhistic" defense of Buddha nature relies upon my explanation of the latter in terms of action and practice, I also consider what kinds of action and practice are considered especially disclosive of Buddha nature.

A final goal of the book is to engage the *BNT* in dialogue with current Western thinking on the concept of human personhood. The concept of Buddha nature is probably the single most important component of East Asian Buddhist concepts of human personhood. As such, to the extent that it is possible to overcome the cultural gap between us, we could profit by hearing this Buddhist response to the perennial and universal question of human being. In Chapter 7 I will engage in cross-cultural philosophy by addressing Western philosophical questions about human personhood to the *BNT*'s Buddha nature concept.

CHAPTER TWO

The Concept of Buddha Nature

A. Taking the Semantic Ascent

"Why did the Buddha speak of Buddha nature?" (787a). In mid-sixth century China, the question of the status of Buddha nature is phrased in this way, and with these words the *Buddha Nature Treatise* begins. The author does not open, as we might expect, with the more straightforward but naive question, What is Buddha nature? Instead, he takes the "semantic ascent"[1] —he directs the focus of the inquiry to the language with which the tradition speaks of Buddha nature and away from the Buddha nature itself. Had the author begun by asking, What is Buddha nature? he would have begged the very questions in which he was most interested. This form of the question presupposes a Buddha nature that "is" "something." But the ontological and metaphysical status of the Buddha nature are two of the issues that the *BNT*'s author feels are most misunderstood by others and on which he focuses from the beginning of the text. By taking the semantic ascent, he structures the question in such a way that no such questions are begged.

Why, then, did the Buddha speak of Buddha nature? The Buddha, says the author, spoke of Buddha nature to help people overcome five shortcomings (inferior mind, arrogance, delusion, slandering the truth, and attachment to self) and to produce in them five virtues (diligent mind, reverence, wisdom [*prajñā*], knowledge [*jñāna*], and compassion) (787a). In short, the Buddha spoke of Buddha nature to help humanity put an end to ignorance and attain enlightenment. This is an important point: The teaching of Buddha nature does not essentially indicate the existence and describe the nature of "something" that "is." Nevertheless, it was important for the Buddha to speak of Buddha nature for the same purpose that all the Buddha's teachings serve; namely, aiding sentient beings in their quest for enlightenment. The author of the *BNT,* like the Buddha (he claims), wants to speak positively of Buddha nature, but without leading the reader to conceive of the Buddha nature as "something" that "is." How he resolves this difficulty is the subject of this chapter.

B. Refutation of Other Views

The author of the *BNT* is concerned that his readers' minds may be full of notions of *ātman* and *anātman,* misconceptions of Buddha nature, and so on and that these ideas will interfere with the correct understanding of Buddha nature he wants to present. Thus he begins by contrasting Buddha nature with such competing conceptions and criticizing the latter, thereby clarifying what Buddha nature is not. Only on this basis, he feels, can he go on to discuss in a constructive manner how the term *Buddha nature* actually does function. Thus we begin with a discussion of what Buddha nature is not, argued in the context of a refutation of competing views.

The author's first move is to refute both the view that the Buddha nature exists and the view that it does not exist. The way in which this is done is typical of the logic of the *BNT.* With respect to Buddha nature, says the author, if you say either that it exists (*you*) or that it does not exist (*wu*) you go astray. Let us consider these important terms.

You and *wu* are two of the most thoroughly studied words in the classical Chinese language, especially in their philosophical meanings. Basically, *you* means "have" or "there is." *Wu* is the opposite, meaning "lack" or "there is not." Thus the terms indicate the presence or absence of a thing or things. Philosophically, *you* and *wu* early took on the extended, abstract senses of existence and nonexistence, something and nothing. These are used, for example, in the Daoist (Taoist) philosophy of Laozi (Lao-tzu) and Zhuangzi (Chuang-tzu). However, *you* is used primarily with regard to concrete things; the *Dao* (*Tao*), *li* (principle), and other such abstractions only occasionally are covered by *you,* but usually are *wu* or neither *you* nor *wu.*[2] "The English word 'Nothing' implies the absence of any 'entity,' the Chinese *wu* only the absence of concrete things. . . . But if the Tao is Nothing, then Nothing is a positive complement of Something, not its mere absence."[3] *You,* unlike other verbs and adjectives, is not negated by the term *bu,* "not," but forms a pair with its contrary, *wu,* "similar to such pairs as long and short, left and right, Yin and Yang."[4] Thus, especially in Daoist philosophy, *wu* may have a positive, constructive content, unlike the English *nothing* or *nonexistence.* That this is so is illustrated by the Daoist teaching that it is in being a combination of something (*you*) and nothing (*wu*) that such things as doors and windows are useful.[5] In fact, *wu* has such a positive nature that in Daoism it is considered the source or *ben* of all manifested things. We shall shortly speak again of this concept, *ben.*

The author's most fundamental concerns in the *BNT* are, soteriologically, to promote practice and change, and, philosophically, to explain reality, human being, and human transformation in dynamic, process-oriented terms that ultimately derive from the experience of practicing Buddhism. On the basis of this agenda, he argues that neither the concept of existence (*you*) nor of nonexistence (*wu*) can account for the point of his interest; namely, that some here and now are realizing their Buddha nature and some are not. Insofar as he wants to encourage the practice of Buddhism, he must criticize the view that there is no (*wu*) Buddha nature, a view that naturally tends to discourage efforts to attain what might be unattainable. Insofar as he is a Buddhist, he sees change as the basic "given" from which philosophy must begin. He therefore must criticize the view that all "have" (*you*) Buddha nature in a substantialist sense.

The concerns for practice and for the imperative of basing philosophy on the givenness of change are mutually related concerns. If, he argues, one says there is no Buddha nature, then one will never be able to attain Buddhahood, as this would mean that there was an unbridgeable gulf between the ordinary being and Buddha, each frozen into its own nature. The corollary to this is that if one says there *is* Buddha nature, then the idea of the change or transformation inherent in practice will be lost. Why practice the Buddha Way if one already is Buddha? Thus, the ideas of both there being and not being a Buddha nature must be rejected, as either equally would freeze reality into a static state of being.

Being and nonbeing are seen as static categories in Buddhist thought. As such they are unacceptable terms for explaining reality because they do not allow for the self-transformation that constitutes the Buddha Way. As our author puts it, neither existence (*you*) nor nonexistence (*wu*) can be "transformed." "What is cannot be destroyed, what is not cannot be produced" (788c). This, of course, applies to Buddha nature as well. Thus, the author says, Buddha nature is nothing "fixed" (*ding*). Reality, and that which constitutes reality, is of a dynamic, everchanging nature. To think of it as "fixed"—whether as being or as nonbeing—is a basic mistake. Ontology takes second place to practical necessity; primary importance is given to what is soteriological, the self-transformation of liberation. Ontological notions serve primarily to provide a theoretical explanation as to how self-transformation or change is possible. In the *BNT,* the basis of this explanation is established with the rejection of the static notions of being and nonbeing.

So far this type of logic sounds like Middle Path logic—the two extremes of being and nonbeing, eternalism and annihilationism, are denied. However, whereas in *śūnyavāda* thought the problem of being and nonbeing is resolved in the dialectics of *śūnyatā* or emptiness, here in *tathāgatagarbha*–Buddha nature thought, the case is rather different. The issue of the being or nonbeing of Buddha nature is concluded in the *BNT* as follows: "In accordance with principle (*Dao li*), all sentient beings universally and aboriginally possess the pure Buddha nature. That there should be one who eternally failed to obtain *parinirvāṇa* is not the case. This is why Buddha nature most assuredly aboriginally exists (*ben you*); the reason being, that is, that it has nothing to do with either being or nonbeing" (788c).

The author begins this passage by appealing to "principle," literally "Way-principle." Thus, though the statement does, as the author notes, refer to scripture (*Tathāgatagarbha Sūtra*), the author also wants to ground his teachings in what he feels simply is true, the way things are, whether or not a Buddha had come into the world to point it out to us. This is typical of *tathāgatagarbha* literature.[6]

The author also wants to indicate with this that what he is saying is an actively affirmative truth; that is, a positive quality of reality, which may be spoken of in affirmative language, however obliquely. He is saying, in effect: The world is not chaotic, we need not be lost in it. There is a principle, discoverable by humans, manifesting the order of the universe. By realizing this principle (more closely, by bringing ourselves into accordance with this principle) we may discover this truth of the universe, which also is the truth of our own nature. This is a reason for rejoicing, and the author of the *BNT* felt it imperative that this be made clear.

What is the meaning of the statement that Buddha nature "most assuredly aboriginally exists"? The aboriginal existence, *ben you,* spoken of here, is altogether different from ordinary existence. Literally, *ben*—"root, source, origin"—plus *you*—"existence, being"—the term contrasts with *you* in the sense of finite existence; that is, the process of coming into being and perishing in time. *Ben you* thus contrasts with both existence, or being (*you*), and nonexistence, or nonbeing (*wu*), both in the finite sense. An interesting parallel can be found in the Daoist concept of *wu.* Daoist thinkers distinguished two senses of the term *wu:* (1) "that primal undifferentiated state that preceded the later state of manifested things (*yu*)[*you*]" and (2) "the perpetual alternation of the absence of something (*wu*) as contrasted to the presence of something (*yu*) [*you*]." The former "was not . . . a mere 'nothing' for it contained all future possibilities for world manifestation."[7] This sense of *wu* also was called *ben wu,* "original or root nonexistence" to distinguish it from the second sense of merely contingent nonexistence.

The term *ben you* used in the *BNT* may have been influenced by the Daoist *ben wu.* In both, the term *ben* is attached to the verb to distinguish the existence or nonexistence in question from the merely contingent variety. Both *ben you* and *ben wu* (independently) stand opposed to the existence-nonexistence pair. *Ben you,* however, does not carry the connotation carried by *ben wu* in the Daoist usage; namely, the sense of referring to that out of which all else emerged in a temporal sense.

Ben you, moreover, plays a role in *tathāgatagarbha*–Buddha nature thought similar in an important way to that which *śūnyatā* plays in *śūnya* thought. In both cases, the two extremes of being and nonbeing are rejected, and we are left with a term that indicates the conceptual insufficiency of those extremes. Yet how different are the "flavors" of the two terms! The authors of the *tathāgatagarbha* literature were intent on putting into some kind of positive language what they took to be the ultimate truths of Buddhism. They clearly felt that the *śūnya* language was negative, or that it would inevitably be perceived as such. In short, we have two linguistic paths, both of which proceed through negation of conceptual extremes, but one of which ends with the term *śūnya* and the other with a "Buddha nature" that "aboriginally exists."

This, then, is *śūnya* dialectics with a difference. According to the *BNT,* both the view that Buddha nature exists and the view that it does not exist are to be rejected because both imply that Buddha nature is something capable of existing as other things exist. To borrow Gilbert Ryle's terminology,[8] to so conceive Buddha nature is to make a category mistake; that is, to conjoin the kind of existence proper to things such as trees and stones with the very different kind of existence pertaining to Buddha nature. One thereby confuses the ontological status of Buddha nature with that of trees and stones. Buddha nature, unlike the latter, is not a thing in the world. Rather, as a term, it serves to affirm the potential of all sentient beings to realize Buddhahood. Thus to say "Buddha nature exists" is very unlike saying "stones exist." To indicate this difference between the two uses of the term *exist,* the author refers to the existence of Buddha nature as aboriginal existence, emphasizing that it has no relation to the ordinary concept of existence or its negation.

The author's next step in clarifying the nature of being of the Buddha nature is to refute the idea that Buddha nature is a kind of own-nature (*svabhāva, zi xing*). The author does this by arguing against the existence of any own-natures at all, as follows.

> For example, what formerly is a seed subsequently produces a grain plant. The "former" and "subsequent" stages of this grain are neither one nor two, neither exist (*you*) nor do not exist (*wu*). If they were one [i.e., the same], then there would be no "former" and "subsequent." If they were different, then what was originally grain could subsequently be a bean. Therefore, they are neither the same nor different. Due to [the confluence of] the destruction of the cause and the production of the effect, own-nature neither exists nor does not exist. [That is,] because the cause perishes, own-nature does not exist, but because the effect is produced, it does not not exist. Because at the time of the cause there is not yet an effect, you cannot say own-nature exists. Because the production of the effect is certainly due to

> the cause, you cannot say it does not exist. In this sense, cause and effect, reflection and understanding reach completion together, and therefore we say there is no own-nature. (793a)

The idea of own-nature is refuted because it does not allow for the process of change as seen in the growth of a plant or in any process having a former and a subsequent stage. The author, as a Buddhist, conceives of an own-nature as being eternal precisely in the sense of unchanging. Therefore any phenomenon or event that in any way is dynamic or in process is judged to be empty of an own-nature. Because, according to Buddhism, all is in flux, nowhere will one find an own-nature. Buddha nature is no exception to this all-encompassing rule.

The author offers us here no new ideas or perspectives. What he gives us is straight Middle Path logic emphasizing the process of flux and the interdependence of cause and effect, of former and subsequent stages. He concludes the section by affirming in the most orthodox manner, "Know, therefore, that all things are Thus truly without own-nature. Only true emptiness is their essential nature" (793c). In this way the author affirms that his forthcoming teachings concerning the Buddha nature do not trespass on the inviolable teaching that there is no own-nature. He anticipates that his teachings may resemble an own-nature view. Hence, early in the treatise he discredits this view in order that such a misunderstanding not develop.

The author next prepares the reader to understand the status of his Buddha nature teachings in the context of the Mahāyāna emptiness doctrine, specifically, the emptiness doctrine of the Mādhyamika two truths (*satyadvaya*) theory. To do so, he must first discredit a certain misunderstanding of the two truths doctrine and then offer his own interpretation of that doctrine. His interpretation is presented in the form of a synthesis of Mādhyamika two truths theory and Yogācāra three natures (*trisvabhāva*) theory.

The Mādhyamika two truths theory teaches that all of reality is encompassed by two levels: the relative or worldly (*saṃvṛti*) and the ultimate or supreme (*paramārtha*). Though ordinarily translated as "truth," the *satya* of *satyadvaya* embraces both epistemological and ontological qualities; it is the key term in a theory of experiential reality. *Saṃvṛti-satya* is said to be whatever is enveloped and obscured; ignorance; existence, understood in terms of the *kleśa*—desire, hatred and delusion; conditioned co-origination (*pratītya-samutpāda*); and the realm of what is empty (*śūnya*). *Parmārtha-satya* is said to be the cessation of the modes of "I" and "mine" and of belief in person; tranquility, understood as the cessation of the personal world; what does not arise or cease and is not dependent; known by wise saints in and through itself; the reality of *saṃvṛti* as its emptiness; the Middle Path; liberation.[9]

Like the Mādhyamika theory, the *trisvabhāva* theory is concerned with experiential reality and thus is simultaneously epistemological and ontological. The *parikalpita* nature is both the commonsense view of the world constructed by the deluded mind and that deluded mind itself; it is the interpretation of experience in terms of the wholly imaginary categories of subject and object, names and concepts. The *paratantra* nature is both the fact of conditioned co-origination (*pratītyasamutpāda*) and the recognition of that fact. Finally, the *parinişpanna* nature is the Thusness of reality and the cognition of Thusness and therefore is perfect and absolutely true.

The author begins this section by announcing that he wishes to "refute the biased views [errors] of beginners on the Mahāyāna path" (793c). The misunderstanding at issue is the view that "according to worldly truth (*saṃvṛtisatya*) all things exist (*you*); according to supreme truth (*paramārthasatya*) all things do not exist (*wu*)" (793c). The misunderstanding of supreme truth (*paramārthasatya*), or emptiness, in a nihilistic manner is especially troublesome to the author here.

This first level of misunderstanding is rejected in favor of the following suggested correct understanding of the two truths. "That all *dharmas* lack own-nature is supreme truth. To speak of the existence of own-nature within [the actuality of] the absence of own-nature is called worldly truth" (793c). The difference between the two truths, then, is not a difference between things existing or not existing, nor is it simply the difference between the existence or nonexistence of an own-nature. Rather, it is emphasized that worldly truth is constituted by falsely speaking of an own-nature as existing when in fact it does not.

No sooner is this second-level understanding of the two truths proffered, however, than it, too, is called into question, especially the understanding of supreme truth given therein. Is it sufficient, the author asks, to speak thus of supreme truth as no more than the *absence* of own-nature? It is not, for in recognizing supreme truth as the *absence* of own nature, we are still speaking and thinking on the level of worldly truth, on the level of the duality of the presence and absence of things, including own-nature. Given that the language and concepts of worldly truth are inherently deficient, they must represent a deficient perspective from which to speak of supreme truth. Therefore, this second-level understanding of the two truths also must be transcended.

We thus are brought to the third and final position, representing the author's own understanding of the two truths. Especially important is his understanding of supreme truth. In expressing this understanding he rejects the dualistic language of being and nonbeing characteristic of the position of worldly truth in favor of his own characteristic formulation: Neither being nor nonbeing is the case.

> The two truths theory cannot be called [a theory of] being (*you*), nor can it be called [a theory of] nonbeing (*wu*), because neither being nor nonbeing is the case (*fei you fei wu*). The reason why the supreme truth can be called neither [a theory of] being nor of nonbeing is that because it negates (*wu*) both person and thing it cannot be called [a theory of] being, and because it reveals (*xian*) the two forms of emptiness [of person and thing] it cannot be called [a theory of] nonbeing [insofar as emptiness is not the same as nonbeing]. The same is true of worldly truth. Because of the discriminating nature (*parikalpita*) it cannot be called [a theory of] being, and because of the relative nature (*paratantra*) it cannot be called [a theory of] nonbeing. Furthermore, supreme truth establishes neither being nor nonbeing with respect to persons and things. [Being and nonbeing] are neither one nor two [i.e., neither the same nor different]. Emptiness [both] is and is not. The same is true of worldly truth. One cannot definitively establish nonbeing [simply] on the basis of the discriminating nature. Nor can one definitively establish being [simply] on the basis of the relative nature. (793c–794a)

The most important point here is that the *wu* or negation intrinsic to the previous two attempts at discussing supreme truth is now eschewed in favor of an approach which rejects the dualistic being vs. nonbeing approach. To establish this point, the author combines the three natures and two truths theories, as follows:

Three Natures	*Two Truths*
discriminating (*parikalpita*) relative (*paratantra*)	= wordly (*saṃvṛti*)
[true (*parinişpanna*)—not named]	= supreme (*paramārtha*)

However, rather than demonstrating the superiority of supreme truth (and, by implication, the *parinispanna* nature) over worldly truth, as usually is the case, he places both truths at the same level: Neither truth "can be called" a theory of either being or nonbeing. In the case of worldly truth, this is because the recognition of the discriminating nature implies an affirmation of nonbeing since the discriminating nature is totally false, whereas the recognition of the relative nature implies an at least partial affirmation of being since the relative nature is partially true—things *are* interdependent. Thus, since both being and nonbeing are affirmed in worldly truth, the two negate each other, and neither can stand.

In the case of supreme truth, being cannot stand because persons and things are negated (*wu*); that is, neither is said to be ultimately real. Yet nonbeing also cannot stand, because the dual emptiness of person and thing after all, is, revealed (*xian*). This indicates for the *BNT*'s author that not only is emptiness or the supreme truth *not* a matter of pure negation or nihilism, but to the contrary, it can, and for soteriological purposes should, be described in the most positive, affirmative terms possible. He wants to demonstrate that supreme truth is not just a negation of worldly truth (the ideas of person and thing); it also functions positively to reveal something. His particular concern is to emphasize the positive quality of this function.

The author concludes by stating that from the perspective of supreme truth, not only do being and nonbeing not apply to the phenomena of experience, they also are neither the same nor different; that is, they are nondual. This may be explained as follows. Because being and nonbeing are denied on the grounds of their being *both* affirmed and denied (e.g., in the case of supreme truth, nonbeing is affirmed with respect to persons and things, but denied with respect to emptiness), clearly their identities, which should be based on mutual exclusion, are jeopardized, and it is no longer possible to see one as the negation of the other. That is, ordinarily, to affirm nonbeing is to negate being, but here one simultaneously affirms nonbeing (thereby implicitly negating being) *and* denies nonbeing (thereby implicitly affirming being). Thus, from the perspective of supreme truth, nonbeing is at once both affirmed and denied, hence it is at once both being and nonbeing. The same applies to being.

Moreover, says the author, emptiness "both is and is not" (*kong you bu you*). This is the final salvo against any who might mistake emptiness for nonbeing. The treatment of emptiness in this text both argues against this particular mistake and opens the way for a discussion of emptiness in positive terms. For the *BNT*'s author, emptiness, or supreme truth, has a positive, "beingful" quality to it. It is not just the negation of worldly truth; it also functions positively to "reveal" something.

In sum, three points have been established in this section.

1. It is incorrect to say either that Buddha nature exists or does not exist, though it is correct to say Buddha nature aboriginally exists, as long as this is understood as an affirmation of each person's potential to realize Buddhahood and not as a kind of existence that can stand in contrast to nonexistence.
2. Buddha nature is not an own-nature; an own-nature cannot be found where a phenomenon, such as a person, is in process. The idea of an own-nature therefore is to be discredited and thoroughly distinguished from the notion of Buddha nature.
3. Emptiness is not merely a matter of negation; supreme truth does not merely negate worldly truth. The contents of emptiness or supreme truth cannot be so limited as to be exhausted by functioning in a destructive manner; there also must be a positive revelation in emptiness. Therefore, (implicitly) because emptiness is not exclusively negative, it need not conflict with a Buddha nature that, though not an own-nature, is affirmed as existing aboriginally.

The import of these three points is this: Though Buddha nature cannot be said to exist or not to exist, it is in accordance with principle to realize that all possess it and hence to affirm it. Note here the key role played by the author's understanding and manipulation of language. When the two extremes of existence and nonexistence (or being and nonbeing) are negated, and as a result the principles of identity (A is A), noncontradiction (nothing can be both A and not A) and excluded middle (everything is either A or not A) no longer are to be relied upon, the laws of language based on those principles likewise are no longer to be assumed. At such a point, we are wide open to a new use of language. Nāgārjuna stepped into this language void and filled it with *śūnya* language. The *BNT*'s author stepped into the same void and filled it with a very different kind of language, a language that could speak positively of such things as Buddha nature and *tathāgatagarbha.* The author makes his point clearly and succinctly in this key passage: "Attachments are not real, therefore they are called vacuous. If one gives rise to these attachments, true wisdom will not arise. When one does away with these attachments, then we speak of Buddha nature. Buddha nature is the Thusness (*zhen ru*) revealed (*xian*) by the dual emptiness of person and things. . . . If one does not speak of Buddha nature, then one does not understand emptiness" (787b). The author is uncompromising on this point. Emptiness is not limited to a negative function. it clears the way only so that something positive, Buddha nature, may be revealed. One who does not affirm Buddha nature simply has not sufficiently penetrated emptiness.

C. The Essence of Buddha Nature

We now turn to an account of the Buddha nature per se, which the author discusses in terms of three concepts: three causes, *trisvabhāva* (three natures), and *tathāgatagarbha.* We will examine each of these in turn.

The Buddha Nature as Three Causes

The three "causes" are three aspects of Buddha nature in its function as cause of the attainment of Buddhahood. The three are given as the cause of attainability, the *prayoga* cause, and the complete fulfillment cause. They are discussed as follows.

> The cause of attainability is the Thusness revealed by the dual emptiness [of persons and things]. Because of this emptiness, one "can attain" *bodhicitta, prayoga,* and so forth, up to the *dharmakāya* at the end of the Path. That is why this cause is called *can attain.*
>
> The *prayoga* cause is called *bodhicitta.* With this mind, one can attain the thirty-seven limbs of enlightenment,[10] the ten stages (*daśabhūmi*) of the bodhisattva, the ten perfections (*pāramitā*), the auxiliary aids to practice,[11] and, at the end of the Path, the *dharmakāya.* This is called the *prayoga* cause.
>
> The complete fulfillment cause is *prayoga.* With this *prayoga,* one attains complete fulfillment of both the cause and the fruit [of Buddha nature]. By fulfillment of the cause is meant virtuous and wise action.

Fulfillment of the fruit is constituted by the three virtues of wisdom, the cutting-off of delusion, and loving-kindness.

Of these three causes, the essential nature of the first is unconditioned Thusness. The essential nature of the latter two causes is conditioned resolution and action.

Within the cause of attainability are three kinds of [Buddha] nature: the nature which dwells in itself, the emergent nature, and the attaining nature. The record says, the nature which dwells in itself is [Buddha nature] in the stage of the ordinary person who has not yet begun Buddhist practice; the emergent nature is [Buddha nature] in the stage of the Buddhist practitioner from the first awakening of mind up to the completion of the Path; the attaining nature is [Buddha nature] in the stage of the person who has completed the Buddhist Path. (794a)

According to this passage, Buddha nature should be understood as three kinds of cause. These three, however, all stem from the first cause, the cause whose nature is Buddha potentiality as such and whose essential character is unconditioned Thusness. This constitutes the text's first fully developed direct statement as to what the Buddha nature is: Thusness making possible Buddhahood. As the description of the three causes proceeds, we can see that this initial urge toward the self-realization of the Buddha nature is the basis that progressively develops into *bodhicitta, prayoga,* and fulfillment, in turn.

The latter two causes, which are based on the first, simply are constituted by various aspects of Buddhist practice, or "conditioned resolution and action."[12] *Bodhicitta,* although not explained in this text, generally is understood as the mind that has awakened to a knowledge of the reality and loftiness of Buddhahood and that aspires to the attainment of that Buddhahood which it glimpses. As such, it represents the beginning of the *bodhisattva's* career. *Prayoga* has a narrow and a more general meaning, both of which we see reflected here. In the narrow sense, *prayoga* refers to preliminary or preparatory practices on the Buddhist path, such things as the thirty-seven conditions and the auxiliary aids. In a broader sense, *prayoga* means progress based on endeavor, that is, Buddhist practice as such. This latter sense is reflected in the preceding text in describing *prayoga* as including the ten stages, the ten perfections, and the eventual realization of *dharmakāya.* The Chinese rendering of *prayoga* is *jia-xing: xing*[2], the active practice or cultivation of the Buddha Way that is *jia,* progressive or additive. It is noteworthy that the author of this text equates *bodhicitta* and *prayoga. Bodhicitta,* or mind of wisdom, is a term that may appear at first to refer to a mental entity of some kind. However, it is equated with *prayoga,* a term that clearly refers to action, practice, and doing. The complete fulfillment of the potential of Buddha nature, moreover, is accomplished by *prayoga,* or Buddhist practice and is manifested in virtuous and wise actions.

Three kinds of Buddha nature are then listed (in the last paragraph of the quotation) and correlated with three stages of development on the path of Buddhist practice. A Buddha nature that "dwells in itself" is the kind of Buddha nature found in those who have not yet taken up Buddhist practice; this Buddha nature "dwells in itself" in the sense that it is latent and not yet manifest. A second kind of Buddha nature, the "emergent nature," is found in all practitioners of Buddhism, from the newest beginner to the *bodhisattva* on the brink of Buddhahood, whereas a third kind, the "attaining nature," represents the stage of the final completion of the Path. Insofar as all of these stages develop from the first cause of Buddha nature, they all are grounded in unconditioned Thusness.

*The Three Natures (*Trisvabhāva*)*

The second category given as revelatory of the essence of Buddha nature is the three natures. In this text, two sets of three natures are discussed, the three natures or *trisvabhāva* (*san xing*), and the three no-natures (*san wu xing*), both classic Yogācāra ideas. The latter are discussed first.

> The three no-natures are: the no-mark nature, the no-birth nature, and the no-reality nature. These three natures together exhaust the Tathāgata nature. In what sense? Together they constitute its essence.
>
> What is meant by the no-mark nature is the fact that all dharmas are just names and words; their own-nature lacks marks and form. The no-birth nature means that all dharmas are brought into being by causes and conditions; they cannot produce themselves. Since neither self nor other completes [production], it is called the no-birth nature. The no-reality nature means that because all things lack the mark of reality, there is no other possessor of reality from which [reality] can be attained. (794a–b)

In the present context, the function of these three no-natures is to identify the essential nature of the Tathāgata, or Buddha, nature with emptiness in order to legitimize it in terms of orthodox theories of the emptiness of all things and to turn aside potential objections that the Buddha nature is a crypto-Hindu entitative mind or soul. We have seen this approach in the text already: Before the author says what Buddha nature is, he is careful to say what it is not. It is quite evident that he is arguing, at least in his own mind but probably also in reality, with more *śūnya*-oriented opponents who would accuse him of un-Buddhist activity.

After these preparatory comments, the author moves on to a discussion of the three natures as such; that is, the *trisvabhāva* of Yogācāra theory: the discriminating nature, *parikalpita svabhāva* (*fen-bie-xing*); the relative nature, *paratantra svabhāva* (*yi-ta-xing*); and the true nature, *parinispanna svabhāva* (*zhen-shi-xing*). He first defines the general meaning of each term.

> The discriminating nature is established on the basis of the use of the language of provisional speech. If there were no such terms, then the discriminating nature would not come into being. Therefore you should know that this nature is merely a matter of verbal expression, in reality it has no essence and no properties. This is what is called the discriminating nature.
>
> The relative nature is the principle (*Dao-li*) that manifests as the twelvefold chain of conditioned origination (*pratītya-samutpāda*). Because it serves as a basis (*yi-zhi*) for the discriminating nature, it is established as the relative (*yi-ta*) nature.
>
> The true nature is the Thusness (*zhen-ru*) of all things. It is the nondiscriminating wisdom realm of the wise. For the sake of purifying the [first] two natures, realizing the third [i.e., liberation], and cultivating all virtues, the true nature is established. (794b)

The three natures theory is important for the understanding of the subject-object relationship it provides. This, of course, is standard Mahāyāna Buddhist material, but it may fairly be said that the three natures theory manifests the Buddhist position on this issue rather clearly. For what exactly is a nature (*xing*[1]), and in what way can there be said to be three of them that somehow constitute reality? Do these natures constitute states of mind or things?

The beginning of an answer to this question may be sought in the following quotation. In answer to the question, "what would be lacking if there were no true nature?" the reply is given, "If there were no true nature, then all the various kinds of pure realms (*jing*[2]) would not be attained (*de cheng*)." (795b). In other words, it is the true nature that makes realization possible. There are three main elements in this sentence: the true nature, the pure realms, and the attaining. Ordinarily, one might assume that the nature in question is constitutive of personhood or subjectivity inasmuch as we know it is fundamentally linked with Buddha nature. If this were assumed, then we would tend to think that the "realms" were something like subjective states of being, attainable only because of the potential represented by the true nature. However, the term used for "realms," *jing*^{2}, ordinarily means the objective realm, one's environment, the objects of one's senses and cognition, precisely in contrast to the subjective realm, which is rendered with the term *zhi*. Therefore, the simple attribution of subjective qualities to the true nature becomes somewhat problematic. Is this true nature then, some kind of quality in the world, objective to persons, that one may or may not discover? The terms for "attaining" also contribute to one's indecision, as they literally mean "obtain" plus "complete, fulfill." Thus we have two possible interpretations for this sentence: (1) If there were no (subjective) true nature, one would never experience certain states of purity; or (2) if there were no (objective) true nature, the "pure" quality of the world would not exist. In fact, both meanings are intended simultaneously.

This passage is an excellent example of the perspective of Mahāyāna Buddhist thought insofar as neither objective reality nor purely subjective states are being referred to as such. Rather, the subject of the sentence cuts across this distinction. It concerns lived reality, or experience, with experience understood as "experience of" something, as immediately and simultaneously subjective-objective: Our experience is subjective in the sense that an element of awareness is present, and it is objective in the sense that there is a "content" in that awareness, we are aware "of something." In this passage, the author is indicating a certain quality that life may have. Life is able to have this quality *both* because the world (objective reality) is the way it is (Thus) *and* because we are the way we are. If either of these qualities were missing, life would not have this quality. Although this may sound to the reader like a complex way of talking about the same subjective states that were earlier rejected, closer examination shows this not to be the case, for this would be to render the sentence according to (1) and to ignore (2). Such a reading would do justice neither to the inescapably objective quality of *jing*[2] nor to the importance of the Thusness of all phenomena or things. Therefore, what the passage is intended to express is the immediately given, lived reality that includes both objective and subjective elements. The author's perspective is one in which the two are immediately and inseparably present.

In short, all three natures indicate ways in which (1) reality presents itself to persons, and (2) persons experience reality. The two elements are inherent in each nature; each has both subjective and objective qualities. The discriminating nature, then, indicates both a deluded person and a fragmented reality, with delusion defined as the experiential reality based on language. The relative nature indicates a person with partial understanding of the way things are and a reality in which all things are interdependent and relative. The true nature indicates both the way things are (Thus) and the undeluded beholding of the way things are. The author of the *BNT,* I submit, describes each of these natures as something "primitive," in the sense that each is given to human experience as a whole, as a unit, and only with reflection upon our experience do we realize that what is given as a primitive whole may be described with terms of subjectivity and objectivity.[13] The union of the two in experience is prior to the separation of the two in analysis. The three natures represent both a person's nature and reality's nature, as an inseparable, primitive unity, in the sense that they are bound together in what is phenomenologically given. Our world is the way it is because of the way we are; we are the way we are because of the way our world is. The two arise together and are mutually creative. However, it is stressed that this interplay may be broken by transforming oneself and the way one perceives the world, something over which one has total control and for which one's responsibility also is total. Thus, by changing the way one thinks-perceives-experiences, one simultaneously transforms not only the way one is (one's "being," in an active sense), but the way the world is as well (the way it presents itself to one). There is no sense that the world is "out there," objective to and separate from me. I create it, and it conditions me: The interplay creates a complex mesh that is not to be broken.

This being said, one still would like further clarification of the ontological status of each of these three natures. The author provides us with such a clarification when he discusses the three natures in terms of the relative "reality" (*shi*[1]) of each nature.

> Each of the three natures is real (*shi*[1]) in some sense. How so?
> 1. The essence of the discriminating nature has eternally been nonexistent (*wu suo you*) and yet it is not the case that it [totally] lacks reality. Why? The names and words [that constitute this nature] stand.
> 2. The essence of the relative nature exists and yet is not real. It exists (*you*) on the basis of deluded consciousness, its organ, and its field, but insofar as it is not Thusness, it is not real (*shi*[1]). Why? Because the idea of conditioned origination stands, in comparison to the discriminating nature it is called existent. But in comparison to the true nature it does not "really" exist (*fei shi you*). This is called existing but not being truly real (*you bu zhen shi*).
> 3. The essence of the true nature is the essence of Thusness (*ru-ru*), in which being and nonbeing are real (*zhen*) because neither being nor nonbeing is the case (*fei you fei wu*). (794c)

Each of the three natures participates in reality to some extent. Given the above analysis of the subjective-objective character that they possess, this perspective was inevitable: All are experiential reality, however delusory. Thus the discriminating nature possesses some degree of reality to the extent that the words which constitute it stand (literally, "are not upside down") as names and words. That is to say, though this experiential reality is fundamentally out of touch with reality as it is (Thus), still one can create a false experiential reality on the basis of verbal cognition-experience. Because a person actually lives and experiences that way, we must admit that it possesses reality to that extent.

In the case of the relative nature, deluded consciousness and conditioned origination are what stand; that is, are experiential reality. This reality is a purely relative reality: more real than the discriminating nature, less than the true nature. This relative reality applies in both an ontological and an epistemological sense: It is relatively more true to see reality in terms of the processes of conditioned origination than in the terms of entitatively oriented verbal cognition—reality is more like that and therefore one's experience is more real. However, this is still delusion and unreality when compared with the true nature.

Another perspective on the relative nature is offered elsewhere in the text: "The relative nature is of two kinds: pure and impure. The impure relative nature comes into being on the basis of discrimination. The pure relative nature comes into being on the basis of Thusness" (794c). We have here a rather different perspective from that just discussed. The first analysis establishes a progression: The relative nature is relatively more real than the discriminating nature and relatively less real than the true nature. According to the present analysis, however, the relative nature, or conditioned origination, actually is the only reality. Insofar as one experiences it in the mode of discrimination, the discriminating nature is operative; insofar as one experiences Thusness, the true nature is operative. In other words, the relative nature, which is the only possible given, is purified by Thusness and sullied by discrimination.

These two perspectives seem somewhat irreconcilable. The author's intention, however, may be within the reach of speculation.[14] The first analysis clearly shows the author's interest to establish the true nature as supreme, to portray the enlightenment it represents as superior to the other two natures. The second analysis returns us to a basic Mahāyāna tenet: There is only one world, the world of interdependent phenomena, which can be experienced in an entirely delusory, partially delusory, or enlightened fashion. The ordinary world is not to be left behind; there is no superior, hidden world of purity to be attained. If the author's concern is to maintain both of these positions, then this awkward double analysis of the relative nature becomes comprehensible. Such reconciliation as there is in the text for these two analyses is found in the statement that the pure aspect of the relative nature is equivalent to Thusness, or the true nature. In this way the relative nature may remain the only reality, whereas in its pure aspect (as supreme Thusness) it in effect transcends itself in its impure aspect.

Finally, the true nature is the "Thusness in which being and nonbeing are real," due to the very fact that "neither being nor nonbeing is the case." The dualistic categories of being and nonbeing both are negated as a preliminary step, but in the end they are reaffirmed via the Thusness intrinsic to them both. That is, being and nonbeing are emptied of any intrinsic reality. What one can see when those categories are out of the way is the Thusness of what is or, in other words, the Thusness of the reality flux. In this way, the discussion of the true nature itself points back to the fundamental reality of the relative nature: Thusness is not transcendent of being and nonbeing, it is their true nature.

How does all of this apply to the concept of Buddha nature? It is important to remember that all three natures are constitutive of the Buddha nature; this is easier to see insofar as there ultimately is one nature, the relative, in pure (the true nature) and impure (the discriminating nature) aspects. The very slight reality accorded the discriminating nature reinforces the signal emphasis given to the omnipresence of Buddha nature. In fine, though, the pure relative nature = true nature gives us our clearest image of the Buddha nature as manifest in a nondistorted fashion. The true nature, like Buddha nature, is fully real yet uncharacterizable by either existence or nonexistence. Its reality is known by its functions: purification of the first nature, liberation, and the cultivation of all virtues. Finally, its nature is equated with Thusness: the realty of things as they are and knowledge of that reality.

Tathāgatagarbha

The final constituent of the essentials of Buddha nature is the *tathāgatagarbha.* Because the latter is itself a close synonym of Buddha nature, this is a crucial component for our understanding of the Buddha nature. For this reason, the entire text on the subject will be presented, interspersed with interpretation. The text reads:

> There are three aspects of *tathāgatagarbha* which should be known: the contained (*suo she zang*), hiddenness, and the container (*neng she zang*).
>
> 1. *Garbha* as that which is contained. The Buddha calls this the Thusness that dwells in itself (*zhu zi xing ru-ru*). All sentient beings are (*shi*[2]) the *tathāgatagarbha* (*ru-lai-zang*). There are two meanings of *Thus* [*ru* in *ru-lai-zang*]. The first is the knowledge of Thusness (*ru-ru-zhi*) and the second is the realm of Thusness (*ru-ru-jing*). Since the two stand together, we speak of the Thusness of Thusness (*ru-ru*). *Come* [*lai* in *ru-lai-zang*] means coming from itself, in coming to arrive, and in arriving to attain. This is what is called *Thus Come,* Tathāgata (*ru-lai*). Hence, although the Tathāgata nature (*ru-lai xing*) is a causal name, it should [also] be a name of fruition. (795c)

Tathāgatagarbha has three aspects, which can be examined one at a time. We begin with the assertion that the term *storehouse* (*zang* in *ru-lai-zang*) can be interpreted as meaning "the contained"; that is, that which is contained within the storehouse. This, in turn, is specified as the "Thusness which dwells in itself." This echoes the passage in the section on Buddha nature as the three causes in which the fundamental cause of attaining Buddhahood is given as Thusness. As in that passage, where Buddha nature as Thusness embraces all sentient beings, here also, as the next line of the text tells us, all sentient beings are the *tathāgatagarbha.* In other words, the essential nature of every person is Thusness and as such all constitute the *tathāgatagarbha.*

Thusness, then, is the fundamental basis of the *tathāgatagarbha.* The author expands on the meaning of this Thusness by identifying it as the sum of two elements: the knowledge of Thusness and the realm of Thusness. The term translated here as "knowledge" (*zhi*) is, as mentioned earlier, a standard term for the subjective, whereas "realm" (*jing*^{2}) is a standard term for the objective. Ordinarily the *zhi* is the cognizer and the *jing*^{2} the cognized. In the case of the knowledge of Thusness (*ru-ru-zhi*) and the realm of Thusness (*ru-ru-jing*), the former is the knowing that accords with the principle of Thusness, and the latter is the known that accords with that principle. Because, the author says, the two "stand together," the term *Thusness* as *ru-ru* is coined to embrace them simultaneously. As such it represents the unity of their mutuality. All of this—the *ru-ru* Thusness with both its subjective and objective constituents—is given in explanation of the single "Thus" of *tathāgatagarbha* (the *ru* of *ru-lai-zang*).

The discussion of *Come* (*lai* in *ru-lai-zang*) brings up the issue of the extent to which *tathāgatagarbha* (and Buddha nature) should be understood as the cause of Buddhahood or as the fruit, Buddhahood itself. The author picks up the thread of standard *tathāgatagarbha* thought, where it often is said (following Sanskrit etymology) that the *garbha* of *tathāgatagarbha* can mean, on the one hand, seed or embryo (i.e., cause of attaining Buddhahood) or, on the other hand, womb or matrix (containing the various Buddha virtues; i.e., fruit or effect). The author believes the term *Tathāgata nature* (or Buddha nature) generally is taken to connote causation and now aims to show that the term equally connotes fruition. He does this by means of an analysis of the word *come.*

The author represents *come* as meaning coming from itself (which the context indicates means from Thusness) and simultaneously arriving and attaining the fruit of liberation. He argues that coming already entails arriving (because one has not come anywhere unless one has arrived somewhere) and arriving already entails attaining (because when one arrives at a place one has attained that new situation). Thus where there is coming there is attaining—where there is cause there is effect. *Tathāgatagarbha,* therefore, is simultaneously the cause and the fruition of Buddhahood. This justifies the earlier statement that all sentient beings, including the unenlightened, are *tathāgatagarbha.*

> What one attains is essentially not two, it is only differentiated according to purity and impurity. In the causal stage, because one abandons the two kinds of emptiness, one gives rise to ignorance. Because it is mingled with the *kleśa,* it [the *tathāgatagarbha*] is called *polluted.* Although it is not immediately manifest, it certainly is due to become manifest, and therefore it is called *attainable.* At the fruition stage, by uniting with the two kinds of emptiness, there is no further delusion, the *kleśa* no longer pollute, and one calls it *pure.* When the fruit is manifest, we call it *attained.*
>
> We can compare it to the nature of water. Water, in its essence, is neither pure nor impure. We only use the words pure and impure in the presence or absence of dirt. When mud and sediment are stirred up the water is not clear. Although it is not clear, the water's pure nature has not been lost. When, by some means, it is settled, then purity is attained. Therefore know that the words *pure* and *impure* refer only to the presence or absence of dirt. It has nothing to do with the nature of the water itself being pure or dirty. One should understand this.
>
> The two kinds of Buddha nature are also like this. Both are the same Thusness. There is no difference in their essence. It is just that when one abandons the principle of emptiness, one arouses doubt and attachment. Because of impurity and confusion due to the *kleśa,* it [Buddha nature] is called *polluted.* When one does not abandon the two kinds of emptiness and the single mark of Thusness, then one does not give rise to ignorance and the *kleśa* do not pollute; therefore one provisionally designates it as *pure.* (795c–796a)

The Buddha nature is always nondual and unchanging: The causal and the fruition stages are not different in any essential aspect. One gains nothing new at the fruition stage; one simply stops alienating oneself from one's true nature. Buddha nature in purity (attainment) does not differ from Buddha nature in impurity (delusion).

> As for the term *garbha* (*zang*), all sentient beings universally exist within the Tathāgata's wisdom (*zai ru-lai zhi nei*) and therefore it is called

> the womb (*zang*). Because the knowledge of Thusness (*ru-ru zhi*) corresponds to the realm of Thusness (*ru-ru jing*[2]), there is certainly no sentient being who is excluded (*chu*[1]). The realm of Thusness is also encompassed (*suo she chi*) by the Tathāgata, and therefore it is called the *contained* [i.e., "embryo," *suo zang*]. Sentient beings are (*wei*) the *tathāgatagarbha.*
>
> Furthermore, *garbha* has three meanings. The first shows the incomparability of the true realm (*zheng jing*), because apart from this ream of Thusness (*ru-ru jing*) there is no other realm that surpasses it. The second shows the incomparability of the true practice (*zheng xing*), because there is no other superior wisdom that may surpass this wisdom (*zhi*). The third makes manifest the incomparability of the true fruit [of practice], because there is no fruit that surpasses this one. This is why we speak of incomparability. Because this fruit encompasses (*neng she zang*) all sentient beings, we say that sentient beings are (*wei*) the *tathāgatagarbha.* (796a)[15]

Beginning with the second paragraph, we find a list of three categories that the storehouse encompasses: the realm of Thusness, Buddhist practice, and the fruit of practice or attainment of Buddhahood. We should note that this list seems to indicate that the items encompassed by the storehouse constitute the so-called storehouse itself. After all, how could any kind of entity hold or contain the realm of Thusness? Therefore, the storehouse is not a kind of shell within which various items accumulate. The storehouse is no kind of entity at all; it is simply the sum total of all those things that it encompasses. The very title of this first section on *tathāgatagarbha* glosses the term *storehouse* with the phrase "that which is contained," proffering the latter as an alternative name for one aspect of the former.

Thus the storehouse, in effect the *tathāgatagarbha* itself, is constituted by these three categories. First is the realm of Thusness, or all of reality truly experienced. Note once again the rejection of a subject-object split here. The *tathāgatagarbha* (and Buddha nature) cannot be purely a principle of subjectivity; it cannot be any kind of self cut off from the world, because one of its components embraces the world—or the realm of Thusness—itself. The second component is Buddhist practice, which is equated with wisdom. Note here that because wisdom is employed as interchangeable with Buddhist practice, it cannot be interpreted as representing any kind of static or substantial basis of subjectivity (such as a pure mind or self). The term *wisdom* is used to represent the kind of subjectivity in action cultivated in Buddhism. In other words, practice is a kind of doing, and wisdom is a particular practice—acting or doing wisely. Finally, the third item constitutive of the storehouse's "store" is the fruit of practice; namely, realization of the Buddha nature together with its virtues. This fruit encompasses all sentient beings; all sentient beings are the *tathāgatagarbha* in the sense that they are all beings whose true nature is Buddhahood.

The first paragraph of the preceding passage emphasizes very heavily the "storehouse" meaning, to the extent of playing on the spatial metaphor by saying that all sentient beings are "within" (*nei*) the Tathāgata's wisdom. However, the very fact that the storehouse is identified with the Buddha's wisdom indicates that the spatial sense is no more than metaphor. Sentient beings are encompassed by the Tathāgata's wisdom in the sense that all possess the *tathāgatagarbha*. Because the knowledge of Thusness and the realm of Thusness correspond to each other, and the realm of Thusness also is encompassed by the Tathāgata, it is not possible that any sentient being not be a part of this universal encompassment. In the two senses that sentient beings are encompassed within the Tathāgata's wisdom and that they are encompassed within the realm of Thusness (recall that Thusness is the essence of the *tathāgatagarbha*) sentient beings *are* the *tathāgatagarbha*. Again, note that sentient beings are said to be that which is contained within the storehouse as well as the storehouse itself. Clearly, the storehouse is its contents.

> 2. Hiddenness. The Tathāgata itself is hidden and unmanifest; that is why it is called a *garbha* [i.e., embryo]. The term *Thus Come* (Tathāgata, *ru-lai*) has two meanings. The first represents the idea that Thusness [itself] is not inverted—that is, we call false thoughts inverted; when there are no false thoughts, we speak of Thusness. The second represents the idea of eternal dwelling. This Thusness nature comes from the [Buddha] nature that dwells in itself. Having come it arrives, and having arrived it attains. The essence of Thusness never changes; in this sense it is eternal. When the Tathāgata nature dwells in the stage before Buddhist practice is begun, it is concealed by *kleśa*. Because sentient beings cannot see it, it is called the *garbha*. (796a)

This passage is relatively straightforward. The basic point is that the storehouse is hidden in the sense that sentient beings who have not yet realized it have no direct, personal knowledge of it. For them it is concealed by the *kleśa* or defilments (delusion, anger, greed, and so on) symptomatic of human ignorance. This is standard *tathāgatagarbha* doctrine. This passage also repeats the theme discussed earlier; namely, that the Thusness nature, or Buddha nature, is the same in the causal and fruition stages. This is concealed from the ignorant by false thoughts and *kleśa*, but the Buddha nature itself is untouched by this condition and dwells in the fullness of its maturity, even in the person who has not yet begun to practice Buddhism.

> 3. The reason for speaking of the *garbha* as container (*neng she*) is that all the countless merits of the fruition stage, when dwelling in the time of the "attainability" stage [the causal stage], are completely enclosed. If we spoke of attaining the nature only when arriving at the time of fruition, that [Tathāgata] nature would be noneternal. Why? It is because there is no beginning of the attainment that we know that [the Tathāgata nature] aboriginally exists. That is why we call it eternal. (796a)

The third meaning of *tathāgatagarbha* as "the container" represents the fulfillment of the Tathāgata nature, the realization of Buddhahood with its infinite Buddha virtues. In fact, however, it is misleading to speak of attaining Buddhahood as the Buddha nature exists aboriginally without beginning. Even before the practice of Buddhism is begun, the Buddha nature is full and complete with all its virtues.

Let us now summarize the most important points concerning the *tathāgatagarbha*. First and foremost, the *tathāgatagarbha* is Thusness. This was expressed in many ways: The first syllable of the word *tathāgatagarbha* (*ru-lai-zang*) was identified with Thusness (*ru-ru*); the first aspect of *tathāgatagarbha,* the contained, was directly identified with Thusness as both the knowledge of Thusness and the realm of Thusness; and the *tathāgatagarbha* was equated with a Buddha nature that, whether polluted or pure, is ever the same Thusness. Clearly, this identification of the *tathāgatagarbha* with Thusness is a central point; what is its significance?

The identification of *tathāgatagarbha* and Thusness means that the *tathāgatagarbha* cannot be a principle of selfhood in a self that is absolutely distinct from the world. We will discuss the concept of Thusness further in Chapter Five, but it is clear even now that Thusness, as the knowledge of Thusness and the realm of Thusness, encompasses both self and world (or better, compels us to revise our notions of self and world by asserting their mutuality and inseparability). The identification of *tathāgatagarbha* and Thusness also means that the essential nature of the *tathāgatagarbha* entails a state of experiential reality in which the world, in effect, manifests itself as it is and is seen as it is. Thusness and *tathāgatagarbha,* then, are principles both of enlightenment and of absolute reality.

A second theme is a list of three components of the *tathāgatagarbha:* Thusness, the practice of Buddhism, and the fruit of practice; that is, realization or liberation. This is highly reminiscent of the list of three cause of Buddha nature we looked at earlier; namely, the cause of attainability (which is Thusness), the *prayoga* cause (or practice), and the complete fulfillment cause (or attainment of the fruit). In both cases we see a very simple model. The essential nature of Buddha nature or *tathāgatagarbha* is Thusness. This is the ground of the possibility of our (successfully) practicing Buddhism. The ultimate outcome of Buddhist practice, of course, is realization of the goal of Buddhism, or the fruit of practice. Buddha nature and *tathāgatagarbha,* then, as Thusness are reality and the correct apprehension of reality. As portrayed in this tripartite scheme, they are the foundation of the possibility of practice, the doing of the practice itself, and the ultimate guarantee of its successful fulfillment.

A third theme of the *tathāgatagarbha* material is the author's emphasis upon the essential identity of the *tathāgatagarbha* in the stages of cause and fruition. Let us recall a passage quoted earlier:

> The two kinds of Buddha nature are also like this. Both are the same Thusness. There is no difference in their essence. It is just that when one abandons the principle of emptiness, one arouses doubt and attachment. Because of impurity and confusion due to the *kleśa,* it [Buddha nature] is called *polluted.* When one does not abandon the two kinds of emptiness and the single mark of Thusness, then one does not give rise to ignorance and the *kleśa* do not pollute; therefore one provisionally designates it as pure. (796a)

This parallels the discussion of the pure and impure relative nature in the *trisvabhāva* section. There is one basic given—here, Buddha nature (or *tathāgatagarbha*); there, the relative nature. If one abandons the all-important principle of emptiness, one produces delusion and thereby effectively lives in pollution. The essential character of the basic given (Buddha nature, relative nature), however, is untouched; it remains essentially pure and unchanged. This talk of purity, though, is ultimately unacceptable. Purity is a relative term and as such has no relation to the unchanging Thusness of Buddha nature.

The final important theme enunciated in this section is the assertion that all sentient beings "are" the *tathāgatagarbha.* Three times in this part of the text we are told that sentient beings "are" the *tathāgatagarbha;* not once are we told that they "possess" it. This is to be understood in the sense that sentient beings are identified with Thusness and as such are capable of being identified with the *tathāgatagarbha,* the storehouse or totality, in effect, of Thusness (as both wisdom and realm, subject and world).

Let us conclude this chapter with a list of five meanings ascribed the Buddha nature in the *BNT,* which may summarize some of the main points of our discussion. Three of the meanings given here are just stated without comment, but the last two are accompanied by the interpretation of the unidentified commentator of the *BNT.*

1. It really exists (*zhen shi you*).
2. It can be perceived by *upāya.*
3. Having been perceived, its merits are inexhaustible.
4. It is [concealed by] the beginningless shell with which it is [both] disunited and united. The commentator says, *beginningless* means that defilements, karma and retribution are all without a start and therefore we say they are *beginningless.* As for *disunited,* because these three are in opposition to the *dharmakāya,* we say they are *disunited.* We say they are *united* because these three arise in dependence on the *dharmakāya.* As for *shell,* these three conceal (*neng zang*) the *dharmakāya* and therefore are called *shell.*
5. The beginningless, excellent nature with which it is associated is its Dharma. The commentator says, it is called *beginningless* because the naturally attained *prajñā,* great compassion, meditation and *dharmakāya* all aboriginally exist. The essence and the functions have never been separate and therefore we say they are associated. As for "the excellent nature with which it is associated is its Dharma," [it is explained thus]. By virtue of *prajñā,* the own-nature of the *dharmakāya* does not change; by virtue of meditation, the nature possesses awesome merits; and by virtue of great compassion, the nature benefits [others]. Therefore we say this excellent nature is its Dharma. (811b–c)

These five meanings more or less summarize the author's view of

Buddha nature. First, he begins with the straightforward statement: The Buddha nature really, truly exists. Here he does not choose to say "it both exists and does not exist," or "it neither exists nor does not exist." It really, truly exists. This, of course, is still in contrast to the status of ordinary phenomena that partake of the unreality of delusion and defilement. Yet to say plainly that the Buddha nature really exists is a good example of the use of language in this text. The attempt to speak positively, if not rapturously, of that which fulfillment of the Buddhist path reveals is certainly characteristic of *tathāgatagarbha* and Buddha nature thought and is one of the main elements of distinction between it and *śūnyavāda* thought. Thus, the Buddha nature really exists: It may function as a constant support for the often wearisome reality of daily Buddhist practice; it offers hope and the assurance that the effort of practice is not being made for "nothing." It attests to the reality of Buddhism's soteriological promise.

Second, Buddha nature can be perceived by *upāya. Upāya* is Buddhist practice. This statement affirms that practice is not the mere elimination of ignorance, but yields positive results.

Third, having been perceived, the merits of the Buddha nature are inexhaustible. This statement, like the first two, is a positive declaration of the intrinsic value of the "Buddha fruit," the fulfillment of Buddhism's soteriological promise.

Fourth, Buddha nature is concealed by the beginningless shell with which it is both disunited and united. This meaning demonstrates why practice is needed if we already possess the Buddha nature. Thus like the preceding statements, it too justifies Buddhist practice.

Finally, the beginningless, excellent nature with which it is associated is its Dharma. Here we find once again very positive language used in discussing the Buddha nature. The "essence" referred to is the *dharmakāya* or Buddha nature. The "functions" are *prajñā,* great compassion and meditation. In saying that these two categories are inseparable or associated, the author intends to convey that they are interchangeable.[16] Thus the "essence" of Buddha nature is its functions; that is, the actions constitutive of great compassion, meditation, and *prajñā* are the "essence" of Buddha nature. Action, then, (or "functions") is the essence of Buddha nature, and the particular character of this action is soteriological: the salvation of oneself and others.

CHAPTER THREE

Soteriology: Buddha Nature as the Practice of Buddhism

Like emptiness, the Buddha nature concept is deeply soteriological; in other words, it fundamentally has to do with the ultimate transformation of the Buddhist practitioner.[1] Buddha nature in its causal aspect is that by which one attains such transformation. In this mode, as we have seen, it is essentially unconditioned Thusness as the foundation of our future Buddhahood, but it also embraces the conditioned action of *bodhicitta* and *prayoga.* In addition to its causal role, Buddha nature is simultaneously the already present fulfillment of the transformed state; this is Buddha nature in its fruition aspect. In its ultimate form it is the *dharmakāya,* perfect wisdom, *nirvāṇa.*

Proximately, then, Buddha nature is the conjunction of means and end: Buddhist practice in all its forms and stages. In Buddhist practice we have the means by which Buddha nature attains self-realization and, simultaneously, the manifestation of the Buddha nature itself in its purity. As the author of the *BNT* sees it, the goal of Buddhism is to realize radical self-transformation; Buddha nature is both the means of this transformation and the manifestation of the transformed state.

A. *Āśrayaparāvṛtti*

The term *āśrayaparāvṛtti* (*zhuan-yi*), literally "transformation of the basis," is a Yogācāra term. In that context, its meaning is explained as follows. *Transformation* (*zhuan,* also "turning," "revolution") has two meanings: "transforming" in the sense of getting rid of something, and "transformation" in the sense of attaining something. *Basis* (*yi*) refers to the eighth consciousness in Yogācāra theory, the *ālayavijñāna.* The latter is the "storehouse" consciousness that stores the karmic seeds produced by past actions, which in turn determine the future dispositions of individuals. In the "transformation" of the *ālayavijñāna,* the seeds of defilements (*kleśa*) and discriminatory knowledge are discarded, whereas the two "fruits" of *bodhi* (wisdom) and *nirvāṇa* are attained. Thus for the Yogācārin, the storehouse, or *ālayavijñāna* itself is what is transformed, or in some understandings, destroyed.

The meaning of *āśrayaparāvṛtti* in the present text is rather different. The author of the *BNT* introduces the *āśrayaparāvṛtti* into his discussion by describing it as the supreme purity revealed when all limitations on the understanding have been removed; it is the "purity of the original nature" (*ben xing*); that is, the Buddha nature. (801b) Thus what is undergoing transformation in the understanding of the *BNT*'s author is not the *ālayavijñāna* but a person's relationship to the Buddha nature. The author builds on this beginning to produce a complex account of the *āśrayaparāvṛtti* notion within the context of Buddha nature thought. We begin with a discussion of four characteristics of *āśrayaparāvṛtti.*

1. The productive basis (*sheng yi*) is the continuing basis of the Buddha's nondiscriminatory Path. If there were no such condition [as *āśrayaparāvṛtti*], the nondiscriminatory Path would not be produced. Because there is reliance on this condition, we name this aspect the basis that produces the Path (*Dao sheng yi*).

2. The destructive basis (*mie yi*) is the utter extinction and nonbirth of all delusions and habits due to their lack of basis [in reality]. Except by relying upon the *āśrayaparāvṛtti*'s utter destruction of delusion, there would be no difference in the extinction of delusion by *śrāvakas, pratyekabuddhas,* and Buddhas. But because they are not the same, we know this [*āśrayaparāvṛtti*] is the basis of the utter extinction of delusion.

3. The fruit of well-matured contemplation. Well and correctly penetrating [Thusness], showing reverence over a long period of time, and uninterruptedly and completely cultivating the Thusness that one knows, these are the fruits of *āśrayaparāvṛtti*. If one is on the Path, *āśrayaparāvṛtti* is the cause. If one has completed the Path, it is called fruit. If the *āśrayaparāvṛtti* were not this fruit of well-matured contemplation, all Buddhas, of their very nature, would have to repeatedly mature their contemplation, repeatedly destroy [the *kleśa*], and repeatedly purify [themselves]. Because this is not so, we know that the *āśrayaparāvṛtti* is the fruit of well-matured contemplation.

4. The *dharmadhātu*'s mark of purity. Because all false thoughts are utterly extinguished in it, this *dharmadhātu* surpasses that which can be expressed in reasoning or in speech. Therefore, we take purity to be a characteristic of the *dharmadhātu*. This is the extinction of the activities of the mind and the cutting off of the way of speech. It is ineffable, because it is the attainment of the unattainable principle of Thusness (*zhen-ru li*). (801b)

The first characteristic illustrates that *āśrayaparāvṛtti* is the basis on which the Buddha Way is founded. Without the *āśrayaparāvṛtti* there would be no Buddhist Path, no practice of Buddhism. It is the condition by which the Path comes into being. The second characteristic draws on the standard *tathāgatagarbha* teaching that all defilements, such as ignorance, are basically unreal, having no basis in reality. In other words, they are simply an absence of truth or reality, rather than the real presence of defilement and as such they are utterly extinct and unborn. The *āśrayaparāvṛtti* is credited with being the basis for this extinct, unborn status of defilement. Delusion has no real status in the "purity of the original nature" (Buddha nature) that the *āśrayaparāvṛtti* is.

Rather cryptically, the author posits this pure *āśrayaparāvṛtti* in which delusion is unborn as the reason for the difference between the paths of *śrāvaka, pratyekabuddha,* and Buddha. Based on the exposition in other parts of the text, his reasoning seems to be that the *śrāvaka* and *pratyekabuddha* think of themselves as having actually destroyed defilements, whereas a Buddha realizes that defilements are unborn and moreover has fully realized the positive nature of the *āśrayaparāvṛtti;* namely, the *dharmakāya.*

In the third characteristic, *āśrayaparāvṛtti* is portrayed as both cause and fruit of Buddhist practice, but most important as the doing of the practice itself, whether in the earlier or later stages. This characteristic, in naming the acts of showing reverence and cultivating Thusness as fruits, even implies that the ability to practice authentically is itself a fruit, thereby blurring the means-ends, or cause-fruit distinction. This naturally leads to the fourth characteristic, in which *āśrayaparāvṛtti* is identified with the ineffable *dharmadhātu* and with Thusness.

In short, *āśrayaparāvṛtti* represents Buddhist practice. As the productive basis it is the basis of the Buddhist Path, a synonym for Buddhist practice. The term *basis,* (*āśraya*) then, does not refer here to a substantive basis, but the basis or foundation of a particular form of action, Buddhist practice. *Āśrayaparāvṛtti* as the destructive basis accounts for the negative aspect of Buddhist practice, the extinction of defilement. In accordance with *tathāgatagarbha* thought, the extinction of defilements is constituted by the realization of their ultimate unreality. The third characteristic, the fruit of well-matured contemplation, represents the positive aspect of Buddhist practice: practice as the *realization* of Buddhist truths. Thus this characteristic, which represents the heart of Buddhist practice as such in all of its stages, emphasizes the Path of Buddhism and Buddhist practice as inherently positive: One attains the maturity of contemplation, reverence, and knowledge. Finally, the *āśrayaparāvṛtti* represents the culmination of Buddhist practice, the realization of Thusness, in a condition of freedom from turbulence and verbalization.

In this way, the four characteristics represent *āśrayaparāvṛtti* as Buddhist practice from its beginnings to its mature fruition. As such, it is consistently portrayed as being of an active character. Any idea that the "transformation of the basis" refers in some literal sense to the transformation of a substantive thing must be rejected for this text in the light of its direct identification of *āśrayaparāvṛtti* with the doing of Buddhist practice.

In a short passage that strongly supports this interpretation, the author goes on to ascribe two general meanings to *āśrayaparāvṛtti:* It stands for separation from desire and the cause of separation from desire. Separation from desire is identified with the Third Noble Truth, Cessation (of suffering, i.e., *nirvāṇa*), and the cause of separation from desire is identified with the Fourth Noble Truth, Path (801b). Again *āśrayaparāvṛtti* is identified with the Buddhist Path and the attainments made by treading that Path.

This theme is further emphasized in a discussion of seven "names" given the *āśrayaparāvṛtti dharmakāya. Dharmakāya* is a term used in this text to represent the Buddha nature in its stage of fruition. In examining the seven "names" discussed in this passage, we will see once again that the *āśrayaparāvṛtti dharmakāya* is a term expressive of Buddhist practice, understood in this case as the transformation inherent in realizing one's Buddha nature.

(1) The first name is *perishing* (*chen mo*); that is, the perishing of the *skandha*-attachment-*skandha* cycle. The five *skandha* give rise to the four attachments[2] and these in turn give rise to new *skandha,* or in other words, rebirth. This is a cycle that can continue indefinitely. However, "Within the *dharmakāya,* neither cause nor fruit exists; therefore we speak of 'perishing' (*chen mo*). Attachments are opposed and cured and therefore are defunct (*chen*). As for the *skandha,* the fruit of retribution is exhausted and so we say they 'are gone' (*mo*[1])" (802c).

(2) The second name is *stillness* (*ji jing*); that is, the stillness of all actions.

> All *saṃskṛta dharma* [conditioned things] are called *actions* (*xing*[2]), because they are conjoined with the four states. These four are birth, change, abiding, and destruction. All *saṃskṛtà dharma,* in relation to the past are conjoined with birth, in relation to the future are conjoined with destruction, and in relation to the present are conjoined with change and abiding. They are called *actions* because they never rest from activity. The Tathāgata's *dharmakāya,* though, is not like this. In the past it was not born, in the future it will not be destroyed. In the present there is no illness and old age. It eternally and tranquilly abides. Unborn, it is called *still* (*ji*[1]); undestroyed, it is called *quiet* (*jing*[1]). (802c)

(3) The third name is *discarding* (*qi she*); that is, discarding remnants. The *śrāvaka* and *pratyekabuddha* have several remnants attached to them, specifically *kleśa* and karma. The Tathāgata's *āśrayaparāvṛtti dharmakāya* has already "crossed over" *saṃsāra* (i.e., discarded karma) and utterly extinguished all *kleśa* and delusion. All paths of spiritual cultivation have been tread. Thus with *saṃsāra* cast aside (*qi*) and putting aside (*she*) the Path (in the sense

of a raft being put aside once one has crossed the stream and its usefulness is past), "the *dharmakāya* alone abides in the fulfillment of the four perfections" (of bliss, self, purity and eternity) (802c–803a).

(4) The fourth name is *transcending* (*guo du*); that is, transcending the two kinds of suffering. Because in the *dharmakāya* there is none of the gross suffering of the *śrāvaka* and *pratyekabuddha,* we use the term *surpassing* (*guo*). Because there is none of the subtle suffering of the *bodhisattva* (i.e., four kinds of rebirth), we use the term *crossing over* (*du*). Thus the *dharmakāya* goes beyond these two kinds of suffering. (803a)

(5) The fifth name is *elimination* (*ba chu*); that is, the elimination of the *ālayavijñāna.*

> The meaning of *ālaya* is [found in the combination of the concepts] "basis" and "hidden." It is the source (*ben*) of *saṃsāra* because it produces the four kinds of taint (mo^2). The four taints are two kinds of *kleśa,* karma, and retribution. The first of the two kinds of *kleśa* is all views. Its origin is in ignorance, and the signless liberation gate is its cure. The second is all *kleśa* other than views. It is originated from desire and cured by the wishless liberation gate. The source of karma is the nature of the ordinary person (*fan fu xing*) because the nature of the ordinary person is [holding] the self view (*shen jian*). The source of retribution is one: All of *saṃsāra* is retribution. It [*saṃsāra*] relies on the *ālayavijñāna* for its source; because it is not separated from this *vijñāna,* retribution is not terminated.
>
> In the *dharmakāya* [however] the two time periods are extinguished by means of two paths, and therefore we speak of "elimination." The two paths are: (1) Nondiscriminating wisdom—this does away with present delusions and purifies the *dharmakāya;* it is called the knowledge of extinction [of one's defilements]. (2) Subsequent nondiscriminating wisdom—this prevents any future delusions from ever arising and fulfills the *dharmakāya;* it is the knowledge that [defilements] shall never arise again. "Plucking out" (*ba*) is the purifying, the extinguishing of present delusions. "Removing" (chu^2) is the fulfillment, the severing of future delusion. Hence the name *elimination.* (803a)

(6) The sixth name is *relieving* (*ji*[2]); that is, relieving the five fears. The five fears are (a) guilt, as when a person does something evil and is filled with dread day and night; (b) fear of the blame of others, as when a person has done something wrong and fears that other persons or gods saw it; (c) fear of punishment; (d) fear of being born into an evil birth, on the basis of one's present evilness; (e) fear of the many virtuous ones—because one's own karma is impure and one's discernment is not deep, one fears those who have accumulated virtue. However, "one who has realized the *dharmakāya* is free of the five fears; thus we say the *dharmakāya* is the relieving of the five fears" (803a–b).

(7) The final name is severing (*duan*); that is, severing the retribution of the six destinies or *gati.*[3] "The term *gati* has many meanings; we will briefly speak of two: . . . (1) the place where sentient beings are reborn; (2) the place where karma acts. With these two meanings the term *gati* is established. The Tathāgata's *dharmakāya* does not return to these *gati* . . . therefore we name it *severing* the six *gati.* We speak of the Tathāgata's *dharmakāya* when there is this condition" (803b).

All of these seven names express the negation of various aspects of the life of bondage and suffering. Severed, undone, extinguished, and overcome are (1) the *skandha*-attachment-*skandha* cycle, (2) determination by the condition of time, (3) karma and *kleśa,* (4) suffering, (5) the *ālayavijñāna,* as the source of *saṃsāra,* (6) fear, and (7) rebirth among the six destinies. These acts of severing and extinguishing constitute the *āśrayaparāvṛtti.* Again its active nature is readily apparent. In fact, all but one of the seven "names" is itself a verb. These seven, then, are names for actions that Buddhist practitioners undertake to achieve.

The *dharmakāya,* on the other hand, represents the stage in which these seven categories of suffering and fear are undone or removed. How is the *dharmakāya* described herein? (1) It has no relationship to causation; (2) it has no relationship to time; (3) it is utterly free of rebirth, *kleśa,* or delusion; (4) it is utterly free of all suffering; (5) freedom from delusion is its purification and its fulfillment; (6) it relieves the five fears; and (7) it is cut off from rebirth. Although all of this is expressed negatively, there are also the statements that (3) the *dharmakāya* alone abides in the fulfillment of the four perfections, and (2) it abides eternally and tranquilly. We shall return later to further discussion of the *dharmakāya*. For now, suffice it to say that the *dharmakāya* does indeed represent the stage of fruition in which the actions undertaken by the *āśrayaparāvṛtti* come to maturity.

What, in the end, is this *āśrayaparāvṛtti*? In the *BNT*, *āśrayaparāvṛtti* is given as manifesting the character of Buddha nature. We have seen that it represents Buddhist practice. Buddhist practice here does not mean any set rituals, meditations, or ethical observances, but rather the process of the self-transformation of the individual progressing from a self-centered, ignorant mode of being-behaving to the selfless, awakened, compassionate mode of a Buddha.

But what, more literally, are we to make of the term *āśrayaparāvṛtti*, "transformation of the basis"? What is this *āśraya* or basis? To answer this question we need to look over the preceding material and ask ourselves what is undergoing transformation. The answer is, the person. Though the *āśraya* concept as used in other texts unarguably is related to the Yogācāra concept of the *ālayavijñāna*, the preceding discussion clearly illustrates that, according to the *BNT*, it is the person who is undergoing transformation. In fact, to transform the *ālayavijñāna* (or "do away" with its negative functions) is only one of seven "names" or functions ascribed the *āśrayaparāvṛtti dharmakāya*. It is but one way of speaking of the process of self-purification and spiritual cultivation represented by the term *āśrayaparāvṛtti dharmakāya*. The seven names are mutually complementary, different forms of language emphasizing various aspects of self-transformation. Thus, to say that *āśrayaparāvṛtti* means the transformation of the *ālayavijñāna* is to choose a traditional form of language, heavily laden with theoretical Buddhist concepts, to speak of the radical spiritual transformation of the person. To speak of the *āśrayaparāvṛtti* as the utter elimination of fear, or the ending of rebirth, likewise accomplishes this end. We are offered a variety of linguistic options to help clarify a process of personal transformation, the effects of which are profound and far-reaching.

In this text, then, *āśrayaparāvṛtti* is best interpreted as (1) the radical transformation of the person, (2) Buddhist practice, and (3) the transformation of the person's relationship to the Buddha nature.

Āśrayaparāvṛtti demonstrates that the affirmation of the Buddha nature is an affirmation of every person's potential to radically transform himself or herself.

B. *Dharmakāya* and *Nirvāṇa*

In the preceding section we said that *dharmakāya* represents the culmination of the process of *āśrayaparāvṛtti* or Buddhist practice; in other words, *dharmakāya* represents the realization of Buddhahood. As such, the affirmation of *dharmakāya* plays the important role of affirming the capability of the self-transformation process to reach a culmination. In what follows, *dharmakāya* and *nirvāṇa* are treated as synonymous terms. Each affirms the reality and the desirability of the Buddhist goal. As such, they represent the terminus of the *āśrayaparāvṛtti* process. As we shall see, however, the *dharmakāya* also stands for "the purity of the original nature" and thus represents the *aboriginal* existence of the Buddha nature. It manifests the eternally true nature of things and is not just the end of a process. As shall become evident, *dharmakāya* and *nirvāṇa* manifest the preeminently positive value associated with the Buddha nature. Thus, they justify the process of self-transformation itself.

First, let us demonstrate that the *dharmakāya* does represent the culmination of Buddhist practice rather than a metaphysical entity. The outstanding characteristic of the *dharmakāya* is said to be "all suffering being at rest." Its "flavor" is constituted by nonbacksliding and serene joy (803b). It is clear from the text that these are qualities that apply to persons, not to any transcendental absolute: "If there is someone who trains in the proper practice and seeks to perceive this truth (*fa*), when he realizes it, he obtains nonbacksliding and serene joy" (803b).

Another approach to the nature of the *dharmakāya* is afforded us by the following challenge to its reality. The objection is raised: "How do you establish these characteristics and meanings concerning the *dharmakāya*? If it is as you say, the *dharmakāya* must be nonexistent (*wu*), since it cannot be apprehended. If a thing is not perceived by the six consciousnesses[4] then surely it is nonexistent, like a rabbit's horns" (803c).

This question erroneously assumes that the *dharmakāya* is a thing that should be empirically perceptible. To defend its reality, the author interprets the question of the "existence" of the *dharmakāya* as a question concerning the possibility of achieving the goal of *nirvāṇa.* This he does by identifying the *dharmakāya* with the "fruit" of *nirvāṇa.* "You say that the *dharmakāya* does not exist because it is not perceived by the six senses. This idea is contrary to the truth. Why? Because one can realize *nirvāṇa* by skillful means. Contemplation, invocation [of the Buddha's name], and correct practice are called skillful means. Because of these skillful means, the *dharmakāya* can be known and can be perceived" (803c). Thus, through proper practices, one can realize *nirvāṇa*— that is, the *dharmakāya*—and thereby know its reality. This is the first reply, and a perfectly pragmatic one: you shall know the *dharmakāya* by its fruit, *nirvāṇa.* "If the *dharmakāya* were nonexistent (*wu*), then all correct practices should be in vain. Taking right views as the foremost practice, and including in addition such good things as morality, concentration and wisdom, the correct practices that one cultivates are not empty (*bu kong*) or fruitless. Because these correct practices do yield fruit, we know that the *dharmakāya* is not nonexistent" (804a). The *dharmakāya* is not nonexistent because it is known in experiential fruit.

This text's approach to *nirvāṇa* is similarly pragmatic. The author begins this section by arguing that *nirvāṇa* is not the end of a process of spiritual cultivation, for then it would be something produced (*suo sheng*). Because it is not caused (*wu yin*) it can be said that it "abides eternally" (805b). This kind of language is typical of texts related to the *tathāgatagarbha* tradition. In this tradition, speaking of eternity is an affirmative language manner of characterizing the unconditioned, which another tradition might prefer to call the unborn. Of more interest to us is the following passage in which the author discusses the practical, functional facets of *nirvāṇa.*

> Because [*nirvāṇa*] abides eternally, surpassing such marks as form, etc., we say it is not form. Because it is not separate from the purity, etc. of the form mark, we say it is not not-form (*fei fei se*). Because it is attained by great meritorious functioning (*da gong yong*)[5] and nondiscriminative wisdom, we say it truly exists (*zhen you*). Because of the Path that is completed by supra-mundane vigor and because it is attained by Buddha, we know it really exists (*shi you*). As the *sūtra* says, "Bhikṣus, this Dharma really exists. It is unborn and does not arise. It is not made and is unconditioned (*wu wei*). Therefore know that *nirvāṇa* really and eternally abides."[6] *This Dharma* is the Tathāgata's *āśrayaparāvṛtti.* That is why it is named the end of *dhāranī;*[7] it is also called yoga. (805c)

The most immediately obvious feature of this passage is its portrayal of *nirvāṇa* (and therefore of *dharmakāya* and *āśrayaparāvṛtti*) in strongly positive terms. Its eternity and reality, moreover, validate the practice of the Buddhist path of which it is the culmination.

The passage begins with a somewhat *śūnyavāda*-like portion, where it is stated that *nirvāṇa* is neither form nor not-form. This, however, is done with an interesting twist. That it is not form is clear enough, but that it is not not-form is due to its identity with purity and the like qualities of form. Such a perspective is characteristic of *tathāgatagarbha* thought with its doctrine of the unreality—that is, the real nonexistence—of all defilements, of anything that might besmirch the purity of what is. Because all impurities, all defilements are unreal, what is—form—is simply Thus, with nothing to mar its Thusness; hence, its unity with *nirvāṇa,* qualitatively as well as ontologically. Note it is not that *nirvāṇa* is emptiness and hence so is ordinary reality. Rather, *nirvāṇa* is purity and hence so is ordinary reality. The affirmative stance of the Buddha nature position is all-embracing.

Throughout the passage, *nirvāṇa* is spoken of in terms of Buddhist practice and the Buddhist Path. Again and again it is emphasized that *nirvāṇa* is real because it is attained, and that it is attained in the practice of the Buddhist Path. At the end of the passage, *nirvāṇa* is directly identified with practice, specifically with yoga, with *āśrayaparāvṛtti* (which, as we saw earlier, is the foundation of the Buddhist Path, the destruction of defilements, the fruit of mature contemplation and the attainment of Thusness) and with *dhāranī* (recollection, meditation, and wisdom). In this context the unnamed *sūtra* asserts that the "unborn" and "unconditioned" *nirvāṇa* really exists. Its eternity, then, its unborn and unconditioned nature, points to its freedom from the conditioned world of samsaric delusion, its identity with nondiscriminatory wisdom and Thusness.

In the end, *āśrayaparāvṛtti, dharmakāya, nirvāṇa* are all terms used to convey various aspects of the dynamics of the Buddha nature. They portray a Buddha nature that, finally, is a metaphor for the validity of the Buddha Way and a justification for Buddhist practice. It functions thus to validate Buddhist practice not by serving as a substantial, metaphysical ground for the mechanics of release nor by glorifying the figure of the Buddha and thus enticing those attracted to practices of worship. Rather, Buddhist practice is validated by attesting to the desirability of the goal (the role of the *dharmakāya-nirvāṇa* part of the Buddha nature concept) and the capability of each person to reach that goal. In all respects, though, the Buddha nature concept revolves around Buddhist practice. The latter is the final raison d'être of the Buddha nature concept. The fundamental message of the Buddha nature concept as expressed in this text is practice, self-transformation, realization.

Several other characteristics of the *dharmakāya* afford us further insight into the soteriological character of this fruition stage of the Buddha nature. First, the *dharmakāya* is characterized as the Middle Path, which is explained as meaning "separation from extremes." Six examples of such negating of extremes are given; we will here examine one.

The section is introduced with the remark, "as there are six sorts of Middle Path, [the *dharmakāya*] removes itself from six pairs of extremes" (809a). In other words, the *dharmakāya* is the Middle Path; that is, the cure for humanity's suffering, the path of self-transforming action. Our example is entitled "the extremes of 'producing' (*you zuo*) and 'not producing' (*wu zuo*)" and is directly concerned with the meaning of practicing the Buddha Way.

> Producing: Someone gets a notion and says, "If I wish to cultivate wisdom (*zhi hui*), I must first produce (*zuo*) a thought, for only then will the matter be completed." Not producing: Someone gets a notion and says, "wisdom is not an activity (*shi*[3]) and not a skill (*neng*). Why? Because discernment (*jie*) and delusion are contradictories; that is, when discernment arises, delusion naturally disappears. It is not the case that discernment actively removes [defilement]. Therefore, I say wisdom is neither an activity nor a skill."
>
> In order to avoid these extremes there is established the parable of the oil lamp. As it says in the *sūtra,*[8] "Kāśyapa, it is like a burning lamp: the lamplight having arisen, darkness is extinguished. And yet although that lamplight did not produce (*zuo*) the thought, 'I am able to extinguish the darkness; the darkness is extinguished because of me,' it is certainly because the light arose that the darkness was extinguished. Therefore, although the lamplight does not produce a thought, it is not true that there is no activity or skill. Wisdom is also thus. It does not produce the thought, 'I am able to extinguish delusion,' and yet it is also true that it is because of wisdom arising that delusion is extinguished. Therefore, know that it is not true that wisdom is neither activity nor skill."

> [Comment] If one says he produces the thought, "I am able to extinguish delusions," this is called *increasing*,[9] and is the extremist [view] of "producing" (*you zuo*). If one says, "when wisdom arises, ignorance self-destructs—and not because of wisdom," this is called *decreasing* and is the extremist [view] of not producing (*wu zuo*). In order to avoid these extremes, we say that the arising of wisdom does not produce thought. As for the production and nonproduction of thought, it is not the case that it [wisdom] produces [thought]; therefore there is no increase. Neither is it the case that it does not produce [change]; therefore there is no decrease. This is called the Middle Path. (809c)

The author's intent in this example appears to be to establish that the *dharmakāya* (or Buddha nature) is active and plays a part in effecting change (in not being *wu zuo*) but that its activity does not take place within the scope of karmic laws of cause and effect (in not being *you zuo*). In negating the latter extreme, the author is indicating that wisdom, though an activity, is nonphenomenal, that is, nonsamsaric, because it is that which cuts through the karmic linkage of cause and effect, rather than being subsumed by it.

Yet it is equally important for the author to establish that wisdom is an activity or functioning (*shi*^{3}), that is, a doing, and that it does have the skill or ability (*neng*) to effect change. It is not fortuitous that wisdom arising, defilements are extinguished; it is definitely because of wisdom's presence that defilements are undone. Yet the author hesitates to speak of this in a directly causal fashion, as causation is the law of *saṃsāra* and karma, whereas wisdom is precisely the breaking of this bondage. To negate the two extremes in question, the author is obliged to walk a fine line. To think in terms of "increasing" or "producing" is to think in karmic or samsaric terms, which do not apply to wisdom, and to think in terms of "not producing" is a "decreasing" or nihilistic kind of thought, inasmuch as the efficacy of the Buddha Way is denied—and this too is inappropriate in the context of understanding the nature of wisdom or the functioning of Buddha nature. The effective and active functioning of the Buddha Way within, though not subject to, *saṃsāra* is the Middle Path that the author describes. The single point that steers him along this path is his understanding of the soteriologically active nature of the *dharmakāya* or Buddha nature.

A second characteristic with soteriological significance ascribed the *dharmakāya* is the fact of the two truths being "neither the same nor different."

If the supreme and worldly truths are the same, then ordinary persons, upon perceiving worldly truth, should penetrate the supreme truth. But if they penetrated the supreme truth, they should be sages [instead of ordinary people]. But as they do not perceive the supreme truth, the two truths are not one.

If you say the two truths are different, than sages, perceiving worldly truth, should not penetrate supreme truth. But if they did not penetrate supreme truth, they would be ordinary people. Therefore, because sages perceive [both truths], [the two truths] are not different. Therefore, we know [the two truths] are neither the same nor different. (809a)

The theme of this characteristic is the harmony between Thusness and phenomenal reality. With respect to the variety of things, "when you consider the penetration of Thusness you cannot say they are different, but because of worldly distinctions, you cannot say they are the same" (809a). On the one hand, because Thusness and phenomenal reality are not different, they are mutually identifiable. Just as "form is emptiness and emptiness is form," so "Thusness is phenomena and phenomena are Thusness." On the other hand, because they are not the same, one is not reduced to the other, and each maintains its own significance.

The example of the two truths broaches the implications of this logic for practice of the Buddha Way. The two truths (or, seeing things aright and seeing things through delusion) cannot be simply identified or there would be no need of practice. Yet they ultimately also cannot be kept distinct, for the *bodhisattva* must act in and through the worldly reality of delusion. The fact, then, that worldly truth and supreme truth, phenomena and Thusness are not the same means that practice and liberation are necessary; the fact that they are not different means that liberation is something real and worth striving for.

A third soteriological characteristic of *dharmakāya* is called *separation from barriers.*

There are three kinds of barrier: (1) the *kleśa* [defilement] barrier—the *arhat* who obtains the wisdom of liberation overcomes this barrier; (2) the *dhyāna* [meditation] barrier—in overcoming this barrier, *arhats* and *pratyekabuddhas* obtain complete liberation; (3) the all-wisdom barrier—this is what the *bodhisattva* path breaks through. By overcoming this barrier, they realize *sambodhi* [the Buddha's wisdom]. In these three stages, the Tathāgata's *dharmakāya* only contends with three obstacles; it is not itself defiled. (810a)

Here we again see the *dharmakāya* discussed in terms of practice and, especially, realization. The *dharmakāya* is constituted in the overcoming of various barriers or milestones of progress in the Buddha Way. At the first stage, the *dharmakāya* is constituted in overcoming defilement. At the second stage, we see a shift in the logic of the concept of *barrier*. The *dhyāna* "barrier" is not something undesirable or polluting (as *kleśa*), but the opposite. "Separating" from this barrier must be accomplished by fulfilling it; this is not so much a barrier as a milestone. The same may be said of the third "barrier," *sambodhi*. The "breaking through" of this barrier is equivalent to the fulfillment of the Buddha path. Thus, in all instances, the *dharmakāya* is constituted by the realization inherent in progressing on the Buddha Way. Furthermore, realization is only a matter of progressing in practice and nothing more. As the *dharmakāya* or Buddha nature is not defiled in any of these stages of practice, neither is it purified in any real way by realization. There is no change in nature on the Buddha path, only various stages of progress in coming to know one's nature.

The fourth and final characteristic of *dharmakāya* cited by the author is "the purity of the *dharmakāyadhātu*" (the realm of the *dharmakāya*). What is this "purity" attributed here to the *dharmakāyadhātu* and invoked so often in this text in speaking of Buddha nature, *dharmakāya,* and the like? The author here fills out the meaning of this term figuratively, using four images—gold, water, space and *bodhi* (enlightenment), each of which is interpreted in four different ways. The explanation of the *dharmakāyadhātu*'s purity is as follows.

1. The first four meanings are (a) the *dharmakāya* is unchangeable, like gold; (b) Thusness is pure, like water; (c) supreme truth is formless, like space; and (d) *mahāparinirvāṇa* is completely manifest, like *bodhi.*

2. The second four meanings are (a) the super powers transform, like gold; (b) compassion nurtures, like water; (c) own-nature [Buddha nature], like space, does not reject sentient beings; and (d) *prajñā* clarifies and purifies, like *bodhi.*

3. The third four meanings are (a) the cause [of enlightenment] is pure and undefiled, like gold; (b) the superior path is cleansing, like water; (c) liberation is freedom from bondage, like space; and (d) the fruit-essence [liberation] is manifest, like *bodhi.*

4. The fourth four meanings are (a) the nature of bliss is to benefit [others],

> as does gold; (b) the essence of purity is limpidity, like that of water; (c) the virtue of eternity is indestructibility, like that of space; and (d) the meaning of *self* (*wo*) is nonattachment, as in *bodhi.* (810a–b)

First notice the string of terms subsumed within the *dharmakāyadhātu* notion: *dharmakāya,* Thusness, supreme truth, *mahāparinirvāṇa,* super powers, compassion, own-nature (or Buddha nature), *prajñā,* the cause of enlightenment, the superior path, liberation, the fruit-essence of liberation, and the four Buddha virtues or *pāramitā* (bliss, purity, eternity, and self). What is found here is a list of the various superlatives used in this text or, otherwise put, a list of the fruits of realization. The "purity" of the *dharmakāyadhātu,* the realm in which Buddhism comes to fruition, then, consists in the absence of defilements in these fruits. Hence, there is no change (a source of suffering), no adherence to forms (a manifestation of ignorance), no binding or attachment. Rather, there is transformative power (the ability to act on behalf of others), the nurturance of compassion, nonrejection of the plight of sentient beings in *saṃsāra,* and so forth. Thus, the two main characteristics of purity seem to be the absence of any defilements in one's own behavior and mental processes and action on behalf of the liberation and welfare of others. This, of course, is none other than the practice and realization of the *bodhisattva* path, as manifest in *prajñā* and *karuṇā.*

C. *Trikāya: Sambhogakāya* and *Nirmāṇakāya*

According to the *BNT,* the *trikāya,* or three Buddha bodies, are related to the Buddha nature as follows. Buddha nature is divided into two "natures": the Buddha nature that dwells in itself (*zhu zi xing xing*) and the emergent Buddha nature (*yin chu xing*). Three Buddha bodies—*dharmakāya, sambhogakāya,* and *nirmāṇakāya*—"all become complete because of these two natures" (808b).[10] In other words, the *trikāya* are subsumed within the Buddha nature. Specifically, the *dharmakāya* is identified with the Buddha nature that dwells in itself, whereas the *sambhogakāya* and *nirmāṇakāya* are identified with the emergent Buddha nature (808c). Thus the *dharmakāya* represents what the Buddha nature is in itself, whether recognized or unrecognized, and the other two *kāya* represent what it is as it comes into its own, so to speak, the Buddha nature in its manifest form of self-knowledge and action for the liberation of others.

Having already discussed the *dharmakāya,* we will examine the *sambhogakāya* next.

> Because of the breadth and greatness of its power and functions, this *kāya* aboriginally possesses three virtues: great wisdom (*prajñā*), great meditation (*samādhi*), and great compassion (*karuṇā*).[11] The essential characteristic of great wisdom is nondiscriminative knowledge (*jñāna*). The essential characteristic of great meditation is uncreated mentation (*wu zuo yi*); i.e., mentation that has left behind [the duality of] leaving [the world; i.e., saving oneself] and entering [the world; i.e., saving others]. The essential characteristic of great compassion is the ability to remove [sentient beings]from [suffering] and save them.
>
> For the mentation of sentient beings to be caused to attain perfect fulfillment, three things are necessary: pleasure in the Dharma, the six super powers (*abhijñā*),[12] and the giving of aid by removing [sentient beings from their suffering]. Thus great compassion removes [sentient beings] from the three evil paths of suffering[13] and establishes people and *devas* in great peace. Great meditation brings about the arising of faithful joy by manifesting the six super powers. Wisdom takes pleasure in the Dharma and realizes liberation. This is what is called the *sambhogakāya.* (810c)

This is the entirety of the text on *sambhogakāya,* a discussion that revolves entirely around the nature of its functioning or activities and has not a single word that implies in any way that the *sambhogakāya* is any kind of substantive entity. It is constituted exclusively by actions, soteriological actions. The characteristics constitutive of this *kāya* are introduced in terms of the greatness of their influence and activities; that is, their power and ability to effect change. Wisdom is constituted by nondiscriminative knowledge, pleasure in the Dharma, and the realization of liberation. Knowledge, pleasure and realization are actions, not things; their meaning perhaps would be conveyed more accurately if they were translated verbally as knowing, enjoying, and realizing. Wisdom, as described here, is a manner of being-in-the-world characterized by nondiscriminative apprehension of what is, the taking of pleasure in the knowledge of what is, and the active self-transformation of realizing freedom. This aspect of the *sambhogakāya,* then, constitutes its soteriological functions for the practitioner.

Meditation is constituted by so-called uncreated mentation (*wu zuo yi*), which means a manner of apprehension and being-in-the-world free of the duality of concepts of self and other, *saṃsāra* and *nirvāṇa*. To be free of such dualistic thinking is both a manifestation of one's freedom and one of the bases that makes possible acts for the benefit of others. It also produces the six super powers that, in turn, result in the development of faithful joy (in others). Paranormal activities, as is implied here, are not ends in themselves, but are justified insofar as they encourage others in the practice of Buddhism. The active, soteriological character of meditation, then, is partially directed toward the salvation of others and partially is a manifestation of the practitioner's own dynamic, liberated state.

Finally, compassion, of course, removes sentient beings from suffering and establishes them in peace. Obviously, this element in the *sambhogakāya*'s makeup is purely constituted by action for the salvation of others. In sum, the *sambhogakāya* is not a thing, entity, or substance of any kind. It is a particular set of actions that manifest the practitioner's own liberated state—in such actions as nondualistic cognizing and paranormal activities—and that aim to release others from bondage.

The following description of the *nirmāṇakāya* bears certain similarities to that of the *sambhogakāya*. "Great compassion is the [*nirmāṇakāya*'s] basis. Meditation transmutes it into manifest form. Wisdom causes it to have five kinds of abilities: (1) it causes the arising of repugnance and fear [towards *saṃsāra*]; (2) it causes [people] to enter the Noble Path; (3) it causes [people] to discard old attachments; (4) it brings about faithful joy in the great Dharma; and (5) it causes [people] to receive the prediction of great *bodhi*" (810c). As for the *sambhogakāya*, here also the three main characteristics given for the *nirmāṇakāya* are wisdom, meditation, and compassion. In this case, compassion is the raison d'être for the existence of this *kāya*, *samādhi* power enables this *kāya* to take form (i.e., incarnate), and wisdom provides the direction for this *kāya*'s actions. Again, as for the other *kāya*, here too this *kāya* is entirely constituted by soteriological functions, this time entirely for the benefit of others. And again there is no thing, entity, or substance of any kind here, only a set of actions.

Following this passage on *nirmāṇakāya* are listed fourteen acts performed for the benefit of sentient beings. These specify the most significant events in the life of the Buddha (birth, leaving home, defeat of Māra, enlightenment, turning the wheel of the Dharma, *parinirvāṇa,* and so on). Śākyamuni Buddha's life as *nirmāṇakāya* is itself portrayed as a compassionate act.

The section on the *trikāya* includes a detailed discussion of the eternity of the three Buddha bodies. I will translate this passage in full because the assertion of eternity produces the suspicion that the Buddha bodies are eternal things. This selection, however, demonstrates quite clearly that although the Buddha bodies are eternal, they are not eternal things. The eternity of the *trikāya* is based upon the same soteriological functioning noted earlier.

> Furthermore, because these three bodies always perform acts of profit to the world, it is said that they abide eternally. This eternal abiding rests on ten kinds of cause and condition. . . .
>
> 1. They are eternal because of the boundlessness of causes and conditions. Having for innumerable eons cast away body, life, and property, they embrace the true Dharma. The true Dharma is boundless, inexhaustible, inextinguishable. In turn, this inexhaustible cause molds the inexhaustible fruit. The fruit is these same three bodies, and thus they are eternal.
> 2. They are eternal because of the boundlessness of sentient beings. At the time [a *bodhisattva*] first gives rise to the thought of enlightenment, he takes the four great vows,[14] and gives rise to the ten inexhaustible vows,[15] [saying] "If sentient beings are inexhaustible, my vow [to save them] is inexhaustible; when sentient beings are exhausted [i.e., all saved], only then is my vow exhausted." Because sentient beings are inexhaustible, the *nirmāṇakāya* is eternally within the world, endlessly guiding sentient beings.
> 3. They are eternal because of the boundlessness of great compassion (*mahākaruṇā*). If all *bodhisattvas* have great compassion and eternally act to save sentient beings, if in their hearts there is no limit to giving aid and they long abide in *saṃsāra* without entering *nirvāṅa*, how much more is the Tathāgata with all his merits consummated eternally present in great compassion! Saving [all beings] with perpetual kindness—how could there be a limit to it? This is why we speak of eternity.
> 4. They are eternal because the four bases of super powers (*ṛddhi-pāda*)[16] are boundless. Even those within the world who obtain the four bases of super powers are able to live long lives of forty lesser eons. How much more, then, can the master of great super powers, the Tathāgata, abide for a million eons, freely living

such a long life and widely delivering sentient beings. This is why we speak of eternity.

5. They are eternal because of the boundlessness of nondiscriminative wisdom. Far from grasping *saṃsāra* and *nirvāṇa* as two, they are always united in the supreme truth. They are both unmoving [a characteristic of *nirvāṇa*] and not departing [from *saṃsāra*] and thus we know they are eternal.
6. They are eternal because they are always in *samādhi*. Even in the world there are those who, obtaining *samādhi*, are impervious to water, fire, embers, drowning, knives, and arrows. How much more will the Tathāgata, constantly in *samādhi*, be incapable of suffering harm! This is why we speak of eternity.
7. They are eternal because they are serene and pure. Serenity is the Diamond Mind, able to do away with the dwelling place of ignorance, with the final thought [upon entering *nirvāṇa*], with impermanence and with suffering. Because there is no suffering, it is called serene. As the Buddha fruit is completely manifested, it is called pure. This path of liberation is therefore called eternal.
8. They are eternal because, although acting within the world, the eight essential things[17] are not sullied. Although the Buddha bodies return to [the realm of those who have] not yet completed the path and are joined with *saṃsāra*, they are not sullied by defilements nor do they have false thoughts. This is why we say they dwell eternally.
9. They are eternal because they are the sweet dew of immortality [*amṛta*]; they are still, and are far distant from Māra [the Lord of Death]. The sweet dew causes people to be long-lived, superhuman, and immortal. The Diamond Mind discards ignorance, the final thought [before *nirvāṇa*] and delusion, and thus obtains the Buddha fruit of eternal bliss. Because there is eternal bliss, there is stillness; and because there is stillness, they are far distant from Māra. To be far distant from Māra is to abide eternally.
10. They are eternal because they are not of the nature of production and destruction. It is not the case that the *dharmakāya* originally did not exist but now exists [i.e., is produced], nor did it originally exist but now does not exist [i.e., is destroyed]. Although it acts (*xing*[2]) within the three periods[18] it is not *of* the three periods (*fei san shi fa*). Why? The *dharmakāya* aboriginally exists; it is not the case that it begins now to exist. It transcends the three periods and so we call it eternal. (811a–b)

For the most part, the ten "causes and conditions" for the eternity of the three Buddha bodies emphasize soteriological factors—practice and action—as the foundation of this eternity. The second and third examples have the eternity of the Buddha bodies rest on the eternity of salvific acts performed by the Buddhas. Assuming that the number of sentient beings is inexhaustible, the vows and great compassion of a Buddha require him to engage in endless acts of teaching and other forms of help. These acts being endless, so are those Buddhas, but only in the sense that a Buddha is an endless series of acts for the welfare of others. This is not different in the Buddhist context, from pointing to the continuity over time of an ordinary person, who also is constituted by his or her acts, without the need to assume an underlying thing performing those acts.

The fourth and sixth examples are alike in invoking the performance of marvels demonstrating transcendence of physical bonds as proof of eternity. This assumes that the practice of yoga develops as a by-product (to the enlightenment which is its aim) certain supernormal conditions, including longevity and imperviousness to accidental harm. This, of course, is a poor demonstration of eternity and only tangentially relevant to this discussion insofar as it implies the Buddhas' freedom from the ordinary limiting conditions of embodiment. This freedom, however, need not point to the existence of any static, entitative thing and should not be so understood. Freedom from ordinary physical limitations is compatible with Buddhas understood as dynamic series of acts realized in a nonordinary manner (which, indeed, the *trikāya* doctrine already assumes).

The seventh and ninth examples together equate freedom from delusion with the eternity of the Buddha bodies. The seventh example identifies eternity with the serenity and purity consequent upon the vanquishing of ignorance, impermanence, and suffering. This means that eternity is a synonym for *nirvāṇa* simply as the negation of samsaric delusion and suffering. This interpretation is confirmed by the identification of this nirvanic condition with the "path of liberation" (*jie tuo Dao*). We may recall in this context the important *BNT* theme that states that Buddha nature is both cause and fruit; *āśryaparāvṛtti* is both the abandonment of desire (the Truth of Cessation; i.e., *nirvāṇa*) and the cause of the abandonment of desire (the Truth of Path).

The ninth example repeats the theme of identifying eternity with freedom from ignorance, adding the metaphorical element of the "sweet dew" of immortality and the mythological figure of Māra, the Lord of Death. The "sweet dew" of immortality is the food of the gods.

In Buddhism it connotes the sweet taste of liberation from *saṃsāra;* that is, life–and–death. It points not to a static state of being (in distinction to dying), but to *nirvāṇa* understood as freedom from life–and–death (as opposed to extinction). The references to the sweet dew and to distancing from Māra thus reinforce the notion of the Buddha's condition of discontinuity with *saṃsāra.* The mention of eternal bliss anticipates a topic (the four *pāramitā*) to be covered in the next chapter. Suffice it to say that this eternal bliss may be understood as bliss *pāramitā,* which in turn is identified with the *samādhi* that overcomes attachment to false emptiness. Attachment to false emptiness is a condition in which one is committed to belief in emptiness as nothingness, or a negative ultimate truth. The *samādhi* overcomes both the attempt to find bliss in *saṃsāra* and this attachment to false nothingness. As such, it is a Middle Path condition beyond dualistic affirmation and negation; in transcending dualism it is blissful.

Finally, the eighth example, like the second and third, refers to the Buddha's compassionate acts for the welfare of sentient beings. Here the point is that this action proceeds without sullying the "eight essential things"; that is, one's own ongoing religious practice and the clarity resulting from it. In the background of this idea is the basic *tathāgatagarbha* doctrine of the essential purity of the *tathāgatagarbha* (here the Buddha body), unsullied by its contact with defilements (here its engagement in samsaric life). This example very directly portrays the action in the world performed by the Buddha bodies as the source of their eternity: The Buddha (or Buddha body) is essentially pure, or fully itself, in the midst of soteriological action.

The above illustrate the most important theme of the ten "causes and conditions" for the eternity of the Buddha bodies; namely, that eternity is necessitated by never ending soteriological practice and action (including both one's own practice and liberation and acting for the welfare of others). There are exceptions to this general pattern. The first reason given for eternity names the eternity of the Dharma as the cause of the eternity of the Buddha bodies, which are the fruit of this cause. The Dharma, of course, is not a substantive metaphysical entity, nor simply the Truth, but also the way things are (empty-Thus) and the path of realization. Thus the Dharma as an epistemological, ontological, practical, and soteriological basis constitutes the foundation of the eternity attributed to the Buddha bodies.

Two other "causes and conditions" of the eternity of the *trikāya* do not seem to speak essentially in terms of soteriological practice and action. These are the fifth, which speaks of nonduality, and the tenth, which is concerned with nontemporality. The nonduality of *saṃsāra* and *nirvāṇa* is due to their mutual emptiness. Therefore, eternity is not grounded here in a substantive metaphysical entity but in its contrary, the absence of such an entity, the emptiness of any attribute posited for either. Nondualistic wisdom is able to realize the nondistinction between the two and hence the Buddhas, in a sense, are able to participate simultaneously in both. In this condition, we are told, lies the Buddhas' eternity. Nondualism based on emptiness, then, is the source of eternity here.

The tenth reason, concerning temporality, is much like the first and fifth. The nature of the *dharmakāya* is neither samsaric (conditioned, produced) nor nihilistic (not existing, destroyed), yet the author of the *BNT,* characteristically, wants to speak positively of it. The key phrase of the tenth reason for speaking of eternity is the statement that although the *dharmakāya* "acts" within the three time periods, it is not "of" them; that is, it is not of a temporal nature. As in the fifth reason, its acts are themselves of a nirvanic nature, though they occur within the framework of *saṃsāra,* here in the sense of temporality. Like the Buddha nature, the *dharmakāya*'s existence is aboriginal—real in a sense having no relationship to either being or nonbeing—and like the Buddha nature, its reality consists in its acts.

In sum, although asserting the eternity of the Buddha bodies, none of the ten reasons for eternity gives evidence of a thing or entity that lasts eternally. Instead, we see the author's characteristic desire to speak positively of the "fruit" of realization; hence, a positive conception of *nirvāṇa* as freedom from ignorance, from time, from every kind of limitation. Very much evident is an emphasis upon the Buddhas as beings who engage in ceaseless soteriological action, both expressing their own enlightenment and acting for the welfare of others. Finally, we see an emphasis on the Buddhas' nondualistic participation in *nirvāṇa* and *saṃsāra,* their Thus-Gone–Thus-Come nature. None of these reasons for speaking of the Buddha bodies as eternal steps outside widely accepted Mahāyāna principles. None of these reasons requires us to construe the Buddha bodies as enduring entities.

D. The Relationship Between Person and Buddha

A Buddhist text's depiction of the relationship between the Buddha and the ordinary person provides significant insight into the soteriology of that text. The *BNT* is no exception to this rule. The relationship between the Buddha and the ordinary person as portrayed in the *BNT* defines the parameters of liberation in the sense that Buddha is depicted here as the supremely liberated person, no more and no less.

The *BNT* typically distinguishes three categories of sentient beings: ordinary persons, *bodhisattvas,* and Buddhas. The *BNT* clarifies the relationship among these three classes by discussing the manner in which Buddha nature can be said to pervade or be differentiated among them.

We begin with the "pervasive" (*tong*) aspect of Buddha nature. The pervasiveness of Buddha nature is seen in the Thusness (*ru-ru*) and the purity of all things. Each of these two qualities, in turn, is further explained. "Worldly Thusness (*su ru*) is true Thusness (*shen ru*); true Thusness is worldly Thusness. The two Thusnesses, true and worldly, are not distinguished as different." As for purity, "There are two aspects to the meaning of purity. (1) There is Thusness (*ru-ru*) within the cause—because the Thusness that has not yet attained the unblemished fruition stage is not itself blemished; and (2) there is the identity of the purity of cause and fruit—because within the cause there is unblemished purity and arriving at fruition there is unblemished purity" (805c).

What we see in both the Thusness and the purity characteristics is the nondifferentiation between ordinary or "worldly" reality (also equivalent to the "causal" stage) and "true" reality (also equivalent to the "fruition" stage.) In short, there is but one Thusness and it pervades all things uniformly.

Having established this unity, the author goes on to discuss the differentiation of Buddha nature among the three classes of sentient beings. "Within this Buddha nature three kinds of sentient beings are differentiated: (1) those who do not perceive and realize the Buddha nature—these are called ordinary persons; (2) those who do perceive and realize the Buddha nature—these are called sages; (3) those whose realization reaches the ultimate purity of this principle—these are called the Thus Come (*Tathāgata*)" (805c–806a). Clearly this categorization scheme is not a *gotra*-type theory in which some persons are innately capable of realization and others are not. It was established in the discussion of the pervasiveness of Buddha nature that Buddha nature is omnipresent; all share in it, and all share equally in Thusness. The present differentiation of Buddha nature among classes simply recognizes the reality of different stages of awareness among humanity and explains it in terms of the degree to which one has realized one's own Buddha nature.

Elsewhere, the text speaks of three "stages" rather than three classes of sentient beings; namely, (1) the impure (i.e., sentient beings), (2) the pure (i.e., *bodhisattvas*), and (3) the supremely pure (Buddhas). To demonstrate that this does not conflict with the assertion of the universal pervasiveness of Buddha nature, a quotation[19] follows, indicating that all three "stages" are constituted by the *dharmadhātu* (the realm of Truth, equivalent to Thusness). The realm of sentient beings, it states, is this *dharmadhātu* when covered by defilements and suffering rebirth. The realm of *bodhisattvas* is this same realm of sentient beings when they have become averse to the sufferings of *saṃsāra* and practice the *bodhisattva* path in reliance on the 84,000 doctrines of the Buddha and all *pāramitā.* Finally, the third stage (that of the Buddhas) is described as follows:

> This realm of sentient beings, having cast off all *kleśa* coverings, gone beyond all suffering and washed away all defilements, being naturally and to the utmost degree clean and pure, being that which all beings desire to see, having entered and dwelled in the subtle and superior ground, the ground of all-knowledge, and of universal nonobstruction [or harmony], having arrived at incomparable ability, and having attained the great, spontaneous power of the Dharma King—I call [beings who achieve this] *Thus Come* (*Tathāgata*). (806b)

It is noteworthy that the *BNT* refers only once here to the *dharmadhātu;* namely, upon introducing the stage of sentient beings. Thereafter, the remaining two stages are introduced as variations of the sentient being "realm," rather than as manifestations of the Dharma "realm." This emphasizes the extent to which the author is thinking of the Buddha as a sentient being. The essential nature of the Buddha and of the ordinary person is the same, whereas the differentiation between the two is purely a matter of practice and its fruit of realization. Both the points of identity and of differentiation, moreover, serve to encourage practice. The identity between person and Buddha is constituted by their shared Buddha nature; this identity serves to encourage practice by virtue of its optimism. The difference between person and Buddha also is constituted by Buddha nature—the degree to which each *makes real* in practice his or her own Buddha nature; to overcome the difference, practice is absolutely necessary. The message is clear: You are Buddha, but you are not Buddha unless you practice. This is no paradox: The Buddhist tradition has always asserted that a Buddha could be identified by Buddhalike behavior, paradigmatically wise and compassionate behavior.[20]

CHAPTER FOUR

Dereification of Self and Mind

In arguing for an understanding of Buddha nature as active, part of my task must be to demonstrate that Buddha nature is not a substantive self or mind of any kind, nor any other kind of thing or entity. Many passages in the *Buddha Nature Treatise* demonstrate this by using a term that sounds as if it represents an entity but then proceeding to dereify the term and demonstrate an active or functional meaning for it.

A. The "Own-Nature" of Buddha Nature

A first example may be found in the *BNT*'s treatment of what it calls the *own-nature* (*zi xing*) of Buddha nature. Language of this sort cannot help but lead one to think, at least initially, that the term is used to refer to a substantive self or mind. This text, however, makes a point of conjoining such a term with descriptions of exactly the opposite import.

In the *BNT* the own-nature of Buddha nature is characterized by three traits (796b–c):

(1) It possesses power like that of the wish-fulfilling *maṇi* jewel, which gives one what one wants on the basis of one's wanting it. The Buddha nature, like this, is naturally self-fulfilling; one cultivates realization of the Buddha nature because the Buddha nature

intrinsically moves toward its own self-realization. (2) It is characterized by nondifferentiation in the sense that ordinary persons, sages, and Buddhas all are essentially alike insofar as the nature of the mind of each is pure and replete with the Buddha virtues, differing only in stage of realization. This shared quality of the minds of all is explicitly compared with emptiness: It is like an earthen, a silver, and a gold vessel; although they differ in form, they are essentially alike insofar as the nature of each is emptiness and emptiness is not subject to differentiation. (3) It is characterized by the nurturant quality of compassion for all.

In all this there is no substantive self or mind, despite the use of "own-nature" language. The first trait portrays one aspect of the dynamic character of the Buddha nature: its tendency to move toward its own self-realization. This is not to be understood as a characteristic that the Buddha nature, as entity, possesses; the Buddha nature *is* this tendency toward self-realization, this soteriological function. Likewise the third characteristic represents action that the Buddha nature is, in this case compassionate action.

The second characteristic attests to the universality of the Buddha nature. This trait may appear to be more troubling for my thesis, insofar as it is based upon the shared purity and intrinsic value of the minds of all ordinary persons, sages, and Buddhas, and thus may seem to imply the existence of a substantive mind constituted by an unchanging, pure essence. But as the reader will recall from other parts of this book, *purity* is explained by such a phrase as nondiscriminative wisdom (i.e., mental functioning free of discrimination: "Because all false thoughts are utterly extinguished in it, this *dharmadhātu* surpasses that which can be expressed in reasoning or in speech. Therefore, we take purity to be a characteristic of the *dharmadhātu*" 801b) and the Buddha virtues, as we shall see, are explained by such things as seeing reality aright and ceaselessly working for the salvation of others. In both cases, substantive sounding terms actually refer to kinds of mental functioning, and we do not find this functioning ultimately depending upon any entity that can be distinguished from the functioning itself. Moreover, in the passage presently under examination, the purity and virtue of the human, sage, and Buddha mind is compared to emptiness. Although the author does not want to imply with this that the sentient mind is lacking in virtue, he does mean to say that its virtue lies precisely in the freedom constituted by its emptiness.

This reading is corroborated by the following excerpt, taken from the same passage. Subsumed within the discussion of the Buddha nature's own-nature, the *tathāgatagarbha* is discussed as follows: "*Tathāgatagarbha:* the meaning of this *garbha* is own-nature. No *dharmas* are outside the Tathāgata's own-nature because its mark is *anātman.* Therefore it is said, all *dharmas* are the *tathāgatagarbha*" (796b). In this passage, far from representing a substantive entity, own-nature is identified with the very contrary of substantive self-identity, not-self or *anātman.* It is this very lack of a substantive self that makes possible the universality of the *tathāgatagarbha.* It is implied that if the *tathāgatagarbha* had a nature of its own of any kind, this nature would differentiate it from other things. Thus its universal nature, paradoxically, rests upon its lack of nature or emptiness and it is this quality which represents its "own-nature."

These three characteristics of the own-being of Buddha nature are further glossed in the text as expressing, respectively, (1) the inconceivability of the Buddha nature, (2) that one should realize it, and (3) the infinity of its virtues (797a). This conveys the idea of the Buddha nature from the perspective of the ordinary person. One understands that one cannot comprehend it, and yet that it is desirable that one realize it, inasmuch as to do so will transform one into an infinitely virtuous (wise and compassionate) person.

We have seen the term *own-nature* used in one other place already; namely, in the analysis of the purity of the *dharmakāyadhātu.*[1] One meaning of this purity was given as "own-nature [which I gloss as Buddha nature], like space, does not reject sentient beings (810a)." Here again we simply see own-nature identified with an essential, characteristic behavior of Buddha nature, compassionate action on behalf of sentient beings.

In the *BNT,* then, no connotation of substantiveness is attached to the own-nature concept. This nonsubstantiveness is a function of understanding Buddha nature as Buddhist practice. The Buddha nature concept serves both to entice people to engage in Buddhist practice and to represent the potential, activity, and fruition of that practice itself. The "own-being" of Buddha nature perhaps is best understood as the distillation of that practice; in representing the essence of Buddha nature, it manifests the essentials of Buddhist practice. Just as the latter convey no substantiality, neither does the former. Because there is no Buddhist practice apart from persons practicing Buddhism, persons in the act of practicing are all there is to be found here as a foundation or "basis" for the edifice of Buddhism.

B. *Ātmapāramitā*

Some of these themes are developed in a more complete form in our second case, the discussion of *ātmapāramitā,* or self *pāramitā.* The self *pāramitā* is one of four *pāramitā*—purity, self, bliss, and eternity—that are understood as meritorious qualities inherent in the *dharmakāya.* The four *pāramitā* are found in *tathāgatagarbha* literature, where they are explained as an extension of early Buddhist teachings, as follows. Theravāda Buddhism characterizes reality with the Three Marks of impermanence (*anitya*), suffering (*duhkha*), and not-self (*anātman*). These were sometimes accompanied by a fourth characteristic, impurity (*aśubha*). The teaching of the Four Marks by the Theravāda was the correction of four "upside-down" views held by the ignorant, who believed that permanence, bliss, self, and purity could be found in *saṃsāra. Tathāgatagarbha* theorists accepted this tradition as far as it went, but asserted that it was incomplete. They then extended this teaching, with a twist characteristic of their logic.

> The four upside-down [views are the following]: Where there is truly nothing eternal (within form and the five *skandha*), giving rise to an eternity view. Where there is truly suffering, giving rise to a bliss view. Where there is truly no self, giving rise to a self view. Where there is truly impurity, giving rise to a purity view. These are called the four upside-down [views]. . . .
>
> In order to correct these four, the four not-upside-down [views] are taught. What are these four? [1] Form and the five *skandha* in past, present, and future will certainly perish; therefore, they are really not eternal. Thus one truly gives rise to the realization of noneternity. [2] At the time of suffering, there is suffering. When pleasure perishes, there is suffering. Thus one abandons the three time periods as suffering . . . and in this produces the realization of suffering.[2] [3] Noneternity is cause. Noneternity is effect. By the completion of cause and effect the dependent nature (*paratantra*) is maintained. Effect is not independent, and neither is cause: whether in past, present, or future it is still not finished with its preceding cause. Therefore the dependent nature is also not independent. Outside of cause and effect there is no remaining *dharma* that could be a self. Therefore no-self is the truth and one produces the realization of no-self. [4] There are two aspects

of impurity, in form and nonform. Impurity in form has three [manifestations]: the beginning, middle, and end. In the beginning when one first enters the womb, the foetus is impure. In the middle, after one has left the womb, eating and drinking, to possess property, and to bear children, all are impure. At the end, after one has left the body and the substance of the body decays, it is extremely impure. As for nonform, whether joy or grief, whether evil or neutral, whether connected with desire, all are tied to thought and passion and are thus nonform. By virtue of this fact, they are also impure. Therefore the sage gains penetrating insight into the three realms [and sees] that all are impure. Thus the five *skandha* are truly impure and one produces the realization of impurity.

These four are all true. Therefore they are not-upside-down. But with respect to the four virtues (eternity, etc.) of the Buddha nature, these four not-upside-downs must again be reinverted. In order to correct the upside-down [quality inherent in the "no-upside-downs"] there are established the four virtues of the Tathāgata's *dharmakāya.* These four virtues are eternity *pāramitā,* bliss *pāramitā,* self *pāramitā,* and purity *pāramitā.* (798a–b)

The teachings of no eternity, no bliss, no self, and no purity, though acknowledged as true, are too negative for the authors of *tathāgatagarbha* literature to leave alone. As always, the latter are concerned to explicitly affirm the positive nature of Buddhist realization. The four *pāramitā* certainly fulfill this role, but they in turn run the risk of appearing too affirmative, too tangible, too much like qualities that an entitative *dharmakāya* possesses.

This issue highlights the importance of the fact that the discussion of the four *pāramitā* is contextualized in the *BNT* (as well as the *Ratnagotravibhāga*) in terms of Buddhist practice. We should recall here that Buddha nature is both cause and fruit of realization and hence practice is both the seeking and the expression of realization. The *BNT* lists four kinds of person with four kinds of wrong view (or barriers to the realization of the truth). These four kinds of wrong view may be cured, respectively, by four practices. These corrective practices or "cures," in turn, are considered "causes" of four "fruits." These four fruits are the four *pāramitā* or perfections, also given as the four Buddha virtues that constitute the Buddha's *dharmakāya.* The relationship of the four *pāramitā* to their respective persons, obstacles and "causes" or cures may be presented in the form of a table.[3]

Of course, the elevation of the characteristics of purity, self, bliss, and eternity to the level of the highest truth by the authors of the *tathāgatagarbha* literature was a radical departure—at least in terms

Person Type	Obstacle	Cure = Cause	Fruit (Pāramitā)
1. *Icchantika*	Disregard and hate of Mahāyāna	Faith and pleasure in Mahāyāna	Purity, *śubha*
2. Non-Buddhist	Adherence to self view	*Prajñā*	Self, *ātman*
3. *Śrāvaka*	Fear of *saṃsāra*	The *samādhi* that overcomes false emptiness	Bliss, *śukha*
4. *Pratyekabuddha*	Disregard for the welfare of others	Compassion (*karuṇā*)	Eternity, *nitya*

of the language used—from the Buddhist tradition beginning with Śākyamuni and continuing through *śunyavāda.* The item of present concern is the perfection of self or *ātmapāramitā.* As there could hardly be a doctrine more central to the Buddha's teaching than *anātman,* absence of self, this new revelation of a perfection of self at the end of the Buddhist path, characteristic of the Buddha's *dharmakāya* itself, was, at the least, a daring use of language. What was intended by it? Here is how the *BNT* explains itself.

> All non-Buddhists, in their various ways, conceive and grasp a self (*wo*) in those things that lack self; namely the five *skandhas,*[4] e.g., form, etc. Yet these things such as form differ from what one grasps as the mark of self; therefore, they are eternally lacking in self. [However,] with the wisdom of Thusness, all Buddhas and *bodhisattvas* realize the perfection of not-self (*anātmapāramitā*) of all things. Because this perfection of not-self and that which is seen as the mark of not-self are not different, the Tathāgata says that this mark of the eternal not-self is the true, essential nature (*zhen ti xing*) of all things. Therefore it is said that the perfection of not-self is self. As the *sūtra* verse says,[5]
>
> The dual emptiness is already pure;
> [In this] is realized the not-self, the supreme self.

> Because the Buddha realizes the pure nature
> Not-self turns on itself (*zhuan*) and becomes self.
>
> All non-Buddhists perceive and grasp a self within the five *skandha*. Overturning that attachment to self as vacuous and cultivating *prajñāpāramitā*, one realizes the supreme not-self that is identical to the perfection of self (*ātmapāramitā*). This is the fruit [of the practice of *prajñāpāramitā*] that you should know. (798c)

The essential point here is that the new teaching of *ātmapāramitā* is not in conflict with the old *anātman* teaching, but on the contrary is the fulfillment of it. The very *anātman* itself, when taken to its extreme (i.e., when perfected) is the *ātmapāramitā*. This teaching is logically parallel to the *śūnyavāda* teaching that emptiness or *śūnya* is the characteristic or the own-being (*svabhāva*) of all things. In *śūnya* dialectics this is a way of stating the apparent paradox that the own-being of all things is to lack own-being. In *tathāgatagarbha* and Buddha nature literature this same apparent paradox is taken as revelatory of the way things are; that is, "Thus." Hence this characteristic of not-self, when seen as revelatory of Thusness, turns on itself, or perhaps better, turns full circle (*zhuan,* to turn around, to revolve) and *as characteristic of the way things are* is indicated with the positive term *self,* which may be taken as meaning "own-being"; that is, the "own-being of Thusness."

Though the language is new, the content of this message is not. What we have here is a variation on the theme enunciated previously, "Buddha nature is the Thusness revealed by the dual emptiness of person and things. . . . If one does not speak of Buddha nature, then one does not understand emptiness" (787b). Non-Buddhists are as wrong as ever in seeing a self in the changing phenomena of worldly flux. Yet the Buddhist who stops with characterizing this flux as empty does not really understand emptiness, unless he or she realizes that this emptiness is a characteristic of reality, and as such, possesses a positive nature. The perfection of the realization of emptiness, or the lack of self in things, is to realize to the fullest extent the qualities of this positive nature. Thus, though *anātman* and *ātmapāramitā* are logical equivalents, what is implied by the author is the inferiority of the former as a term indicative of the vitalizing potential of spiritual realization. That is, there is a soteriological difference, but no logical difference, between the two terms. Thus *ātmapāramitā* is no more a substantive entity than is *anātman,* and the *dharmakāya* (or Buddha nature) represented by *ātmapāramitā* is consequently likewise free of substantiality.

Perhaps even more significant is the pivotal role played in the table by the third column items, in the case of *ātmapāramitā,* wisdom. Each of these—faith, wisdom, *samādhi,* compassion—is an action. In each case this action is identical with, or better, constitutes, the perfection. In the case of *ātmapāramitā,* the wisdom of realizing the lack of self in all things constitutes the perfection of self. The same principle applies in the case of each of the four perfections. Consider the fourth perfection, eternity. Exactly as we saw in the discussion of the *trikāya,*[6] the perfection of eternity is demonstrated here to be constituted by the act of compassion. As indicated in the table, the *pratyekabuddha* is prevented from becoming a Buddha by his or her disregard for the welfare of others. This obstacle is overcome by the cultivation of compassion. The suffering and delusion of sentient beings is endless, so the compassion required of a Buddha also must be endless. It is this limitlessness of a Buddha's compassion that constitutes the Buddha nature's perfection of eternity. It is *nothing but* infinite compassion. There is no eternal "thing," Buddha nature or other. There is simply an unrelenting series of acts.

Elsewhere in the text, the author directly defends the use of the term *ātmapāramitā* by drawing on one of the most orthodox of Mahāyāna themes.

> There are two kinds of cause and condition [due to which] we say that the Tathāgata's *dharmakāya* possesses *ātmapāramitā.* First, because it is distantly separate from non-Buddhist one-sided grasping of a [self] view, there is no attachment to self [implicit in this concept]. Second, because it is distantly separate from what the Two Vehicles [*śrāvaka* and *pratyekabuddha*] one-sidely grasp as not-self, there is no false grasping of not-self. Because both views are eliminated, we speak of *ātmapāramitā.* (799b)

In case there is any doubt as to the meaning of these words, the author soon comments on this passage (along with his parallel treatment of the other three *pāramitā*), declaring: "This is obtaining entry into the Dharma gate of nonduality" (799c). In support, the *BNT* quotes the *Śrīmālādevīsūtra.* The quotation specifically addresses the eternity *pāramitā,* but the author's comment applies equally to the other three *pāramitā* as well. " 'If you view all events as nonEternal, this is called nihilism. It is not called a correct view. If you view *nirvāṇa* as constantly present, this is called eternalism. It is not a correct view.' This is why the Tathāgata's *dharmakāya* is separate from these two views and is named the great eternity *pāramitā*. . . . This is attaining entrance through the Dharma gate of nondualism, which is neither one nor two" (799c).

In short, this is Middle Path thinking: One-sided negation of self misses the Middle Path as much as does one-sided affirmation of self. *Ātmapāramitā* occupies the Middle and corrects both. In this criticism of dogged adherence to *anātman* there is an echo of the author's disquiet with those who overemphasize emptiness. He does not miss any opportunity to assert that negation cannot be the culmination of the Buddhist Path.

In this context, it is useful to recall that early Buddhism also was concerned with an incorrectly one-sided understanding of the *anātman* doctrine. The following is a quotation from the *Sabbāsava-sutta* of *Majjhima-nikāya*, No. 2.

> When he [the unwise person] reflects unwisely in this way, one of the six false views arises in him:
>
> 1. I have a Self: this view arises in him as true and real.
> 2. I have no Self: this view arises in him as true and real.
> 3. By Self I perceive Self: this view arises in him as true and real.
> 4. By Self I perceive nonself: this view arises in him as true and real.
> 5. By nonself I perceive Self: this view arises in him as true and real.
> 6. Or a wrong view arises in him as follows: This my Self, which speaks and feels, which experiences the fruits of good and bad actions now here and now there, this Self is permanent, stable, everlasting, unchanging, remaining the same for ever and ever.[7]

The *ātmapāramitā* of the *BNT* thus is squarely in the venerable Buddhist tradition of denying that *anātman* means "there is no self" in the simple dualistic sense of a denial of the view "there is a self." *Anātman* can be equated with neither of the dualistic poles; it is a Middle Path doctrine that, as both the *BNT* and the *Majjhima-nikāya* quotations well show, is intended to produce freedom altogether from any kind of view whatsoever on self, whether positive or negative, to which one could become attached. In this context, the *ātmapāramitā* language of the *BNT* should be seen as a corrective to what was perceived as the excessively negative language of *śūnyavāda* and should not be seen as taking up a position on the positive side of the dualistic pole.

C. Self

A different, but also striking, use of the term *self* already was seen in the discussion of the purity of the *dharmakāyadhātu.*[8] There one of the meanings of this purity was given as "the meaning of *self* (*wo*) is nonattachment, as in *bodhi*" (810b). The thinking behind this statement seems to be closely related to that of the *ātmapāramitā,* in which "self" is identified as "the perfection of not-self," via the power of *prajñāpāramitā,* meaning the realization of the emptiness of things. The author of the *BNT* seems to want to "sunyatize" or negate the theory of *anātman* just as *prajñāpāramitā* negates any possibility of a self theory. In both of these explanations, the term *self* is identified with intellectual and emotional nongrasping; that is, acts of mental freedom. One implication of this position is that grasping a doctrine of *anātman* as Truth is not representative of liberation—hence the tendency in this text to play rather freely with words like *ātman, anātman, anātmapāramitā,* and *ātmapāramitā.*

The most important point to be made about this passage for our purposes is that *self* consists in the act of nonattachment. Though negatively stated, this is an act insofar as it is composed of the propensity to behave in a nonattached manner. It should be recalled, moreover, that this "perfection of self" language is used in the context of a discussion of practice, and in fact the "perfection of self" is given as one of the fruits of practice. Hence, the perfection of not-self that is self is the person (as series of acts) transformed by virtue of Buddhist practice culminating in realization.

D. Pure Mind

Our fourth case concerns the notion of "pure mind" and its substantiality or lack thereof. We may examine this notion in the context of a discussion of two practices, the cultivations of the Principle of Thusness and of the Plenary Thusness. Here we will see the interrelatedness of the teachings concerning Thusness, Buddhist practice, the true understanding of mind, and the positive value readily ascribed to reality.

> The cause of abandoning desire obtains completion when conjoined with two practices. These two practices are the cultivation of the Principle of Thusness and the cultivation of Plenary Thusness. In the world there are only two things to be known: people and things. One who is able to penetrate these two [kinds of] emptiness eternally realizes the true pinnacle of Thusness. Hence this is called the Principle of Thusness. The ultimate Plenary Thusness probes the source, attains to the [true] nature, and penetrates the source of the *dharmadhātu;* thus it is spoken of as the ultimate.
>
> The cultivation of the Principle of Thusness does not misuse persons and things. Why? Because people and things are, from the beginning, characterized by the utmost wondrousness (*miao ji*) and by tranquillity. They neither increase nor decrease in number; they have nothing to do with either being or nonbeing (*li you li wu*). The mark of tranquillity indicates that the own-nature is pure, all delusions being, from the beginning, unborn. Seeing the dual emptiness [of people and things] is what is called the mark of tranquillity. The inherently pure mind (*zi xing qing jing xin*) is called the Noble Truth of Path. The nongrasping of the pure mind in which delusion never arises is called the Noble Truth of Cessation. (802a)

This passage is begun with the virtual equation of emptiness and Thusness in the Principle of Thusness. Then, in line with the "Thusness is what is revealed by emptiness" theme of this text, the author goes on to indicate that a kind of positive knowledge follows on the heels of the realization of emptiness; namely, in the cultivation of Plenary Thusness. The latter, then, is the fullness of the former; the former is the gateway, the latter, the realm into which one enters through that gateway.

The Thusness of people and things may be seen from two perspectives: (1) From the ultimate standpoint, it is simply the utmost wondrousness; and (2) from the mundane standpoint, in which thoughts of delusion and nondelusion arise, one describes it as tranquil (i.e., pure), all delusions that might sully the purity being not real. These qualities are ascribed to persons and things as they are here and now, not as they might be. It is not that these things have to be "purified." Rather, if one sees correctly, one will realize that all things already are not only "tranquil" (this is a *śunyavāda*-like insight), but also the utmost in wondrousness, marvelousness, excellence (*miao*). The latter insight is characteristic of Buddha nature thought and the *BNT*.

The crucial point of the passage for our present concern is found in the final two sentences: "The inherently pure mind is called the

Noble Truth of Path. The nongrasping of the pure mind in which delusion never arises is called the Noble Truth of Cessation." Here we see one of the rare references in this text to something called *mind* (*xin*). However, this "mind" is immediately identified, in the first sentence, with the fourth Noble Truth, Path. As we saw in our discussion of *āśrayaparāvṛtti*,[9] the Truth of Path is equated with the "cause of abandoning desire"; that is, the cause of realization (801b). Because the author links this cause of realization with the fourth Noble Truth, we may know that this "mind," as cause, is cause in the same way that *bodhicitta* and *prayoga* were said to be causes of Buddha nature,[10] by representing effort, or the treading of the Path itself. Thus, this "mind," as cause, is the activity involved in realization. From the Buddha's day on, the Path is not a thing to be tread, but a way to behave, a compendium of attitudes, endeavors, and behaviors. Hence the "mind" of this context is not a substance in any sense, but a way of being, the way a person "is" who is on the Path.

This reading is confirmed by the second sentence, where the third Noble Truth, Cessation (earlier identified with "abandoning desire"), is identified, not with "mind" this time, but with its equivalent, a certain action or manner of mental functioning, negatively stated as "nongrasping." Thus, "cessation" is realized by the cessation of a certain behavior, grasping, or in other words, the attainment of mental behaviors free of grasping. In short, though the term *mind* is used, it is to be understood as a manner of being and a set of mental behaviors, rather than as a substantial entity.

E. *Dharmakāya* and "Self"

Fifth, we may consider a passage in which the author discusses nine instances of *prapañca*, or false theorizing, concerning the self (*wo*). These are all negated by the functioning of the *dharmakāya*. Thus the latter, far from being a self, serves rather to deliver us from views of self and represents the absence of such views. The nine false theories concerning the self are as follows (summarizing 803b–c):

1. The theory that a self pervades all five *skandhas*.
2. Taking one of the five *skandhas* as the self.
3. All nihilistic and eternalistic views.

4. The theory that the self will not be reborn. This is a nihilistic view.
5. The theory that in the realms of desire and form the self exists as form (*se*). This is an eternalistic view.
6. The theory that in the formless realm the self exists as either perception, mind, or Dharma. This is an eternalistic view.
7. The view that in all three realms (desire, form and the formless), with the exception of the heavens of no thought and neither thought nor nonthought, thought is the self. This is an eternalistic view.
8. The view that nonthought is self; that is, in the heaven of no thought, the grasses, and trees, and so on are self. This is an eternalistic view.
9. Taking the Akaniṣṭha heaven (the last *dhyāna* heaven) as self.

The section concludes: "Because [persons] with these variously deluded minds will not attain *nirvāṇa,* these [views] are called *prapañca.* When one gains insight into and realizes the *dharmakāya,* no further *prapañca* arises" (803c).

Here we see the *dharmakāya* as freedom from views of self. In each of the nine cases, it is the self view that binds. The *dharmakāya,* then, is in effect the Noble Truth of Cessation with respect to any and all forms of *prapañca,* which here means self view. Thus here in the *BNT* with its affirmation of *ātmapāramitā,* as in the most orthodox Nikāya or *prajñāpāramitā* text, it is theories of self and attachment to self that bind us. Buddha nature thought, like the rest of Buddhism, aims to release us from this bondage. The *dharmakāya* (or Buddha nature), as the Truth of Cessation, represents the active releasing from bondage that constitutes the Buddha Way. Hence not only is Buddha nature not a substantive entity, not a self or an entitative mind, but the cessation of all self views. As such, its character is active and soteriological.

F. Mind

Sixth, we need to look at the *BNT*'s use of the term *mind* (*xin*). This text does not often use this term and where it does, it often could substitute a term such as *person* without any appreciable change in meaning. For example, in the discussion of the eternity of the *trikāya*[11] the phrase *Diamond Mind* was used. Let us look at that passage again. "[The *trikāya*] are eternal because they are the sweet dew of immortality (*amṛta*); they are still, and are far distant from Māra. The sweet dew causes people to be long-lived, superhuman, and immortal. The Diamond Mind discards ignorance, the final thought [before *nirvāṇa*] and delusion, and thus obtains the Buddha fruit of eternal joy" (811b).

The Diamond Mind here mentioned is evidently no "Mind" such as is construed in an idealistic monism, but on the basis of the textual evidence appears to represent the person of realization; that is, the person fulfilling the Buddha Path. This "mind"—or person—is shown solely in the acts of dispelling ignorance and suffering and enjoying the fruits of serenity and joy that result. Thus we are not presented here with a monistic Mind of idealist metaphysics nor with a dualistic mind opposed to a body. What is portrayed is an acting person.

Another example again requires us to look at a passage already seen. "The own-nature, pure mind is called the Noble Truth of Path. The nongrasping of the pure mind in which delusion never arises is called the Noble Truth of Cessation" (802a). In this case, though something called a *pure mind* is mentioned, it is immediately identified with two of the Noble Truths, already indicating that it cannot be taken as a substantial thing. Rather, by virtue of the two Truths that it represents, it is an expression for the series of acts that constitute engaging in practice of the Buddha Way, and for the "nonact" of nongrasping. The identification of pure mind with nongrasping is an echo of the equation of true self and nongrasping noted earlier. In both cases, a substantial sounding term, *mind* or *self,* is rendered nonsubstantial by its identification with behaviors and actions.

The single instance of use of the term *mind* that is the most difficult to explain as nonsubstantial is found in a passage of the *BNT* borrowed from the *Tathāgatagarbha Sūtra,* giving nine similes for the condition of the *tathāgatagarbha* in the midst of defilement. The fourth of these similes likens the "mind" covered by defilement to the conditions of pure gold fallen into filth (807c). This simile, taken from what is considered the earliest text of *tathāgatagarbha* thought, reflects the lack of sophistication of that text, the similes it employs being somewhat clumsy attempts at conveying a doctrine so difficult that the *Śrīmālādevī Sūtra* simply labels the problem "inconceivable" and goes on: the doctrine, that is, of the relationship between wisdom and ignorance. In this simile, the "pure mind" does seem to bear substantial qualities, especially in its comparability to pure gold as a thing occupying space and capable of being physically covered. By borrowing this simile, the *BNT* inherits the problems associated with it, including the implication that it affirms a substantive mind.

However, immediately following the statement of the simile, a few remarks are added that make it clear that no substantiality should be assumed here. After rendering the simile of the pure gold fallen into filth, the text continues, "The person free of desire is also like this; the defilements on the surface of the mind (*shang xin fan-nao*) pervert the *manas*. That is why this simile is related" (807c). In characteristic fashion, the author of the *BNT* relates the simile of the gold to the condition of the practicing Buddhist, explaining the former as a metaphor for the latter. It is the teaching about the human condition that is being promoted here, whereas the simile with its apparent metaphysical implications is not to be taken as any more than an attempt to clarify the former. Where it misleads (and it does mislead to the extent that it implies substantiality) it is not to be adhered to. As a carryover from the clumsy mode of expression of the *Tathāgatagarbha Sūtra* it is incorporated into the *BNT*. However, the author of the *BNT* attempts to bring the simile into line with his effort to clarify the human condition and the path of Buddhahood. Thus, the example of pure gold fallen into filth likened to the "mind" amidst defilements is an apt simile insofar as it sheds light on the human existential condition. However, like all similes, its fit is not perfect, and we should not permit the simile to extend so far as to indicate any substantiality to a human "mind," a notion that runs counter to the teaching and perspective of the *BNT*.

CHAPTER FIVE

Ontology: Monism vs. Nondualism

Is Buddha nature–*tathāgatagarbha* thought a variety of monism? This question has been discussed in the literature by a number of scholars in the recent past, many of whom believe that it is monistic. Obermiller, for example, states that the *Ratnagotravibhāga,* a *tathāgatagarbha* text closely related to the *Buddha Nature Treatise,* is an "exposition of the most developed monistic and pantheistic teachings of the later Buddhists."[1] Nagao states, "the tathāgatagarbha seems to me to occupy a supreme position—a position akin to that of Brahman or Ātman, or other 'Absolute Being,' in Brahmanical philosophy."[2] In his introduction to the *Ratnagotravibhāga,* Takasaki asserts that "for explaining the possibility of anyone's acquiring . . . Buddhahood, . . . monistic philosophy was used as the background."[3] Ogawa[4] and Yamaguchi,[5] on the other hand, view *tathāgatagarbha* thought as an extension of the line of thought leading form the concept of conditioned origination (*pratītyasamutpāda*) to *śūnya* thought. Thus, they do not see it as monism. Finally, Ruegg stresses that *tathāgatagarbha* thought is not monism because it is based upon nonduality, rather than monism.[6]

First, it is necessary to specify the meaning of the term *monism* as it will be used here. Generally speaking, there seem to be two meanings to the term, a stronger and a weaker.[7] According to the stronger meaning, all of reality can be reduced to one basic substance, in the sense of something with independent existence or a nature of its own. This form of monism includes both materialism and idealism. The weaker sense of monism holds only that all of reality can be explained in terms of a single principle or that one can make statements about reality as a whole. There obviously is a great deal of difference between these two meanings, and in fact very many varieties of philosophical and religious thought would have to be considered monistic according to the second definition. Even Mādhyamika (*śūnya*) thought itself would have to be considered monistic in terms of the weaker definition, inasmuch as it speaks of all of reality in terms of the single principle, *śūnyatā*.

Interestingly, when Obermiller describes *tathāgatagarbha* thought as monistic, he in fact is linking it with Mādhyamika thought, which he explicitly labels *monistic.*[8] Thus he is discussing both *tathāgatagarbha* and *śūnya* thought in terms of the weaker sense of monism. As noted earlier, however, Ogawa and Yamaguchi avoid characterizing *tathāgatagarbha* thought as monistic precisely by elucidating *tathāgatagarbha* thought in terms of *pratītyasamutpāda-śūnya* thought.

Now if one wanted to deny that *tathāgatagarbha* thought is monism in the sense that Obermiller meant it (i.e., the weaker sense), one could not do so by means of comparing it or linking it with *śūnya* thought. Nor could one do so in terms of *pratītyasamutpāda,* because this too is an attempt at explaining all of reality by means of a single principle. I take it, then, that the weaker sense of monism is not at issue here, and that the stronger sense is what we are concerned with. This is the form of the issue to which Ogawa, Yamaguchi, Ruegg, and Nagao were addressing themselves.

The question, then, is this. Does Buddha nature–*tathāgatagarbha* thought establish an Absolute comparable to the role played in Brahmanical Hinduism by Ātman-Brahman? Is the Buddha nature, in short, close kin to the Ātman-Brahman of Hinduism? Do the two perform similar functions in the two systems? Is this variety of Buddhism, then, a form of crypto-Hindu thought, reflecting more the influence of Hinduism on Buddhism than the internal dynamic of Buddhism's working out of its own sources?

Without explicitly comparing the two sets of teachings, I shall argue against the view that the Buddha nature thought of the *Buddha*

Nature Treatise can be conceived as a variety of monism akin to Brahmanical absolutism. I will structure my argument around a consideration of five themes found in the *BNT*, the language of which seems to indicate that the Buddha nature is a substantive entity or absolute. Following the analysis of these themes, I will return to Gadjin Nagao's contrary view that the *tathāgatagarbha* is a form of "Absolute Being" and discuss his views in the light of my own understanding of the *BNT*.

Some of the apparently monistic concepts and themes present in the *BNT* are the following:

1. The very common statement, essential to all *tathāgatagarbha*–Buddha nature thought, that sentient beings "possess" or "are" the *tathāgatagarbha*–Buddha nature.
2. The concept of the Buddha virtues or *pāramitā, viz.*, purity, self, bliss, and eternity, attributed to the *dharmakāya*.
3. The concept of the pure nature and its lack of essential relationship with the *āgantukakleśa*, or adventitious defilements; the latter are said to be *śūnya*, in the sense of "unreal," whereas the former is said to be *aśūnya*, in the sense of "real."
4. Statements (related to the preceding) that *tathāgatagarbha*, Buddha nature, *dharmakāya*, or *dharmadhātu* "really exists" (*shi you*) or "aboriginally exists" (*ben you*).
5. Statements that the *tathāgatagarbha* or Buddha nature is beyond cause and conditions and is eternal, quiescent, unborn, unchanging, and so on.

These indicate the locus of the issue; all five themes are to be found in the *BNT*. Although initially they do seem to indicate that the Buddha nature (or its equivalent, *tathāgatagarbha, dharmakāya, dharmadhātu*, etc.) is a substantive absolute, I will argue against this interpretation. How then are these passages correctly to be interpreted? I will suggest three kinds of readings appropriate to these passages: (1) Some will appear to be fundamentally soteriological in intent, and thus have nothing to do with either monism or nonmonism; in other words, some passages may carry no ontological import at all, but may be of an entirely different order. (2) Other passages that do have ontological import may be understood as nondualistic,[9] rather than monistic. (3) Finally, some passages may be seen as discussing actions, rather than substances, and thus, again, are not of ontological import other than negatively. Various combinations of these three themes will be found in the five types of passage to be discussed.

It will be useful to remember from the beginning a passage from the *BNT*, quoted earlier: "Buddha nature is the Thusness revealed by the dual emptiness of person and things." This passage indicates not only the difference between *śūnya* and Buddha nature thought, but also is central to an understanding of the latter as nondualistic rather than monistic. The equivalence of the Buddha nature, *tathāgatagarbha, dharmadhātu,* and so on with Thusness is key because Thusness is not a monistic concept. The word for Thusness in Chinese, *ru,* means "like, as." "*Ju* [*ru*], 'like, as much as,' comparing qualities and actions rather than things, is related to *jan* [*ran*], 'thus' (like this, as much as this). As a noun, one may take *ju* [*ru*] as 'being as (not "what") it is.'"[10] Although it does have an ontological quality to it, Thusness refers to *how* something is, rather than *what* it is; it speaks of an adjectival quality of things rather than a nominative thingness as such. All it means is that things are "as they are." In a sense it is a pure tautology, a simple "thus" attributed to all things. As *The Awakening of Faith in the Mahāyāna* says,[11] the word *Thusness* is not a term that has the qualities or attributes of being "this" or "that"; it is a word by which words are undone, a word that points at our language and indicates that it will not do. Yet the term *Thusness* does not have the negative connotations of *śūnya,* a term that functions in a similar way to "undo" language. Hence to equate the Buddha nature with Thusness is to indicate that there is something positive about it—one wants to say it is "real," it "exists"—but the use of the term *Thusness* serves to remind us that the direction in which our minds begin to move upon hearing the terms *real* and *exists* will not be a totally appropriate one.

The main points of the Thusness concept as used in the *BNT* may be summarized as follows.

1. Thusness is that which is revealed by emptiness. It is the true nature of reality that one is capable of seeing once all previously existing ideas and habits of perception have been cleared from one's mind by the discipline of emptiness.
2. It is the conjunction of persons correctly perceiving the world as it is, and the world presenting itself to persons as it is. It is

therefore nondualistic—it is prior to a division of experience into the categories of subject and object or mind and world.

3. Thusness allows positive language to be used in discourse about the nature of reality. In both a linguistic and an ontological sense it is affirmative of phenomenal reality. Whereas *śūnya* dialects emphasize what is not the case, positive Thusness language emphasizes what is the case. Ontologically, what truly is, is affirmed in Thusness.
4. Thusness is not dualistic, because a commonsensical belief in separate, individual entities is negated by the emptiness through which one passes on the way to Thusness. Nor is it monistic, because reality does not reduce in Thusness to any single principle; Thusness is not a thing, nor even a principle that can be conceived as an all-embracing One, as it functions solely as a pointer to the true apprehension of what it. Thusness is nondualistic, because it negates both dualism and monism.
5. The term *Thusness,* as used in the *BNT,* has a soteriological function and as such epitomizes the optimism of Buddha nature thought. It represents the goal of the religious life as eminently deirable and real, without setting the practitioner up to be attached too soon to any specific notions of what that goal is like.

Let us now turn to the apparently monistic themes just enumerated and see what can be made of them.

A. All Sentient Beings Possess the Buddha Nature

First we need to discover what is intended by the repeated contention that sentient beings "possess" or "are" the Buddha nature. As was seen earlier, this does not indicate that persons possess "something" and that by virtue of that "something," they are able to complete the Buddha Way. In the chapter on Buddha nature, we saw that the author directly refutes the supposition that the Buddha nature is an *ātman,* making it clear that it is not something to which one can straightforwardly attribute existence, not something that simply "is." On the positive side, it is characterized by such things as *bodhicitta-prayoga,* the true nature (*pariniṣpanna-svabhāva*), and *tathāgatagarbha. Bodhicitta-prayoga* is Buddhist practice or progress on the Buddha Way. The true nature is identified with the Thusness of all things, incorporating both the way reality presents itself to persons and the way persons experience reality. The term *tathāgatagarbha* was subjected to a complex analysis through which two particularly salient ponts became apparent: (1) The statement that sentient beings are the *tathāgatagorbha* is based on Thusness. (2) The storehouse (the *garbha* or *tathāgatagarbha*) is constituted solely by that which it contains; namely, the true realm of Thusness, true practice or wisdom, and realization of Buddhahood. In sum, the Buddha nature, as an amalgam of these three constituents, is shown to be (1) identifiable with Thusness, thus ontologically nonsubstantial, and (2) the active practice and realization of Buddhahood. Buddha nature, therefore, essentially is constituted by action and hence is a kind of "doing" rather than a substantial thing; as Thusness, it is the inseparable conjunction of reality presenting itself to persons "Thus" and persons experiencing reality "Thus." There is no place for a substantial absolute here.

Remember also that the statement, "all beings possess (are) the Buddha nature–*tathāgatagarbha*" is interchangeable with the statement, "all beings are capable of realizing Buddhahood." As the *BNT* says, "In accordance with principle, all sentient beings universally and aboriginally possess the pure Buddha nature. That there should be one who eternally failed to obtain *parinirvāṇa* is not the case" (788c). *Buddha nature* means "potential Buddha"—not as a type of being, but as practice (i.e., realization) that is an action or series of actions. It is in accordance with the principle of the Way—Thusness—that this be so. Thusness is all embracing, it excludes no one. All are capable of performing this act, seeing things Thus, seeing reality present itself Thus.

B. The *Pāramitā*

The second theme concerns the Buddha virtues or *pāramitā*.[12] These are presented in the *BNT* as the end-product of a soteriological process, and this is the key to their proper interpretation. They are the "inversions" of the four views to which they correspond and are constituted by the four practices used to correct the errors. Thus, for example, purity *pāramitā* is not a quality that the *dharmakāya* possesses per se. Rather, it is the inversion of disparagement of the Mahāyāna and is constituted by faith in the Mahāyāna. Thus its meaning is entirely soteriological; it is defined entirely in terms of practice.

As for the *ātmapāramitā*, the same principle holds. It is simply the result of the cultivation of *prajñāpāramitā* and the inversion of attachment to *anātman*. The *BNT* portrays this in terms of three stages of practice. The erroneous stage is that in which one sees a self in phenomenal existence. This is overcome in the second stage, in which one realizes that there is no self to be found in phenomenal existence. The third stage is the perfection, or the logical extreme one might say, of the second: Now one sees that this characteristic of not-self is the true, essential nature of all phenomena (this is still in accord with *śūnya* thought) and as such may justifiably be called *self* (798c). This third stage discussion of a "self," then, really is no more than an extension to the logical extreme of the perspective of the second stage. As such, it is seen as the culmination of *prajñāpāramitā* practice. Moreover, although the term *self* may seem to echo the perspective of the first, erroneous stage, the content of the third stage is in fact the opposite (or the inversion) of that of the first.

Another point to note concerning the use of the term *self* as a *pāramitā*, (as well as the use of the terms *purity, bliss,* and *eternity*) is its usefulness—soteriologically—for shock value. Recall how the *Heart Sūtra,* for example, earlier negated such things as the Four Noble Truths, wisdom, *nirvāṇa,* and so on. In the case of both *śūnya* and *tathāgatagarbha*–Buddha nature thought, language is being used to "sunyatize." Both the *Heart Sūtra* and the *BNT* take the terms that are used in the Buddhist community of the time (for the authors of the *prajñāpāramitā* literature this was the Four Noble Truths, etc.; whereas for the *tathāgatagarbha*–Buddha nature theorists, it was precisely the terms used in the *prajñā* literature themselves). A purpose in both cases, perhaps, was to shock the Buddhist community. For the *tathāgatagarbha*–Buddha nature theorists, the idea was to shake anyone who had a too-secure or too-simplistic understanding of *śūnyatā;* that is, anyone who "grasped" *śūnyatā* as the "Truth." Yet perhaps they believed that anyone who really understood *śūnya* thought would not be shocked or dismayed by this move, insofar as the *tathāgatagarbha*–Buddha nature theorists were simply further applying the identical principle of *śūnyatā.*

On a purely linguistic level it is undeniable that there is a rather "beingful" quality to the four *pāramitā* ascribed to *dharmakāya*. However, one would be no more justified in believing that the four *pāramitā* refer to the substantive characteristics of an entitative thing than one would be justified in attributing an "unbeingful" nature to the meaning of *śūnya* terms. Both suspicions are equally mistaken on a purely philosophical level; though, if *tathāgatagarbha*–Buddha nature theorists are right, there is something to these attributions on the emotional level. These differing emotional connotations are the effect of the kinds of language used by the two systems. As we have seen, the author of the *BNT* regards the positive form of language as a more effective *upāya*.

Furthermore, it is evident that, in addition to representing the end-product of a soteriological process and being a peculiar use of language, the *pāramitā* are ontologically nondual. Let us take the self *pāramitā* again as an illustration. Note that the not-self is equated with the self: "this mark of the eternal not-self is the true, essential nature of all things. Therefore it is said that the perfection of not-self is self" (798c). This paradoxical language reveals the workings of nondualistic thinking as follows. The perfection of self is found in overcoming the dualism of self and not-self. The self *pāramitā* is the true and essential nature of all things (sounds like a self) at the same time that it is the utmost negation of self, *anātmapāramitā*, the perfection of not-self. This is a good example of the perspective of Thusness, the Thusness revealed by emptiness. Self is utterly negated, it is completely empty, and yet this is how things "are"—one ends on this positive note. This is the truth of things, the essence of things; yes, they *are* "Thus." Thusness, though, always proceeds by way of emptiness. One must first negate the commonsensical realist perspective, emptying this perspective of its view of things as discrete entitites, but then realize that not only is form emptiness (as *śūnyavāda* might be accused of emphasizing), but that emptiness also is form and not apart from it. One returns very solidly to form, remembering its emptiness, but recognizing it as the totality or fullness of what is.

Just as the duality of self and not-self is transcended with the nondualistic term *perfection of self,* so the duality of form and emptiness is transcended with the nondualistic term *Thusness*. Buddha nature thought as taught in the *BNT* is grounded in the perspective and language of Thusness: a nondualistic ontology expressed in positive-sounding language. After all, one can almost imagine the Buddha nature theorists musing, once nondualism is realized, it might as well be expressed in positive-sounding language as in negative-sounding language, inasmuch as the former is a superior encouragement to practice, giving the (correct) impression that there is something worth striving for at the end of the path.

Ruegg's masterful study was important in pointing out the significance of the distinction between monism and nondualism for participants in the debate concerning whether or not *tathāgatagarbha*–Buddha nature thought is a form of monism akin to Brahmanism.[13] In monism (in the strong sense), all phenomena in their manifold plurality are reduced to the transcendent One. In nondualism, phenomena are not thus reduced: Their plurality remains real. Such is the case in the Buddha nature thought of the *BNT*. There is no One to which phenomena could be reduced. Form is emptiness and emptiness is form; there is nothing else apart from the plurality of phenomena. They are empty, but they *are* "Thus." The perspective of Thusness is the very opposite of monism insofar as the immediate givenness of the plenitude of phenomena is the locus of Thusness.

C. *Śūnya-Aśūnya*

Our third problem area concerns the pair of terms *śūnya* (empty, and in this context, "unreal") and *aśūnya* (nonempty, and here, "real"). The latter term is associated in the *BNT* and other *tathāgatagarbha*–Buddha nature texts with the *tathāgatagarbha,* the Buddha nature, and the *dharmakāya,* which are said to be innately "pure." In addition, to explain the condition of ordinary persons who are ignorant, confused, and greedy, the concept of the *āgantukakleśa,* or foreign, adventitious defilements, is used. Although the *tathāgatagarbha* (Buddha nature, *dharmakāya)* and the *āgantukakleśa* have existed agelessly in conjunction, they have no essential relationship with each other. Persons' delusions and hatred are said to have no basis in reality, but to be the unreal products of ignorance. Thus, a person is "really" the pure *tathāgatagarbha* or Buddha nature, but falsely ("unreally") thinks of himself or herself otherwise because of the activities of the unreal *kleśa.*

Some examples of this kind of thing in the *BNT* follow. In the very beginning of the *BNT* we are told, "Attachments are not real, therefore they are called vacuous. If one gives rise to these attachments, true wisdom will not arise. When one does away with these attachments, then we speak of Buddha nature" (787b). Attachments are not real (*bu shi*); Buddha nature is. Again, "If the *dharmakāya* were nonexistent (*wu*), then all correct practices should be in vain. Taking right views as the foremost practice, and including in addition such good things as morality, concentration and wisdom, the correct practices that one cultivates are not empty (*bu kong*), or fruitless. Because these correct practices do yield fruit, we know that the *dharmakāya* is not nonexistent" (804a). *Dharmakāya,* the practices that lead one to it, and the fruits of those practices are neither nothing (*wu*) nor empty (*kong*). Again, "training in the Way is not a vain error (*bu kong guo*)" (805c). Finally, quoting the *Śrīmālādevī Sūtra,* the *BNT* asserts, "World Honored One, the *tathāgatagarbha* is not empty (*bu kong*) because of the wisdom that it does not abandon and from which it is inseparable, as well as the inconceivable and incalculable Buddha virtues. [Therefore] we know that the *tathāgatagarbha,* because of the Tathāgata's virtues, is not empty" (811c–812a). Here it is stated as plainly as one could wish that the *tathāgatagarbha* is not empty due to the reality of the Buddha virtues or *pāramitā* (purity, self, bliss, and eternity).

As seen in the discussion of the first issue, the term *tathāgatagarbha* or Buddha nature does not refer to anything substantial, but rather indicates each person's potential to achieve Buddhahood (this being a matter of activity) and identifies each person as Thusness (hence, as ontologically nonsubstantial and nondual). Moreover, although the text says that the *tathāgatagarbha,* the *dharmakāya,* and the Buddha virtues or *pāramitā* (purity, self, bliss, and eternity) are *aśūnya,* this does not mean that they exist in any substantial sense. Rather, the attribution of the *aśūnya* qualifier can be seen as part of the inversion process exemplified by the four *pāramitā.* Thus, just as purity is the inversion of the impurity perceived in phenomena, so the *aśūnya* nature of this purity is the inversion of the *śūnya* nature of the impurity. In fact, it would have been inconsistent for the *tathāgatagarbha*–Buddha nature theorists not to ascribe *aśūnyatā* to the *dharmakāya* and *pāramitā:* As we saw in the case of the self *pāramitā,* not-self is the property that "really" (in an *aśūnya* manner) describes phenomena, and it is because of the *reality* of this property that one may speak of the self *pāramitā.* In this sense, the *śūnya-aśūnya* concept presents nothing philosophically new that was not already present in the notion of the *pāramitā.* Whereas the *pāramitā* express the contents of the culmination of practice, the *aśūnya* notion is a linguistic tool used to further emphasize the reality of the fruits of that practice.

Another way to understand the term *aśūnya* is to realize that the logic of the *BNT* follows the pattern of *śūnya* thought, but adds a characteristic twist of its own. According to *śūnya* thought, *śūnya* is empty of any own-mark; that is, *śūnya* is empty of the mark of *śūnya* and therefore it is not graspable as such.[14] Mādhyamikans use *śūnya* to destroy all views; they "sunyatize" *śūnyatā* to deconstruct the latter, to be clear that *śūnyatā* is not Truth nor a valid view. *Tathāgatagarbha*–Buddha nature theorists, in contrast, say that because *śūnya* is empty of the mark of *śūnya,* it must be said of *śūnya* that its emptiness is real. This strikes one as exceedingly strange logic at first. Yet the move made by these theorists parallels in form, though not in content, that of the Mādhyamika: In both, *śūnya* is "sunyatized." For *tathāgatagarbha*–Buddha nature thought, though, when one "sunyatizes" *śūnya*, one inevitably ends up with *aśūnya.* The logic is straightforward: to "sunyatize" *śūnya* is to introduce *aśūnya.*

In other words, it is by virtue of the very unreality of all things that one must say that their unreality is real. The two are two sides of one coin. It is by virtue of the dynamics of emptiness that we must speak of the nonempty; the former necessitates the latter. In my view, there is no distinguishing this kind of dynamic from the Mādhyamika dynamic that equates *nirvāṇa* and *saṃsāra.* There too it is not a matter of substantialist monism, because emptiness is and must be form, every bit as much as the reverse is true. It is not a matter of one reducing to the other, but of each indicating the necessity of the other. The dynamics of *tathāgatagarbha*–Buddha nature thought are virtually the same as in *śūnya* thought, though the particular forms these take appear at first to be diametrically opposed.

As for the relationship between the "pure," not-empty Buddha nature or *dharmakāya* and the empty (unreal), adventitious defilements, it may not be out of place here to comment briefly on the philosophical status of this relationship. The relationship between the pure Buddha nature or *tathāgatagarbha* and the impure defilements is undeniably a philosophically weak point in this theory.[15] The *BNT,* for its part, has little to say about this relationship. Other *tathāgatagarbha* texts that address the relationship directly explain it by not explaining it; that is, by saying that the relationship is inconceivable.

Let us, however, speculate as to another possible avenue of interpretation not found in the texts themselves. We may approach the issue experimentally by considering this doctrine as an attempt to express what is experienced in practice. If this doctrine is looked upon as a statement of an existential, rather than a purely notional, truth, it might appear to be more philosophically respectable. A possible interpretation is as follows. Defilements and ignorance are infinite; if one tries to "cure"' them on their own level, as it were, attempting one by one to eliminate the various manifestations of this pervasive set of dispositions (a selfish act here, a hostile act there), one will never succeed in bringing the matter to an end. Rather, one must pluck out this set of dispositions by its roots, "overturning" (as in *āśrayaparāvṛtti*) the whole person who so behaves. Thus, the gulf represented in *tathāgatagarbha* theory between the "pure" nature and the adventitious defilements may represent the hiatus found in a person's own practice of self-transformation between deluded acts, on the one hand, and nondeluded acts, on the other: two sets of experienced reality in a single person that are so opposite in nature that one may be unable to conceive of any real relationship, any point of contact between the two.

The virtue of this kind of interpretation is that it fits many scholars' belief that Yogācāra thought, in general, is based upon Yogācāra meditative practice. Moreover, the implications for our present issue of monism also are significant. As I have stressed repeatedly, Buddha nature is not an entity of any kind. Nor, for that matter, are *kleśa.* Buddha nature is Thusness and certain kinds of actions. *Kleśa* are other kinds of actions. Insofar as neither is an entity, there is no possibility of the two relating as things relate; there is no question of one entity displacing, coexisting, or being a manifestation of another entity. Thus there is no question of a need to find a philosophically sound way to conceptualize the relationship between a monistic Buddha nature entity and a *kleśa* entity, the type of question, that is, that causes endless trouble for Indian philosophers in their attempts to relate the real Brahman-Ātman with the world of *saṃsāra*. If the relationship between Buddha nature and *kleśa* is purely a matter of the relationship in practice between two sorts of behaviors, the Yogācāra experience would seem to be that the two sets of behavior do not relate; there is an unbridgeable hiatus between the two. The practitioner leaps over the gulf experientially upon realization of Buddha nature without ever "relating" deluded behavior to the enlightened. It must be admitted that the texts themselves do not put the matter this way and this interpretation is pure speculation. It is, however, consistent with the position of the *BNT*.

D. Buddha Nature Exists Aboriginally

Our fourth point is related to the third. There are passages in our text that describe the *tathāgatagarbha*, Buddha nature, or *dharmakāya* as really existent (*shi you*) or aboriginally existent (*ben you*). Again, do these indicate that the Buddha nature is something substantial that "exists"? The answer to this question is similar to that indicated in the *aśūnya* issue. Partially, it is a matter of interpretation: To say that the *tathāgatagarbha* or Buddha nature "exists" is to say that there is truth to the claim that all can attain Buddhahood. Partially it is a matter of the Thusness perspective and of preferred language use: If the *tathāgatagarbha* or Buddha nature, as Thusness, transcends the two poles of being and nonbeing (i.e., if it is nondual), one may as well say that it is real, it exists, as say that it does not exist, especially when cognizant of the encouraging nature of the former statement for the practitioner.

This position is well illustrated in the *BNT*. In the section refuting Hīnayānist views, the author first refutes both the view that the Buddha nature exists (*you*)—because that might lead some to immediately identify themselves with the Buddha, without going through the effort of practicing the Buddha Way and actually becoming a Buddha—and the view that the Buddha nature does not exist (*wu*)—because this might lead others to expect that no matter how much they practiced, they never could become a Buddha. He concludes with the following: "In accordance with principle (*Dao li*), all sentient beings universally and aboriginally possess the pure Buddha nature. That there should be one who eternally failed to obtain *parinirvāṇa* is not the case. This is why Buddha nature most assuredly aboriginally exists (*ben you*); the reason being, that is, that it has nothing to do with either being or nonbeing" (788c).

The decision to say that the Buddha nature exists aboriginally appears to be a pragmatic one; this is the statement that will most encourage practice. Yet it is also quite clear that this does not mean that the Buddha nature "exists" in the normal sense; aboriginal existence has nothing to do with either being or nonbeing. Why? Because it has to do with persons' actions or practice of the Buddha Way, which is not essentially something ontological, and because it has to do with change or transformation, with what appears "Thus," which is never thinglike but always in flux. The ontology of flux essentially is related to the soteriology of practice. Hence to say that the Buddha nature (aboriginally) "exists" is the very opposite of giving it a substantial or thinglike character. Rather it is to encourage practice, to indicate the primacy of practice, and simultaneously to deny of reality that it accurately can be described with the terms and concepts of being and nonbeing. As with persons, so with things. The "dual emptiness" of persons and things reveals what might be called the "dual Thusness" of persons and things. This very revelation of the Thusness (of both) is the Buddha nature that "aboriginally exists." Reality and persons are not ultimately separable in this kind of thought; both are part of the vision of Thusness that is always expressed in positive terms. The language of existence is preferred, in a context that emphasizes the inapplicability of dualistic existence-nonexistence concepts.

E. Unborn and Unchanging

The final form of expression apparently indicating that *tathāgatagarbha* or Buddha nature involves a substantialist monistic theory is found in those passages stating that the *tathāgatagarbha, dharmakāya, nirvāṇa,* or Buddha nature is beyond cause and conditions, is unborn, quiescent, eternal, or unchanging. For example, the *BNT* declares, "The Tathāgata's *dharmakāya* . . . eternally and tranquilly abides. Unborn (*wu sheng*), it is called 'still'; undestroyed (*wu mie*), it is called 'quiet' " (802c).

Also, "The *dharmakāya* is unchangeable, like gold" (810a). And finally, *nirvāṇa* "eternally abides (*chang zhu*)" (805c). Do not these passages indicate that we have here a monistic substance, capable of transcending the law of conditioned origination (*pratītyasamutpāda*)? This seems to be a negation not only of *śūnya* thought, but of early Buddhist thought as well.

However, rather than being a negation of such basic Buddhist thought, this sort of language is the logical extension of it. The *prajñāpāramitā* literature, for example, says that all *dharmas,* or things, are "unborn." In *prajñā* thought, all things are unborn because there is no own-nature (*svabhāva*) to be born or to die. It is by virtue of the dynamics of *śūnya* (based on the principle of *pratītyasamutpāda*) that this qualifier "unborn" is logically necessitated. The theory of *pratītyasamutpāda* indicates that all things come into existence (are "born") due to causes and conditions, and yet, by virtue of that very principle, everything is said to be empty of own-nature (insofar as they are dependent), hence unreal (not truly existent as independent entities), hence incapable of birth and death or for that matter of not being born and not dying. Thus, the meaning of *unborn* is "unrelated to the dualism of birth and no-birth"; it is necessitated by every step of *pratītyasamutpāda-śūnya* thought.

The exact same process is at work in *tathāgatagarbha*–Buddha nature thought, for the authors of this literature intend no difference in the purely conceptual content of the terms *unborn* and *eternal.* Both mean "outside the realm of cause and condition"; both are based on and necessitated by *pratītyasamutpāda-śūnya* thought. If one were to call the *tathāgatagarbha*–Buddha nature theorists' "eternal" attribute beingful, one would also have to call the *prajñāpāramitā*'s "unborn" attribute nihilistic. Both labels would be inappropriate, as both the "eternal" and the "unborn" attributes are intended to manifest nonduality. The difference between them is that the *prajñāpāramitā* does so in apparently "negative" language, whereas *tathāgatagarbha*–Buddha nature thought employs apparently "positive" language.

In sum, our five problem areas are resolved as follows. Ontologically, they indicate nondualism rather than monism. They are marked by a world-view in which reality is conceived in terms of actions rather than substances, and by frequent use of "positive" sounding language, the meaning of which does not differ essentially from the more "negative" sounding language of the *śūnya* tradition. Often they are soteriological, rather than strictly philosophical, in intent.

One recent challenge to the preceding understanding that *tathāgatagarbha*–Buddha nature thought, as represented by the *BNT,* is not monistic should be noted. The eminent scholar Gadjin Nagao, in his study, "What Remains,"[16] labels the *tathāgatagarbha* as a monistic pure being. He proceeds by comparing several texts on the subject of emptiness and nonemptiness. Of these texts, one is from the Nikāya, three are from the Yogācāra school (and are written by Vasubandhu and Asaṅga), and the fifth is the *Ratnagotravibhāga,* a text closely related to the *BNT*. Nagao concludes that the latter's concept is different from that of the other texts. It is valuable to study his remarks, because the references he makes to the *Ratnagotravibhāga* are all to themes shared by the *BNT*.

In the former four texts, says Nagao, "what remains" in emptiness are hindrances to realization (such as the body or discrimination), whereas "what remains" in the *Ratnagotra* are the "pure" Buddha qualities (virtues). In the *Ratnagotra,* he says, it is a matter of "arithmetic subtraction"; once you have "destroyed" the *kleśa,* all that remains is "pure being."[17] Thus, he sees the *tathāgatagarbha* as a monistic pure being, which remains when the defilements have been "subtracted." Furthermore, he states that this position of the *Ratnagotra* is "fatal," because it would seem to lay the foundation for the notion that *kleśa* and *bodhi* are identical.[18] The implication is that this notion threatens the continuation of practice of the Buddha Way.

Let us examine this matter more closely. Nagao speaks of "destroying" the hindrances, but in the *Ratnagotra* and the *BNT* the hindrances are unreal, they do not exist—how could they be destroyed? (The *BNT* itself makes this point directly.) Moreover, he speaks of the Buddha virtues as "transparent" pure being. Thus, he interprets the *aśūnya* notion as meaning that the Buddha virtues are utterly distinct and separate from *śūnya.* Yet we have seen that the term *aśūnya* is used in the *BNT* to represent the inversion that is the fulfillment of *śūnya.* In fact, this is the logic of the *BNT* throughout: Buddha nature also is revealed by way of *śūnya. Śūnya* is the basis of everything in the *BNT;* nothing is apart from it—the *aśūnya* end of the path is the fulfillment of it. Nor can the notion of "arithmetic subtraction" stand scrutiny. One cannot subtract "nothing" (i.e., the nonexistent defilements) from "neither nothing nor something" (i.e., Thusness). The logic of the *BNT* is based on the nonduality of

Thusness and clearly is not a matter of eliminating an undesirable element and ending with a positive "something."

Finally, Nagao's fear that the *tathāgatagarbha* theory will lead to the identification of *kleśa* and *bodhi* (delusion and wisdom) and thereby eliminate the theoretical justification of practice is forestalled in the *BNT*. Of course, Nagao is right, in a sense, insofar as he has put his finger on the weakest point of *tathāgatagarbha*–Buddha nature thought: the relationship between the "pure" *tathāgatagarbha* and the defilements that cover it (or in other words, the relationship between wisdom and delusion). However the author of the *BNT,* for one, is at pains to demonstrate why the Buddha nature doctrine not only is no threat to practice, but actively justifies and encourages it. This is one of the central themes of the text. For example, the author argues that one cannot say either that the Buddha nature exists or that it does not exist precisely because of the necessity of encouraging practice and emphasizing its desirability. The latter also stands out as the formative motive behind the writing of the *BNT*. The Buddha nature itself, especially as *āśrayaparāvṛtti,* is directly identified with Buddhist practice. Thus Nagao's fear, although justifiable, is not borne out in the context of the *BNT,* the core theme of which is the inestimable value of Buddhist practice and the very identification of Buddha nature with practice.

I conclude that the Buddha nature thought of the *BNT* should not be understood as monistic.

CHAPTER SIX

Engaging in Spiritual Cultivation

As I have emphasized throughout this book, the *BNT* articulates the Buddha nature concept as a metaphor for Buddhist practice. This approach allows the author to affirm the Buddha nature without positing the existence of a reified self akin to the Ātman of Brahmanism. Moreover, the identification of Buddha nature and Buddhist practice, coupled with the glorification of the former, powerfully validates and encourages the undertaking of Buddhist practice. What, then, of this practice itself? How, in practical terms, does one engage in practice so as to realize the Buddha nature that one already is? Or, because cause and fruit are identified in the Buddha nature, perhaps we should ask, what actions are paradigmatic of the self-expression of Buddha nature? Does the *BNT* give us any guidance on this subject?

There is a good deal of material in the *BNT* on engaging in Buddhist practice, ranging from quite down-to-earth, mundane advice on the kind of friends one should seek, through a discussion of various *bodhisattva* practices, up to quite abstract material on the most advanced of the *bodhisattva bhūmi.* All of this material seems to fall well within the norms of well-established Mahāyāna practices; indeed, some of it draws from early Buddhist traditions. Though the *BNT* offers this material in a disorganized fashion, scattered here and there throughout the text, I propose to begin with the advice given to the beginner and then focus on the material that seems to be the focal point of the author, the material that seems directed to the audience of Mahāyāna practitioners to whom he addressed himself. I intend to select the most practically oriented material of this sometimes quite abstract discussion.

To begin, the foundations of successful Buddhist practice are quite straightforward and commonsensical.

> There are two insights: insight into the suffering and faults of *saṃsāra;* and insight into the bliss and merits of *nirvāṇa.* By a person's factor of purity, by his or her pure nature, these insights attain completion. This "factor of purity" is [composed of] (1) a constituent of merit; (2) a constituent of liberation; (3) a constituent of penetration [of Thusness].
>
> (1) Merit: Good roots from former lives can influence this life. When all roots are complete, one can bear the Dharma vessel.[1] (2) Liberation: Having been a virtuous disciple already in the past, one can influence future lives and attain the fruit of liberation. (3) Penetration: One can penetrate Thusness by means of the Noble Path.
>
> These [three] are called the *factor of purity.* With the factor of purity as the condition and the pure [Buddha] nature as the cause, people complete these insights. It is not done without cause and condition. (800a)

Here the role of conditions as valid components of the Buddhist Path is stressed. Though the unconditioned Buddha nature itself is singled out as the "cause" of attaining insight, it is clear that, in the author's mind, this cause alone, exalted though it may be, will not come to fruition without the active presence of the basic Buddhist necessities—merit, virtue, and the treading of the Noble Path—as conditioning influences.

The mundane foundations of Buddhist practice are further elucidated in the following discussion of the "four *cakras*" or four wheels, four commonsensical conditions for success in the practice of Buddhism.[2]

> The four *cakras* are (1) to dwell in a country that is in accord with the Dharma; (2) to rely upon Dharma friend(s); (3) to possess self-discipline of one's own mind; (4) to have planted good roots in past lives. . . .
>
> (1) To dwell in a good place is [to live] in a place where a good person lives, cultivating correct practice. If one lives there, constantly seeing this person, one will attain an enlightened mind. (800a)

(2) The second *cakra* is to be near a Dharma friend (*kalyāṇamitra*). A *kalyāṇamitra* has seven characteristics, summarized as follows. She or he is (1) giving, (2) honorable, (3) trustworthy, (4) able to speak effectively, (5) able to endure, (6) able to speak of the profound Principle, and (7) able to give peace to good friends and to establish them in good conditions. These seven characteristics are embraced by three more general qualities, all of which a *kalyāṇamitra* must possess: (1) sympathy, (2) intelligence, and (3) patience. Śākyamuni is the paradigm of the *kalyāṇamitra* (800b).

> (3) [The third *cakra* is] to possess self-discipline of one's own mind. The correct teaching and practice is at the time of hearing, no scattered mind; at the time of thinking, no disparaging mind; at the time of cultivating spiritual practice, no inverted mind. If one doesn't discipline one's own mind, a good [dwelling] place and a *kalyāṇamitra* are of no use.
>
> (4) [The fourth *cakra,*] to have planted good roots [i.e., merit] in the past, is the constituent of liberation. Cultivate good roots. Good roots are faith, *śīla,* hearing, giving, and wisdom. Faith is Right Mindfulness (*samyaksmṛti*) of the Three Jewels. *Śīla* means not to stray from the good Path. Hearing [encompasses] one's own hearing, causing others to hear, not causing others to hear what is contrary [to the Truth], and not being an obstacle to others' hearing. Because of these four kinds of hearing, today the world is able to hear [the Dharma], reflect upon [the Dharma], and cultivate spiritual practice. [Hearing] can be a sufficient Dharma vessel for [these] three modes of attaining wisdom. [Next,] giving is of two kinds. Because one has in the past given material things to others, today one's desire is vanquished. Because one has in the past given of the Dharma to people, today one's ignorance is destroyed. . . . Therefore by this cause and condition, one attains the fruit of liberation. [Finally,] regarding wisdom, because in former lives this person has already chosen, reflected upon, and understood the Three Jewels and the Four [Noble] Truths, in this life she or he attains [the ten knowledges, from] worldly knowledge through exhaustive knowledge and no-birth knowledge.[3] (800b)

The text goes on to say that without merit from past lives, the other three *cakras* are of no use. Moreover, if any of these four *cakras* is lacking, liberation will not be attained (800c).

The first two *cakras* indicate the importance of having both a teacher and a practicing community, however small, around one. One needs exposure to the Dharma from such people, instruction by example as much as by word. Although Śākyamuni is the paradigmatic *kalyāṇamitra,* others may fill that role to a lesser extent. The list of characteristics of a *kalyāṇamitra* gives the practitioner practical guidance in determining what is a spiritually wholesome and what an unwholesome influence, whom she or he should seek or shun.

The third *cakra* is self-discipline of one's own mind. The first element in this *cakra,* "no scattered mind" at the time of hearing, refers to a disciplined mind, a mind that has been disciplined by calm or concentration such that the practitioner is capable of listening to teaching on the Dharma with undivided attention. This, then, is advice to cultivate concentration; this is the foundation of meditation practice in early Buddhism, but here this concentration is the foundation of listening practice.

The second element in the third *cakra* is "no disparaging mind" at the time of thinking. This stops short of something we will discuss later; namely, cultivation of "faithful joy" in the Mahāyāna. Here the author limits his advice to an admonition that the practitioner not take lightly or carelessly dismiss the teachings received, when he or she pauses to reflect upon them, but rather, open-mindedly and seriously consider their value.

Finally in this *cakra,* we have "at the time of cultivating spiritual practice, no inverted mind." This means simply that when one engages in spiritual practice, sincerity is essential. One's intentions, motives, values, and so on should be in harmony with one's actions.

The fourth and last *cakra* advises us to cultivate good roots, which are defined as faith, *śīla,* hearing, giving, and wisdom. Faith here is simply the maintenance of mindfulness of the Three Jewels. *Śīla* is mentioned only in passing, apparently indicating that it is assumed and virtually goes without saying. Hearing, in contrast, is very much stressed. This is reminiscent of Mahāyāna *sūtra* emphasis upon the importance of spreading the new (Mahāyāna) word; this Mahāyāna *śāstra* author appears to feel the same urgency. The inclusion of giving, both material and spiritual, in this list returns us to a traditional foundation of practice. By portraying giving as a practice with both material and spiritual elements and with both practical and spiritual consequences, the author succeeds in representing it as a practice for everyone, in all circumstances, with any aspiration. Finally, wisdom, as discussed here, would seem to be not so much itself a "good root," but rather the fruition in this life of the good roots of faith and practice sown in former lives. However, because the wisdom discussed is Hīnayānic wisdom, the author implies that Hīnayānic wisdom is a good root for the cultivation of Mahāyānic wisdom.

Such are the foundations of successful spiritual practice. I would judge that none of what we have covered so far is targeted by the author as a point that he especially wants to emphasize. This has all been more in the way of background that he assumes already is possessed by people coming to him for the instruction found in the *BNT*. It is a kind of summary of essential faith, moral discipline, mental concentration, merit, and supporting conditions. Note that very little has been said about meditation. Indeed, ordinary discursive thought in the form of reflection upon the Buddha's teachings has been endorsed. This indicates that the *BNT*'s author accepts the traditional idea that the cultivation of faith—in the sense of a degree of confidence and trust in the Buddha, his teaching, and the community he founded—and morality—in the sense of self-control, generosity to others, and virtue of all kinds—must precede the cultivation of meditational practices per se. Discursive reflection upon the Dharma is one of several essential ingredients in the early stages of practice, helping to determine whether one will engender the faith, effort, and discipline necessary to the treading of the Noble Path.

We now turn to more advanced practices that typify the form of spiritual cultivation advocated by the *BNT*. The following practice, the foundations of which were introduced in Chapter Four, is a four-part practice composed of the cultivation of faithful joy in the Mahāyāna, *prajñā,* meditative concentration, and *mahākaruṇā.* Because this practice is tied to one of the most emphasized themes of the text, it stands out as especially significant. The basic idea is as follows:

> There are four [classes] of people—the *icchantika,* the non-Buddhist, the *śrāvaka,* and the *pratyekabuddha*—who, because of four kinds of obstacle, do not see the Buddha nature. What are the four obstacles? (1) The *icchantika*'s obstacle is disregard and hatred of the Mahāyāna. To correct this, the Buddha taught the *bodhisattva* practice of cultivating faithful joy in the Mahāyāna.
>
> (2) The non-Buddhist's obstacle is giving rise to a self view with regard to all

> *dharmas*. To correct this, the Buddha taught the *bodhisattva* practice of cultivating *prajñāpāramitā*.
>
> (3) The obstacle of the *śrāvaka* is to fixedly grasp onto the thought of *duhkha* with regard to *saṃsāra*, such that [*śrāvakas* develop] a mind that is disgusted with and fearful of [*saṃsāra*]. To correct this, the Buddha taught the *bodhisattva* practice of cultivating the *samādhi* that destroys [false] emptiness. Those on the first [*bodhisattva*] stage and above can attain this *samādhi* and destroy such views as the false emptiness view. When one enters this insight, [one sees that emptiness] is neither identical with being or nonbeing, nor separate from being and nonbeing. To illustrate: it is like the insight into both absolute and worldly [Truths] at the eighth stage. . . .
>
> (4) The *pratyekabuddha*'s obstacle is disregarding activities benefiting sentient beings and creating a mind that rejects sentient beings. To correct this, the Buddha taught the cultivation of the *bodhisattva*'s *mahākaruṇā*. The activity of the *bodhisattva*'s *mahākaruṇā* is to benefit others. This shows that the *pratyekabuddha* only has an individual insight into cause and condition. He has no mind to save others, hence no *mahākaruṇā*. The *śrāvaka* is also like this.
>
> To overcome these four obstacles, we take faithful joy and the rest as four kinds of cause. By having all *bodhisattvas* cultivate these causes, they attain the pure *pāramitā* of the supreme *dharmakāya*. These are called the causes of the Buddha nature's purity. Such persons attain the name *Buddha's child*. (797c–798a)

The endorsement by this text of the quaternity of faithful joy in the Mahāyāna, *prajñā*, meditative concentration, and *mahākaruṇā* is taken from the *Ratnagotravibhāga*. The latter text, however, only names the four practices without commenting on them. The *BNT* devotes considerable space to the development of these ideas. Thus both the *Ratnagotra* material and the creativity of the *BNT*'s author shaped the formulation of the four practices that we will discuss here as the practices especially emphasized by the *BNT*.

Cultivation here translates *xiu-xi*, which connotes consistent and repeated engagement in practices intended to nurture one's spiritual potential. The concept of Buddhist practice we see reflected in this scheme requires a multifaceted approach in which one nurtures several human capacities conducive to spiritual growth. This four-part program of Buddhist practice reflects the traditional Buddhist idea of *bhāvanā*, spiritually nurturant practice inclusive of a multitude of forms.[4] Meditation alone is not all there is to Buddhist practice; rather, meditation is one of several kinds of practice that address the various aspects of human being, all of which are helped by guidance and nurturance. In the present case, faithful joy addresses our emotional and volitional faculties; *prajñā* and meditative concentration as discussed herein address primarily the nature of our consciousness, inclusive of our noetic and perceptual faculties; and *mahākaruṇā* addresses our instrumental and active faculties.

Though *śīla,* moral discipline, is notably absent from this list of qualities to be cultivated, we have seen that the basic moral disciplines already are assumed as prior practices readying one for the practices specifically encouraged in this text. This reflects the traditional concept of moral discipline as the foundation of practice. Of course, an element of morality also is implicit in *mahākaruṇā,* though this is not morality in the sense of restraint or discipline. *Mahākaruṇā* is spontaneous engagement in the world for the sake of the salvation of others.

In sum, then, in our author's mind, the four *cakras,* inclusive of the traditional disciplines of self-restraint, giving, and so on, are the first steps in practice. Then, at the stage on which he focuses, come faithful joy as a kind of foundation for Mahāyāna practice, specific *prajñā* and meditation exercises, and finally, compassion. Let us look further at the particulars.

The four practices that have been highlighted are the "causes" of three virtues, as follows: "The cultivation of faithful joy in the Mahāyāna is the cause of the purity of the *dharmakāya;* this should be known. The cultivation of *prajñā* and meditative concentration (*chan ding*) bring about the virtue of a Buddha's wisdom; this should be known. The cultivation of the *bodhisattva's mahākaruṇā* is the cause of the virtue of loving kindness; this should be known" (801a). Furthermore,

> The cultivation of faithful joy in the Mahāyāna is like a vessel in which there is limitless meditation and wisdom (*ding hui*). Because it is completely filled with the Great Jewel [the Dharma], it resembles a vessel.
>
> The cultivations of *prajñā* and mediative concentration are incomprehensible; since they are the foundation of [the *dharmakāya*'s] merits, *prajñā* is like a pure jewel and meditative concentration is like a wish-fulfilling jewel.
>
> The cultivation of the *bodhisattva's mahākaruṇā* is like pure water because a single taste nourishes all sentient beings in the world. (801a)

Let us consider the key terms in these practices. *Faithful joy* is a compound Chinese term *xin le,* composed of "faith" + "joy, bliss," and meaning faith and pleasure in the Dharma or the happiness inherent in Buddhist faith. The term is used by the Pure Land and Yogācāra schools, each in its own way, but here its meaning is best understood from its use as a corrective practice for the *icchantika. Icchantikas* hold an "upside-down" view: they find joy and pleasure in *saṃsāra* and in the five *skandha*—whose nature is truly *duhkha,* the opposite of pleasurable—and for this reason turn their back on Buddhism. The *icchantika* who seeks joy in *saṃsāra* is destined to be disappointed and should drop the "upside-down" view motivating such an attempt. The *BNT*'s author argues, though, that to see *saṃsāra* as *duhkha* is only half a correction. In the Mahāyāna one can find a joy that is based upon something real, namely, the Buddha nature, which is both freedom from *duhkha* and the positive realization of the four great virtues including "bliss *pāramitā.*" The *icchantika*'s search for joy per se is not misguided; it is misguided only insofar as it is doomed to failure because the *icchantika* is seeking joy in *saṃsāra,* where none is to be found. Thus faith in the Mahāyāna is joyful or pleasurable because it gives a reliable and constant joy, rather than a doomed and constantly eroding pseudo-joy. This faith is not a creedal faith nor a faith in some transcendent Good. Faith in Mahāyāna is existential release from the sorrow of seeing one's fleeting joys forever slipping through one's fingers. This is what the text means in speaking of faithful joy as "purity": letting go of the false, of the delusory and sorrow-producing dream, coupled with the freedom and joy attendant to realizing the real. What is false cannot produce joy; what is real, can. Hence, Mahāyāna faith is joy.

Faithful joy is compared to "a vessel in which there is limitless meditation and wisdom (*ding hui*)" because "it is completely filled with the Great Jewel [the Dharma]." Faithful joy is the vessel, the Dharma vessel; it is that which makes possible the carrying forward of the Dharma. Without faith, one would not engage in meditation and consequently not attain wisdom. The Dharma is embodied in all of these—faith, meditation, and wisdom—and without any one of them, the Dharma would not exist.

The cultivations of *prajñāpāramitā* and meditative concentration are grouped together as the jewellike causes of Buddha's wisdom.

The cultivation of *prajñāpāramitā* is a two-tiered practice that refers, first, to practice to engender in the non-Buddhist recognition that there is no self in *saṃsāra* and, second, to the deepening of this insight into realization of the self *pāramitā* nature of this universal nonexistence of self.

The third item in the set of four is named less definitely than the other three. It usually is named as the *samādhi* that destroys false emptiness, but sometimes, more generally, as meditative concentration. The latter is *chan ding,* literally *dhyāna-samādhi.* Both *dhyāna* and *samādhi* are used in a variety of ways by different groups and at different times. *Dhyāna* may be used in a specific sense as transic absorption (in several well-defined levels), or it may refer to meditation in general, mental cultivation, or the examination of the mind and mental objects, especially in a condition of mental stillness. *Samādhi* tends to refer to the cultivation of mental concentration, the stilling of the activities of the mind, the development of one-pointedness of mind. The compound *chan ding* means the combination of these two.

The *samādhi* that destroys false emptiness is a specific cultivation recommended for a specific purpose: as a cure for those who are attached to a one-sided, nihilistic view of emptiness. This *samādhi* is related by our author to the attainment of passage through the "emptiness liberation gate." The usual understanding of the latter is that it is simply insight into the emptiness of all things on the basis of conditioned origination. Our author, however, understands it as a gate representing freedom from a negative view of emptiness.

> There are arrogant people who grasp emptiness as a view. This is the real emptiness true liberation gate. This emptiness liberation gate, arising from grasping emptiness, is [attachment to the view that] all things are nonbeing; all is emptiness. This attachment to emptiness is contrary to reality. Because it is contrary to reality, both cause and effect, that is, the two Truths of Path and Principle, are lost [in it]. Having become attached to this emptiness, one falls into false nothingness. This kind of attachment arises by means of emptiness and in this way produces a false view. [Generally speaking,] all false views can be extinguished by means of emptiness. But this view arises on the basis of emptiness and therefore cannot be corrected. Because of such a person, the Buddha said, "Kāśyapa, if a person gives rise to a self view, though that view is as large as Mt. Sumeru, I promise to sanction him. Why? Because [that view] can be destroyed. But

> this emptiness view of the arrogant person is like one-quarter of the tip of a hair. I quickly rebuke it and certainly do not promise sanction."[5] (797b)

The apparent fact that there were people who understood emptiness in a one-sided, negative manner has been discussed with concern several times in this text. Consider the placement of this "*samādhi* to destroy false emptiness" in the company of this quartet of practices. Faith is universally accepted as the starting point for a Buddhist practitioner. It is axiomatic that one must have a certain amount of confidence and trust in the Buddha's word and in the Path before one will be willing to take the first step on that Path. *Prajñāpāramitā,* of course, is the foundation of Mahāyāna thought and practice, and compassion is equally universally accepted. In this company of unquestionable pillars of the Mahāyāna Path is entered this particular *samādhi.* Obviously a matter of focal concern finds expression here. The *samādhi* that destroys false emptiness is the fulfillment of the thematic statement cited earlier: "Buddha nature is the Thusness revealed by the dual emptiness of person and things. . . . If one does not speak of Buddha nature, then one does not understand emptiness" (787b). Without realization of Buddha nature, emptiness has not been understood. The cure for those stuck halfway is the *samādhi* that destroys false emptiness. This *samādhi* is called an *insight* (*guan*). It is an insight constituted by a nondualistic, hence nonnegative apperception of the true nature of emptiness as "neither identical with being or nonbeing, nor separate from being and nonbeing." Despite its importance, this *samādhi* is not loftily out of reach. Those on the first *bodhisattva* stage and above, that is, anyone who has engendered *bodhicitta,* the Thought of Enlightenment, can attain it. Insofar as this insight "is like the insight into both absolute and worldly [Truths] at the eighth [*bodhisattva*] stage," its consequences, quite evidently, are found in the practitioner's freedom from a dualistic view of *saṃsāra* and *nirvāṇa,* such that he or she courses without obstruction in both. As the *BNT* typically puts it: "These people all travel the Path of the equality of *saṃsāra* and *nirvāṇa* (*ping deng zhi Dao*). They dwell in the condition of not-dwelling. Although they course in *saṃsāra,* they are not sullied. Although they course in *nirvāṇa,* they are also not 'pure' [in a dualistic sense]. But because of *mahākaruṇā,* they do not reject *saṃsāra;* because of *prajñā,* they do not reject *nirvāṇa*" (797c).

Thus when one passes through the emptiness liberation gate (thanks to the *samādhi* that destroys false emptiness), *mahākaruṇā* lies directly ahead.

Mahākaruṇā is "great compassion." It is linked, appropriately, to the Buddha's virtue of loving kindness (*en*) and is likened to pure water, due to its ability to nourish all. I will postpone further discussion of this term until the rest of the textual material on *mahākaruṇā* is introduced later.

The set of four practices is further elucidated as follows:

> There are four aspects to the meaning of *child of the Buddha:* cause, condition, basis, and completion. (1) There are two causes [of realizing one's status as "child of the Buddha"]: Buddha nature and faithful joy. Of these two, Buddha nature is unconditioned; faithful joy is conditioned. Faithful joy as that which attains Buddha nature is the cause of completion because it manifests and completes the true cause nature [i.e., Buddha nature]. Faithful joy as *prayoga* is the productive cause because it gives rise to all practices. (798a)

Note here the sensitive and useful distinction drawn between *asaṃskṛta,* unconditioned Buddha nature, and *saṃskṛta,* conditioned faithful joy. This distinction holds in fruitful tension two aspects of Buddha nature theory that could seem mutually contradictory.[6] On the one hand, the identification of Buddha nature as unconditioned and as the ultimate source of realization (of Buddha nature) is fundamental to this text. Moreover, it is consistent with the idea that Buddha nature is both cause and effect and as cause already is perfect and complete. On the other hand, the author of this text very much wants to validate Buddhist practice in the ordinary, mundane sense, and this is nicely accomplished with the validation of conditioned faithful joy—the acknowledgement, in other words, that the practitioner is intentionally engaging in specific acts chosen because they promise to lead one to the desired goal, acts tested by tradition and found to be effective to that end. This tension between the inherent perfection of the Buddha nature and the necessity for practice becomes, of course, a major paradox in Chan, resulting occasionally in a breakdown of the tension such that one pole of the paradox, the necessity of practice, is rejected. As we have seen, in the *BNT* Buddha nature is identified with Buddhist practice; thus neither the inherent perfection of Buddha nature nor the necessity of practice can be foresworn without the loss of the central theme of the text. The author deftly handles this tension here by the simple device of naming both conditioned practice and unconditioned Buddha nature as the dual causes of realization. Note that faithful joy is the "productive cause" precisely because it produces practice.

> (2) The condition [of realizing one's status as "child of the Buddha"] is *prajñāpāramitā.* Because it is the condition of all unconditioned merits, it produces the individual *bodhisattvas.*
>
> (3) The basis [of realizing one's status as "child of the Buddha"] is the *samādhi* that destroys [the grasping of a false] emptiness. The attachments of a person who takes pleasure in being (*you*) are severed because there is [in being] no condition for 'having' bliss, purity, etc. The *bodhisattva* who cultivates the *samādhi* that destroys [the grasping of a false] emptiness can remove that grasping [to emptiness] by the power of this *samādhi.* That is why the *bodhisattva*'s *dharmakāya* is firm, rather than weak. (798a)

Here the grasping of, or attachment to, emptiness is set up as a parallel to the grasping of being. The act of grasping itself is the problem, and this is overcome by the *samādhi* that destroys false emptiness. This freedom from all forms of attachment makes the *bodhisattva*'s *dharmakāya* strong, and thus this *samādhi* can serve as the foundation or basis of one's status as child of Buddha.

"(4) The completion [of realizing one's status as "child of the Buddha"] is the *bodhisattva's mahākaruṇā,* because it profits others in endless engagements. Because Thusness is limitless and *sattvas* are innumerable, the profiting activities [of *mahākaruṇā*] also are limitless" (798a).

This statement on *mahākaruṇā* follows the pattern we by now expect, so let us pass immediately on to a subsequent passage in which a great deal more is said of *mahākaruṇā,* including some very interesting things. "The meaning of *mahākaruṇā* has three aspects: its essence, its greatness and the distinctions [between it and *karuṇā*]. 1. Its essence is *prajñā. Prajñā* has two aspects: nondiscriminating, supreme wisdom and discriminating, worldly wisdom. We take discriminating wisdom as the essence of *mahākaruṇā,* because *mahākaruṇā* is the condition of the uplifting of sentient beings" (796c). To link *prajñā* and *karuṇā,* or wisdom and compassion, is the standard Mahāyāna message. This passage, however, goes beyond this familiar slogan to examine the functional implications of this linkage. Usually *prajñā* is considered to function in a nondiscriminating, nondualistic manner; indeed, it has been so labeled many times in this text. Here, however, *prajñā* is attributed two aspects: "nondiscriminating, supreme wisdom and discriminating, worldly wisdom." This in itself is remarkable; we are told here in unmistakable terms that *prajñā* is inclusive of, though not limited to, discriminating, worldly wisdom.[7] Moreover, discriminating wisdom is regarded as the "essence of *mahākaruṇā,* because *mahākaruṇā* is the condition of the uplifting of sentient beings." Thus when *prajñā* is labeled the *essence* of *mahākaruṇā,* it is really discriminating, worldly *prajñā* which the author has in mind. Of course, this is enlightened discrimination, but discrimination nonetheless. This makes intuitive sense. The *bodhisattva* must grapple with the existential condition of sentient beings, which prominently includes discrimination, to be of any help to the latter. Moreover, the *bodhisattva*'s disinclination to turn his back on *saṃsāra,* discussed earlier, naturally entails that he also not turn his back on worldly wisdom; that is, the wisdom that functions in the context of *saṃsāra.*

> 2. There are five aspects to the meaning of the greatness [of *mahākaruṇā*]. . . . (1) [It is great because its practice incorporates] giving supplies for body and spirit (*saṃbhāra*): the two practices of *saṃbhāra* [i.e., material and spiritual giving] can produce great happiness, virtue, wisdom and meditation. (2) [It is great] because its mark is the ability to have insight into the three forms of *duhkha*[8] and to save all sentient beings [from *saṃsāra*]. (3) [It is great] because of its place of practice: it takes the three worlds of sentient beings as its place.[9] (4) [It is great] because of its impartiality: it gives rise to an impartial mind regarding the condition of all sentient beings. (5) [It is great] because of its supremacy: nothing surpasses this spiritual cultivation. (796c)

The first aspect of the greatness of *mahākaruṇā* makes clear that both spiritual and material giving are part of compassion. These two forms of giving are not even ranked, but referred to by a single, inclusive term. The "impartial mind" mentioned in the fourth aspect refers to a mind that regards all persons as inherently equal, specifically in the sense that no person is more or less deserving than any other of the *bodhisattva*'s compassion, of relief from suffering, of material help and of spiritual instruction.

> 3. There are eight distinctions [between *karuṇā* and *mahākaruṇā*]. (1)

> Distinction in inherent nature: the boundlessness of *karuṇā* has nonanger as its nature; *mahākaruṇā* has nondelusion as its nature. (2) Distinction in mark: *karuṇā* has the suffering inherent in *duhkha* as its mark; *mahākaruṇā* has the three *duhkhas* as its mark. (3) Distinction in place of activity: *karuṇā* has the desire realm as its field; *mahākaruṇā* penetrates all three realms. (4) Distinction in stage: *karuṇā* takes the fourth *dhyāna* as its stage;[10] *mahākaruṇā* takes the no-outflow Tathāgata fruit as its stage. (5) Distinction in the sphere [in which it is expressed]: *karuṇā* [is manifested by] ordinary persons and [those in] the Two Vehicles [*śrāvaka* and *pratyekabuddha*]; *mahākaruṇā* [is manifested] only by *bodhisattvas* and Buddhas. (6) Distinction in virtue: *karuṇā* takes freedom from desire and from the desire realm as its virtue; *mahākaruṇā* takes freedom from desire and from all three realms as its virtue. (7) Distinction in [efficacy of] salvation: *karuṇā* only has the heart-mind to relieve suffering, it does not take action to relieve suffering; *mahākaruṇā* has both the heart-mind [to relieve suffering] and the activities [to that end]. (8) Distinction in being ultimate and nonultimate: *karuṇā* can relieve suffering for a short while, but it cannot truly save; *mahākaruṇā* can eternally save because it never abandons [the suffering]. (796c–797a)

The primary objective of this list of distinctions obviously is to show how and why *mahākaruṇā* is superior to *karuṇā*. Many of these points are self-evident, but a few require some comment. According to the first distinction, though *karuṇā* is "boundless," its inferiority as compared to *mahākaruṇā* is related to their difference in essential nature: *karuṇā*'s nature is essentially nonanger, whereas that of *mahākaruṇā* is essentially nondelusion. The idea, evidently, is that anger may be eliminated while some delusion remains, but if delusion is uprooted, anger has no foundation and cannot arise. The idea of *karuṇā* as freedom from anger is consistent with the fourth distinction, in which *karuṇā* is associated with the fourth *dhyāna*, which is characterized by freedom from emotion or, in other words, equanimity, and by mindfulness. The sixth distinction adds that *karuṇā* also involves freedom from desire. Thus it would seem that freedom from desire and freedom from anger go hand in hand and that the two are expressed positively in equanimity.

The seventh and eight distinctions seem at first to be mutually inconsistent, but I believe the point is as follows. The seventh distinction shows that *mahākaruṇā* does not separate the compassionate heart-mind from compassionate acts. In the case of *karuṇā*, however, various conditions can interfere with the expression in action of a compassion that is sincerely felt. There are plenty of cases in which a person feels *karuṇā* but does nothing. This is explained by the point with which this discussion of *mahākaruṇā* began: the essence of *mahākaruṇā* is *prajñā*. What could interfere with the expression in action of a compassionate feeling? Contradictory feelings, such as one of many forms of self-interest, or perhaps the inability to determine a useful course of action are sources of such blockage, and these are the kinds of things that *prajñā* would eliminate. The eighth point is similar: all the compassion in the world is no guarantee of effective action; *prajñā*—discriminating, worldly wisdom, that is—is necessary to know the right action to take under the circumstances at hand in order to help others along the Path toward ultimate liberation.

But please note, though *karuṇā* is throughout compared with *mahākaruṇā* to the detriment of the former, nowhere is it said that *karuṇā* as such should be dismissed. Such an idea would never occur to the author of the *BNT*. To the contrary, *karuṇā* may be inferior but it is still "boundless." It may be the practice of ordinary persons, *śrāvaka* and *pratyekabuddha*, but its expression in action is still *saṃbhāra*. It may be a relatively early stage, but it is still part of the Buddhist path; it constitutes "good roots" planted now that will bear fruit in one's own spiritual practice in the future.

Let us leave the quaternity of faithful joy, *prajñā*, meditative concentration, and *mahākaruṇā* and turn to a final set of passages that also are characteristic of the *BNT*'s instructions on practice. These passages are introduced in the context of a discussion of *āśrayaparāvṛtti*, which the reader will recall is a synonym in this text for the Buddha nature understood as Buddhist practice. The *āśrayaparāvṛtti*, we are told here, is constituted by two categories; namely, the abandonment of desire, which is equivalent to the Truth of Cessation, and the cause of abandoning desire, which is equivalent to the Truth of Path. This shows very clearly that *āśrayaparāvṛtti* is both cause and fruit of realization. For present purposes, we will concentrate on the causal aspect of *āśrayaparāvṛtti*.

"The cause of abandoning desire embraces the Path of seeing Truth and the Path of spiritual cultivation; these are for the purpose of attaining the *dharmakāya*" (801c). This refers to a traditional scheme of stages of practice on the Buddhist Path. According to this scheme, there are three stages of practice. The first is the Path of seeing. This stage is initiated with the arising of the Thought of Enlightenment and corresponds to the first *bodhisattva bhūmi.* The second stage is the Path of spiritual cultivation, which consists of cutting off delusion and developing further insight into the Truth; it corresponds to the second through the tenth of the *bodhisattva bhūmi.* The third stage is that of one who has realized the ultimate and has nothing further to learn; it is manifested in the Tathāgata fruit. Here the *BNT* tells us that the "cause of abandoning desire" embraces the entire Buddhist Path, short of the final stage, at which there is nothing further to learn. The passage continues by speaking of the goal of practice and that which obscures it:

> We speak of the nondiscriminating wisdom of this realm [of *dharmakāya*] as resembling the sun, in three ways. Because of its no-outflow purity, it resembles the disc of the sun. Because it completely illuminates all realms, it resembles the sun's brilliance. Because it can oppose and cure all that clouds the Truth, it resembles the sun's rays.
>
> Comment: "all that clouds the Truth" refers to thought in its entirety, and the adversities of *kleśa,* karma, and retribution. "Thought in its entirety" takes *kleśa*-seed as cause, desire for the objects of the five senses as condition, and incorrect thought as simultaneous cause. Together these three are called *thought in its entirety.* They cloud and conceal Reality [such that one] does not see it and does not know it. Upon the arising of the one realm of the *dharmakāya* that is free from desire, you will see and know this. (801c–802a)

Ultimately, then, the "cure" for delusion is the *dharmakāya* itself, just as we saw above that the ultimate "cause" of realizing one's status as Buddha's child is the unconditioned Buddha nature. But just as we saw in that context that conditioned faithful joy also had an essential role to play, so here certain practices are recommended.

> How does one see and know the Tathāgata's *dharmakāya* that is free from desire? [One sees and knows it] in the Reality of thinking in which one sees neither thoughts nor objects. Objects are called *parikalpita-svabhāva.* Thoughts are called *paratantra*[*-svabhāva*]. Because one sees neither the *parikalpita-* nor the *paratantra-svabhāva,* it is called *parinișpanna* [*svabhāva*]: seeing and knowing the one realm [of *dharmakāya*].
>
> Moreover, thoughts are persons [as subjects]; objects are *dharmas.* Not to see persons and *dharmas,* thoughts and objects, is called the *two*

> *emptinesses.* The Tathāgata sees and knows all *dharmas* like this because he has penetrated the *bhūtatathatā* and [realized] the universal sameness [of all things]. The nonincrease and nondecrease of subject and object is called *insight into universal sameness.* This insight can overcome obstacles to seeing Reality As It Is (*zhen shi*). As inclusive of the Path of seeing and the Path of spiritual cultivation, it is the general cause of the Tathāgata's attainment. (802a)

In other words, in this formulation, insight into the emptiness of both subject and object is virtually the be all and end all of Buddhist practice. From the beginning of Buddhist meditation theory, it consistently was held that insight (*vipaśyanā,* Ch. *guan*) rather than concentration (*śamatha*) was the key to the attainment of enlightenment. Concentration was a tool for the better production of insight. This emphasis on the importance of meditative insight lies behind the meditation teachings given in the *BNT.* In the present passage, "insight into universal sameness" is stressed as the key to enlightenment. In the quaternity of practices discussed earlier, the "*samādhi* that destroys emptiness" was uniquely emphasized, and this *samādhi* was specifically identified as an "insight."

In this context, we should note that there always is a very close fit between the meditative insight practices recommended by a text and the philosophical views expressed in that text.[11] This is clearly evident in the *BNT.* We already have seen that the "*samādhi* that destroys emptiness" is the practical fulfillment of the *BNT*'s stress upon the necessity of attaining positive realization by way of the negations of *śūnyatā.* Similarly, the stress here upon "insight into universal sameness" brings out the importance in the *BNT* of Yogācāra philosophy. In the latter, adherence to the belief in both the self and the objective world constitutes delusion. As the above quotation indicates, the eradication of this delusion frees one to see Reality As It Is; that is, another "positive realization." When recommending the "*samādhi* that destroys emptiness," the author is particularly targeting persons with negative views of *śūnyatā,* a very troubling and prominent form of delusion from the author's point of view. The "insight into universal sameness" is more universally recommended for anyone with the commonsensical, "realist" view entailing an existential commitment to a universe composed of "selves" and "things."

> In this sense, the cause of abandoning desire attains completion when conjoined with two practices. These two practices are the cultivation of the

> Principle of Thusness and the cultivation of Plenary Thusness. In the world, there are only two things to be known: people and things. One who is able to penetrate these two [kinds of] emptiness eternally realizes the true pinnacle of Thusness. Hence this is called the *Principle of Thusness.* The ultimate Plenary Thusness probes the source, attains to the [true] nature, and penetrates the source of the *dharmadhātu;* thus it is spoken of as the ultimate. . . .
>
> The knowledge of Plenary Thusness: The ultimate and exhaustive knowledge of all realms is called the *knowledge of Plenary Thusness*. . . . All Tathāgata *dharmas,* in this sense, are called *Plenary Thusness.* The first stage *bodhisattva* attains these two [forms of] knowledge [i.e., knowledge of the Principle of Thusness and of Plenary Thusness]. Because she or he penetrates the all-encompassing *dharmadhātu* principle, both *saṃsāra* and *nirvāṇa* are known. (802a–802b)

To realize *dharmakāya,* then, one cultivates two kinds of knowledge, of the Principle of Thusness and of Plenary Thusness. Knowledge of the Principle of Thusness is knowledge of Thusness as such: the positive realization of the true nature of all things, by way of *śūnyatā*'s negating of conventional views. Knowledge of Plenary Thusness takes this fundamental realization and extends it by probing its contents vis-à-vis the entire universe, the *dharmadhātu.* Thus to know the Principle of Thusness is to know the fundamental principle; knowledge of Plenary Thusness is the application of that principle to all things, or the infinite particularization of the general.

> These two [forms of] knowledge are self-realized; the knowledge is attained by oneself having attained understanding, it is not attained from another. Only by oneself does one attain realization; it is not caused by another. This is called self-realization of knowledge and correct views.
>
> Moreover, these two [forms of] knowledge have two marks. . . . Nonattachment is to see the inherent purity of the realm of sentient beings. It is the mark of the knowledge of the Principle of Thusness. Nonobstruction means limitless penetration of all realms and limitless insight into them. It is the mark of the knowledge of Plenary Thusness. Again, these two [forms of] knowledge have two meanings. . . . The knowledge of the Principle of Thusness is the cause; it is the cause of the production of *saṃsāra* and of *nirvāṇa.* The knowledge of Plenary Thusness is fruit insofar as in this principle is completed all-sufficient knowledge of the Tathāgata's ultimate and worldly *dharmas.* (802b)

Realization of the Principle of Thusness, then, recalls us to the *pāramitā* of purity: the world is not inherently flawed, as the *śrāvaka* believes. With the realization of Thusness, one can see the lotus in the mud. This realization is characterized by nonattachment, which I interpret as meaning nonattachment to both *nirvāṇa* and *saṃsāra,* due to the realization of their intrinsic nondifference. Nonobstruction is described as the Tathāgata's all-knowledge; it is knowledge of all realms and all *dharmas,* on both the worldly and the ultimate levels. In these two realizations, then, we see the characteristic *BNT* emphases on the goodness of the world, the positive nature of realization, and the harmonious mutual validity of worldly and ultimate knowledge. This double validation of the worldly and the ultimate results in practice in a person who would be nonattached and nonobstructed in both the mundane and the supreme realms. Such a person also would be adept in the practical wisdom of *mahākaruṇā.*

CHAPTER SEVEN

Buddha Nature and the Concept of Person

Buddhism has a profound and thoroughly developed set of teachings on human being. One might well argue that the question of human being is the question par excellence with which the Buddhist tradition as a whole struggles. According to the traditional account, the point of departure for the Buddha's own search, discoveries, and teachings was the dilemma of the human condition. Moreover, vast numbers of Buddhist texts speak out of or address human experience as such, consciously focusing upon it as source of both question and answer. Nonetheless, many questions a modern Westerner asks as a matter of course about human being are not directly addressed in the Buddhist texts. Of course there are important reasons for this. Our concept of and assumptions about human individuality are profoundly different from Buddhist views of the same. Our two worlds of discourse about the value and meaning of incarnate, finite existence, the course of history, the meaning of suffering, and the nature of possible human greatness are set up on entirely different foundations. Thus for a contemporary Westerner to ask the question, What is a person? What is human being? of a Buddhist text is to set oneself up to receive an answer that does not satisfy the intent of the question. Yet, although Buddhist views and assumptions differ so markedly from our own, Buddhist texts reveal in their own way a preoccupation with the human condition as intent as that of our own hyperindividualistic, anthropocentric culture.

With such a shared fixation, it is inevitable that persons on both sides of the cultural boundaries will attempt to gain light from the other side on this subject, despite the incommensurability of each other's questions and answers. This chapter is such an attempt. Herein I will engage in dialogue the *BNT,* in an attempt to wrest from the text answers to two categories of questions: its view of the ontological nature of human being and its view of the existential status of human beings. In the course of the discussion I will ask such questions as, What roles do individuality and freedom play in the view of human being portrayed in this text? What value, if any, does an individual human personality possess? Is there anything of value in human history?

Clearly, the text itself does not speak in these terms; these are the questions of a twentieth-century, philosophically inclined American. Acknowledging that the text itself neither speaks this language nor shares my concerns, in this chapter I will put my questions to the text and attempt to extract from the text its implications for the subject of my concern. In other words, I cannot claim that the author of the *BNT* makes the statements I will give as responses to my questions about human being, but I do claim that these views are implicit in and follow from the statements he made about Buddha nature. Granting that human freedom requires us to expect the unexpected, I nonetheless believe that, if the author of the *BNT* were here today and could engage in dialogue with me, as long as my interlocutor remained consistent, something close to the views I will articulate in the course of this chapter would emerge.

First, let me specify that I use the world *person* as an equivalent of "human person." Insofar as I am seeking to discover what the text has to say about the nature of human being, there is, at first glance, a somewhat poor fit between this intention and the concept of Buddha nature. The bottom-line statement in the Buddha nature textual tradition is "all sentient beings (*sattva, zhong sheng*) possess the Buddha nature." Entailed by the Buddha nature concept in particular and the Buddhist perspective in general is the view that human beings as a class belong in the larger world of sentient existents and should not be singled out as ontologically discontinuous with regard to other existents. This is a very important and well-known point in Buddhist thought: human beings are not an ontologically separate class, insofar as sentient beings migrate among the six destinies (the realms of hell beings, demons, hungry ghosts, animals, humans, and gods) in dependence upon their karma. The dominant Western belief that humans are a special class, distinct forever from animals below and God above, of course, stems from the Biblical tradition.

On the other hand, Buddhism always has recognized that there is a unique feature of the human condition that although it does not put us in an entirely separate class, does make the human race special with respect to Buddhist soteriology. This special feature is the capability we have to understand our condition and respond in such a way as to radically alter the parameters of our existence. This may account for the fact that in the *BNT,* the text repeatedly speaks in terms of the three categories of ordinary persons (*fan fu*), *bodhisattvas* or sages (*pu sa* or *sheng ren*), and buddhas (*fo*) (e.g., 806b). Thus in the mind of our author, too, it is necessary to single out human beings (or at least anthropomorphic beings) to speak of our condition and our potential. Because the text repeatedly uses this framework for its analysis, there is no great gap between its perspective and my question, What is a (human) person?

What is a person, according to the *Buddha Nature Treatise*? There are two dimensions to this question, an existential dimension and an ontological-metaphysical dimension.[1] To discover what a person is according to the latter dimension requires of us that we clarify what it means to say that a person "exists." What is the nature of this existence? What is the meaning of the word *person* in the phrase *personal existence?* To ask what a person is in an existential sense is to ask what behaviors—in the broad sense of all physical and psychological acts—are characteristic or paradigmatic for human persons. How would we characterize the essence of human character? What possibilities belong intrinsically to human beings, and in what way are these possibilities actualized? Of course, because the text does not pose these questions in this way, it also does not answer them in an explicit manner. What follows is my own interpretation of the implications of the textual material for these questions posed from the outside, by a person who lives in a culture dominated by another world-view.

A. The Ontological-Metaphysical Dimension

There are two main points to the *BNT*'s understanding of the ontological nature of a human person: First, a person is not an entity of any kind, but consists of actions; and second, a person does not exist in contradistinction to a world, but is correctly conceived as inseparable from world. We will begin with the first point.

When I say that the author of the *BNT* speaks of the ontological nature of a human being as a series of acts, I mean that he identifies the person with a particular series of physical and psychological acts and indicates that this is the entirety of the person; there is no entity that performs the acts. This, of course, is the classic Buddhist position from very early times.

The following examples, culled from previously discussed passages, will demonstrate the way in which the *BNT*'s views apply to a concept of the person. I can do no more than give a handful of examples; if one were to read the *BNT* itself, one would find that this perspective of the person as a series of actions pervades virtually every line of the text. Moreover, the text does not struggle toward this position as toward a conclusion, but speaks out of this perspective as a starting point.

First example, the true nature, as a term descriptive of Buddha nature and hence of human being, is explained in terms of three kinds of action: purification (of the deluded and relative natures), liberation, and the cultivation of the Buddhist virtues. It is not a thing, but these acts.

Second example, the second component of *tathāgatagarbha* is given as Buddhist practice, which is equated with wisdom. Because wisdom is employed as interchangeable with Buddhist practice, it cannot be interpreted as representing any kind of static or substantial basis of subjectivity (such as a pure mind or self). Practice is a kind of doing, and wisdom is a particular practice—acting or doing wisely.

Third example, *āśrayaparāvṛtti* is defined as Buddhist practice. Naturally, this means it is of an active rather than an entitative nature. Because *Buddhist practice* here means the process of self-transformation of the individual progressing from delusion to awakening, the *transformation of the basis* means the transformation of the person. The Buddha nature, then, is not that which lives the Buddhist life; it is the active, verbal doing or living of the life.

Fourth and final example, the text identifies the Buddha nature with the four *guṇapāramitā,* or supreme perfections, one of which is *ātmapāramitā,* perfection of self. Although this sort of language makes the Buddha nature sound like an entity par excellence, the text removes the possibility of such an understanding by explaining *ātmapāramitā* as the active realization of the emptiness of all things; in other words, it simply gives the name *ātmapāramitā* to experiential *prajñāpāramitā*. "All the non-Buddhists perceive and grasp a self within the five *skandhas*. Overturning that attachment to self as vacuous and cultivating *prajñāpāramitā*, one realizes the supreme not-self which is identical to the self-*pāramitā* (*ātmapāramitā, wo bo-le-mi*). This is the fruit [of the practice of *prajñāpāramitā*]" (798c).

The second important theme concerning the ontological nature of the person is the view that a person does not exist in any way separate from a world. The perspective of the *BNT* is plainly opposed to any such subject-object split. In the *BNT*, personal being always is continuous with the being of a world. The *trisvabhāva* are three ways (actually two, insofar as the three reduce to a pure and an impure *paratantra*) in which the person experiences what is given (the world) and what is given (the world) presents itself to the person. In fact, even this way of speaking fails to do justice to the continuity between person and world. A person is a series of events that, in the language of subjectivity, are called experiences. But experience, in fact, is not a matter of pure subjectivity. Experience is always "experience of" something. Experience ordinarily is conceived as the point of contact between a subject and an object. But in the *BNT* these two are portrayed as a single, primitive given, unified in itself, and divisible only upon secondary analysis. Ontologically, then, a person is this primitive given: an experiential world or a personal world.

The inseparability of subject and world is conveyed also in the concept of Thusness. This is captured rather nicely in the following passage: "All sentient beings are (*shi*^{2}) the *tathāgatagarbha* (*ru-lai-zang*). There are two meanings of 'Thus' (*ru* in *ru-lai-zang*). The first is the knowledge of Thusness (*ru-ru-zhi*) and the second is the realm of Thusness (*ru-ru-jing*). Because the two stand together, we speak of the Thusness of Thusness (*ru-ru*)" (795c). Here we see the conjunction in the single term *ru-ru* of the knowledge of Thusness (*zhi*, a standard term for the subjective) and the Thusness "realm" (*jing*, a standard term for the objective). Although ordinarily the *zhi* is the cognizer and the *jing* the cognized, in the case of

Thusness, the two "stand together," and the term Thusness as *ru-ru* is coined to embrace them simultaneously. As such it graphically represents their inseparability.

Finally, in a section devoted to the elucidation of the Middle Path, the author of the *BNT* provides an example intended to discredit the practice of "discriminating the grasper and the grasped and considering them to really exist." In other words, the intention here is to discredit the idea of discrete subjects and objects.

> Discriminating grasper and grasped and taking them really to exist: In the *sūtra,* the Buddha uses a magician as an illustration to draw us away from these two extremes.[2] "Kāśyapa, it is like a magician who conjures magical images. The tigers that he makes turn around and devour the magician. Kāśyapa, when *bhikṣus* whose method of contemplation is like this contemplate an object, what appears [to them] is merely empty. Hence, there is nothing to the 'real' and no reality to the false."
>
> How then can one escape the extremes [of grasped and grasper], and by relying on the *manovijñāna* (*yi shi*)[3] create consciousness-only wisdom? Consciousness-only wisdom (*wei shi zhi*) is the wisdom [constituted by the understanding that] all sense data [*guṇa*] lack an essence. When this consciousness-only wisdom is perfected, it turns around and extinguishes its own root; namely, *manovijñāna.* How is this? Because the sense data lack essence, *manovijñāna* is not produced. With the *manovijñāna* not produced, consciousness-only wisdom self-destructs. *Manovijñāna* is like the magician; consciousness-only wisdom is like the magical tiger. Because *manovijñāna* produces consciousness-only wisdom, when the contemplation of consciousness-only is perfected, it can turn and destroy *manovijñāna.* Why? Because sense data lack being (*wu*). Thus *manovijñāna* is not produced, just as in the example the magical tiger turns and devours the magician. As Aryadeva says in verse,
>
> Throughout the three realms,[4] the origin of *manovijñāna*
> Is always to be found in sense data.
> When one perceives that sense data have no essence
> Existing seeds are naturally extinguished.
> (809b–c)[5]

This example ably demonstrates the text's assertion of the nonduality of the grasped "object" and the grasping "mind." The argument adheres closely to Yogācāra doctrine. Yogācāra agrees with Mādhyamika that all sense data are inherently unreal, that is, lacking in any nature of their own, and that a Buddhist should practice in order to realize this. The peculiarly Yogācāra point is that sense data are unreal because they are produced by the mind. It is crucial to realize, though, that the mind likewise is produced by the sense data. If there were no sense data "objects," there would be no cognizing of sense data and hence, immediately, no cognizer qua separate self.

Thus we rely on the *manovijñāna,* or ordinary consciousness, to produce so-called consciousness-only wisdom, the knowledge that sense data or phenomena lack essence, hence ultimately lack reality. In other words, starting from the stage of ordinary consciousness at which the practitioner finds himself or herself, as a skillful means one engages in unspecified meditative practices that enable one to see the nonexistence of essences in phenomenal reality. Once one has done that, however, this new awareness one has engendered possesses the power to turn on that which produced it, ordinary consciousness, and destroy it. Why? Consciousness-only wisdom sees there are no object-things "out there." It, in effect, directs *manovijñāna* to see this. With no objects from which to separate itself, *manovijñāna,* in turn, becomes incapable of discriminating itself as a separate thing with its own self-contained essence-identity. In other words, if there are no objects, there can be no subject; the existence of each is completely dependent upon the existence of the other. Thus *manovijñāna,* as a sense of a separately existing self, is destroyed. Once this happens, though, the so-called consciousness-only wisdom self-destructs. Why? First, it was simply a skillful means for the purpose of undoing the self-delusion of *manovijñāna.* Second, its existence was derived from *manovijñāna;* the latter produced it.

What, then, is the nature and status of the subject in this theory? It is clear that with sense data as its cause, the *manovijñāna* consists totally in cognizing activity. That is, no sense data, no cognizing; no cognizing, no cognizer. The cognizing, then, is the cognizer; in other words, there is no entity-cognizer here, only acts of cognizing that produce an illusory sense of self. As for consciousness-only wisdom, it is plain that this is far from an ultimate in this text. It is no more than a skillful means that self-destructs once its task is accomplished. Moreover, the very words *consciousness-only* (which are the words the text uses) are misleading as used in the *BNT.* Though the phrase is appropriate inasmuch as the sense data "objects" lack an independent essence and hence are unreal, or do not exist, the real teaching of this passage is that the cognizer and the cognized, subject and object, are interrelated even to the extent of being mutually dependent. They arise and disappear together. Hence, *consciousness-*

only does not mean "consciousness—yes, objects—no" (and certainly not "mind—yes, matter—no") but rather, it implies "cognition only" or "cognizing only," with both "consciousness" qua mind and sense data qua objects of consciousness negated.

As an illustration of the ontological status of a human person, this example indicates several things.

1. It manifests the nonduality of cognizer and cognized, or subject and object. It does not reduce objects to an ultimate subjective base, but asserts the absolute dependence, relativity, and ultimate unreality of both.
2. It demonstrates the active nature of the person; there is no "mind" here, but certain kinds of cognitions and wisdom.
3. The practical consequences of "consciousness-only wisdom" consist in the elimination of delusion. Thus, as an illustration of Buddha nature, we see again in this example an emphasis on the teaching that Buddha nature means the practice (or engagement in the activity) of becoming Buddha. This activity, again, is what a person is.

Incidentally, as representative of the *BNT*'s stand on the nondualism of subject and object, this example reinforces the argument of Chapter Five that the position of this text cannot be idealistic monism. Subject and object are mutually dependent: mutually unreal in delusion, inseparably self-revelatory in Thusness. This is nondualism.

B. The Existential Dimension

Let us now take up the question of human personhood in the existential dimension. A little reflection quickly will reveal that, in the view of the *BNT*'s author, one cannot speak of the human character or of paradigmatic human behavior as such without one preliminary point. Existentially, human beings are of two basic types: deluded and enlightened. Once one has divided humanity (in which category I include the *BNT*'s three divisions of ordinary beings, sages, and Buddhas) into these two camps, one then can proceed to make meaningful statements about characteristic human behaviors.

As evidence of this, recall the author's treatment of the classic Yogācāra concept of the *trisvabhāva,* the three "natures" that, as we have seen, represent three ways in which persons perceive worlds and worlds present themselves to persons. In working through these three natures, our text stressed the reading according to which the middle nature, *paratantra,* is divided into two subcategories, an impure and a pure *paratantra.* The former is identifiable with the nature of delusion, *parikalpita,* whereas the latter is identified with the pure *parinispanna.* In this way the tripartite *trisvabhāva* theory becomes a theory that divides humanity into two categories.

The characteristic that assigns persons to one category or the other is so-called purity and impurity, or delusion and enlightenment. Our author has in mind a model of human being in which deluded beings transform themselves into enlightened beings upon the pivot of *āśrayaparāvṛtti,* which I earlier translated as "the transformation of the person" but which I can now translate as "conversion,"[6] in the sense that *āśrayaparāvṛtti* converts the person from a deluded being into an awakened being. Thus we have two categories of person, before and after *āśrayaparāvṛtti.*[7]

1. Before "conversion," then, we have the "impure" or deluded existential mode of human being. What characterizes human being in this mode? In whichever existential mode a person finds himself or herself, a human being always is identifiable with Buddha nature. The significance of this for the deluded person is twofold. There is the universally valid promise of eventual Buddhahood. More interesting for present purposes are the Buddha nature doctrine's implications for a theory of human nature. If the Buddha nature is the essential nature of a human being, then there is, on this level and in this context, a universal sameness shared by humanity at the core of our identity. We are all intrinsically enlightened and compassionate beings and not just in potential but always and already in present reality, though all appearances and self-knowledge may be to the contrary while in the deluded existential mode. To the extent that this hidden reality is not yet manifest, though, the sameness that it implies is all the greater. We can speak of it only as wisdom and compassion and cannot specify its character further; active manifestation is required for that.

On the other hand, what does distinguish us one from another are our individual karma and *kleśa,* the past history and defilements that together are responsible for the creation and constitution of our bodies as well as what we in the West, from a very different perspective, call our various personalities. To the extent that a person exists in the deluded existential mode, that person's individual character traits, beliefs, habits, tendencies, values, mannerisms, and so forth simply are *kleśa.* They are all based upon a fundamentally deluded or warped perspective upon oneself and reality and could not exist as they are without that foundation. They also, from the perspective of Buddha nature thought, are unreal and ultimately nonexistent. The text tells us many times that the *kleśa* have no basis in reality.

We therefore have a situation in which persons in the deluded existential mode can be differentiated one from another only by virtue of the *kleśa* that constitute their personalities and have constructed their bodies, but the *kleśa* themselves are unreal and therefore cannot serve as any real basis of differentiation. The *kleśa,* therefore, have no value in constituting a person's identity. In the existential mode of delusion, then, a person can truthfully be identified with the universally identical Buddha nature but cannot truthfully be identified with the distinctive *kleśa* that constitute that person's individuality.

The implications of this are as follows. Within the purview of Buddha nature thought, the person in the deluded existential mode is ahistorical and lacking in individuality. History and individuality are composed by the *kleśa* that constitute a person's personality; because these are simply negligible, so are history and individuality as pertaining to persons in the deluded existential mode. Second, autonomy and freedom are largely, though not entirely, negligible for the deluded person. Most of the deluded person's actions are driven by karma and as such identifiable with the realm of *kleśa* and utterly lacking in real freedom. However, there is one important exception to this statement. The drive to spiritual freedom impelled by the Buddha nature is an act of authentic freedom. Buddha nature and Thusness, having nothing to do with the realm of karma and *kleśa,* can serve as the basis of acts of real freedom. Hence, to the extent that one acts in such a way as to free oneself of karma and *kleśa* one's act is free. To the extent that one's actions are the product of past karma and *kleśa,* those actions are not free. By definition, though, the deluded person has not yet undergone "conversion." Such a person therefore will be defined largely by unfree acts.

In sum, the person in the deluded existential mode is not a

person as we ordinarily use the term. There is no real historicality or individuality accruing to the "person" and precious little freedom. What we consider to be the basis of individual personhood is written off as unreal. What is real is the universal sameness of Buddha nature; in this sameness, individual personhood, as we ordinarily use the term, cannot be found. Thus before "conversion" and while in the existential mode of delusion, a person is not a person.

2. What, then, of the person after "conversion," the "pure" or enlightened person? Again we must begin by stating that the person is the Buddha nature. Thus also in the existential mode of enlightenment there apparently is this degree of universal sameness. But how far, in this mode, does this sameness extend? The fact that we are all the Buddha nature means that we are all characterized by clear seeing and altruistic behavior. But persons in the enlightened existential mode, unlike persons in the deluded mode, have made this Buddha nature manifest in real acts of clarity and altruism. This manifestation in action, therefore, brings the Buddha nature into the realm of particularity and individuality. No two acts of clarity or compassion are alike. Hence once the Buddha nature moves into the realm of manifestation it no longer is appropriate to speak of universal sameness, because the Buddha nature is no more than those particular acts of clarity and altruism and no entity of any kind.

In other words, the person is the Buddha nature as manifest in particular actions and only as manifest in those actions. Thus history and individuality, which were lacking in the deluded existential mode, enter the constitution of the person now, in the enlightened existential mode. The particular behaviors, mannerisms, even the personality of the person, now possess reality and value. Moreover, the actions of the person now possess complete autonomy and freedom. What the person does (physically, psychologically) has no relation to the world of karma and *kleśa* but is entirely a spontaneous manifestation of the always free Buddha nature. The person, then, is really and fully a person at this stage, after "conversion" and upon entry into the enlightened existential mode.

I must emphasize this remarkable point: "Conversion" and enlightened behavior not only do not rob a person of individuality, but in fact constitute its very possibility for the first time. Compare this with the classic position of the Hindu *Upaniṣads* in which, upon enlightenment, the person loses whatever individuality he or she had by merging into the Oneness of Brahman-Ātman, "as when rivers flowing towards the ocean find there final peace, their name and form disappear, and people speak only of the ocean."[8] The position of Buddha nature thought is the precise converse of this. Buddhist practice constitutes the possibility for discovering and actualizing individuality for the first time. One becomes a person upon enlightenment. One gains freedom. The history that one constructs with one's particular actions is a real thing.

This, in the end, is the result of the position epitomized in the *Buddha Nature Treatise*'s line that states that Buddha nature is manifest in Thusness; one *realizes* it: "Attachments are not real, therefore they are called vacuous. If one gives rise to these attachments, true wisdom will not arise. When one does away with these attachments, then we speak of Buddha nature. Buddha nature is the Thusness (*zhen-ru*) revealed (*xian*) by the dual emptiness of person and things. . . . If one does not speak of Buddha nature, then one does not understand emptiness" (787b).

In the view of the *BNT,* Buddhist practice gains one something, and that something is reality: One finds reality in oneself and in one's world. And this reality possesses absolute value. Just as the logic of Buddha nature thought compelled the author ultimately to speak of an *ātmapāramitā* in which the negativity of *anātman* and *śūnyatā* was simultaneously inverted and fulfilled, so here the negativity of the karma and *kleśa*-based realm of history and individuality is inverted and transformed into a realm in which history and individuality are real and valuable. Here though, unlike the *anātman-ātmapāramitā* inversion, the history and personhood that one creates are something new. *Ātmapāramitā* is simply the completely adequate understanding of *anātman.* The free acts of a real individual creating himself or herself moment by moment are the construction of a historical world that never before existed, even in potential.

3. We need now to consider the existential status of the pivot between the two existential modes of delusion and enlightenment; namely, *āśrayaparāvṛtti* or conversion. The status of *āśrayaparāvṛtti* is not worked out as fully in the text as one would prefer, but in the end if falls into the category of the existential mode of enlightenment. *Āśrayaparāvṛtti,* it is said many times, is "pure": it is the purity of the *dharmadhātu,* the purity of the Buddha nature. As pure, it falls squarely on the side of enlightenment. It also, however, is identified

with Buddhist practice: It is the basis of the Buddha Way; the foundation of the extinction of delusion; the fruition of practice as manifest in goodness, reverence, and knowledge; and it is the attainment of Thusness. In these respects, its nature might at first seem to be one transitional between delusion and purity, but that in fact is not the case. When, as the text says, one is "on the Way," *āśrayaparāvṛtti* is the cause. When one has "completed the Way," it is called *fruit.* Nonetheless, this *āśrayaparāvṛtti* finally must be understood as belonging totally on the side of purity and enlightenment, in short, of fruition. It is cause in the same way that the Buddha nature is cause: it always is fully complete with all its virtues intact. It serves as cause of one's being "on the Way" or, in other words, as cause of the Buddha Way in the sense that, like Buddha nature, it is the purity of Thusness impelling one to practice Buddhism, impelling one to seek freedom and the realization of personhood. *Āśrayaparāvṛtti* is capable of serving as a pivot between the two existential modes precisely because it is purity in the act of causing one to be on the Buddhist Path. Like *bodhicitta,* which also is identified with the Buddha nature, it can be a first act on the Buddhist Path. But even as a first act, it already is completely pure; it is purity that moves one to perform that first act of stepping onto the Path, and the act itself is constituted of purity.

There is in this notion that *āśrayaparāvṛtti* is identifiable both as purity and as Buddhist practice an anticipation of Dōgen's later concept of Buddhist practice as realization. In the *BNT, āśrayaparāvṛtti* is called *pure* both in its role as cause and as fruit. But, as we have seen, as cause it already is in full possession of its character as fruit. We have here, then, a notion in which every authentic act of Buddhist practice is itself of the nature of fruition, the nature of the end of the Path, of purity or realization. A genuine act of Buddhist practice, whether the first awakening of the desire to practice, an advanced state of *samādhi,* or the dedication of oneself to the salvation of others in perpetuity, always is a manifestation of Buddha nature as such, which always is of the character of full and complete clarity and altruism. Purity and Buddhist practice, then, are alike. Thus *āśrayaparāvṛtti,* although always of the nature of purity and fruition, nevertheless can be identified with Buddhist practice.

Now insofar as the crucial event that separates the deluded existential mode from the enlightened existential mode is the act of conversion, *āśrayaparāvṛtti,* this conversion itself must be crucial to the concept of personhood embraced by the *BNT*. This act of conversion that engenders real personhood is in effect the foundation of personhood. If any statement can apply to both modes of the existential dimension, and thus epitomizes the existential nature of human beings as such, it is that we are beings whose nature is to transform ourselves, to undergo radical transformation at the very foundation of personhood; namely, at the foundation of act-genesis. The deluded existential mode is the drive—however convoluted—toward that event, whereas the enlightened existential mode is the dynamic manifestation of that event, the ongoing manifestation of free personhood.

C. A Final Question

A final, and important, question remains to us. When we combine our insights on the existential and ontological aspects of human personhood as suggested by Buddha nature thought, one apparent inconsistency remains. Buddha nature thought universally affirms "all sentient beings possess the Buddha nature." If, though, as I have argued, Buddha nature is not an entity, but rather certain kinds of acts and if in the deluded existential mode such enlightened acts by definition do not appear, what is the status of Buddha nature for the person in delusion? If, in short, Buddha nature is not an entity and if it is not manifest in acts while one is deluded, in what sense can it be said to be there at all for the deluded person? It would seem that Buddha nature could not be present under such conditions. Yet the Buddha nature tradition specifically asserts that the deluded also possess Buddha nature. How can this be?

The beginning of an answer to this question is the acknowledgement that in the deluded existential mode Buddha nature is really just a promise. When, from time to time, the deluded person acts freely out of Buddha nature, then in that act of "purity," Buddha nature is fully manifest, fully realized. Outside of such moments, it is only a promise. That this must be so can be seen when one places Buddha nature thought in the larger context of Buddhist philosophy. In Buddhism, "reality" always means "experiential reality." To ascribe reality to anything outside experience would certainly violate the most basic Buddhist principles. So to the extent that, in delusion,

Buddha nature is outside experiential reality (our experiential reality is the concealing *kleśa*), it is not in any real way present. It is present only as promise. In this light, we can look once again at the passage quoted earlier from the *BNT:* "Attachments are not real, therefore they are called vacuous. If one gives rise to these attachments, true wisdom will not arise. When one does away with these attachments, then we speak of Buddha nature" (787b). While the attachments are experientially present, we do not speak of Buddha nature. Only when wisdom is experientially present do we speak of it.

This view is confirmed by Sung Bae Park in his study of doctrinal and patriarchal faith, when he writes: "Whereas doctrinal faith is the commitment that 'I can *become* Buddha,' patriarchal faith is the affirmation that 'I am *already* Buddha.' Therefore, patriarchal faith is not to be regarded as a 'preliminary' to enlightenment, as is doctrinal faith, but as equivalent to enlightenment itself. To arouse patriarchal faith is to become instantly enlightened."[9] Thus insofar as the patriarchal faith that "I am *already* Buddha" is equivalent to the realization of enlightenment, one cannot authentically affirm "I am already Buddha" until one is enlightened; that is, until one experientially knows one's Buddhahood. The same is true of the affirmation, "I, a deluded person, possess the Buddha nature."

These statements take us close to the solution of our problem. While in the deluded existential mode, Buddha nature is present as promise in two senses, which must be distinguished. First, of course, is the promise of future Buddhahood affirmed for all. Second, and more important for the present question, is the promise that Buddha nature is present to the deluded person *now* in the sense that it can and will appear in its fullness and purity *now* if only the deluded person will open his or her eyes and see it. Thus to say that Buddha nature is present "only" as a promise while in the deluded existential mode is not to negate that it is, in fact, present and real at all times and in all conditions. But it is up to the deluded person to see that reality, to "realize" the reality of the Buddha nature for him or herself now, in the present moment.

In this context, we should recall that in the *BNT* the Buddha nature is consistently identified with Buddhist practice. Thus all appearance of contradiction or inconsistency is removed when we think of Buddha nature as equivalent to the *Buddhist practice* of those still enmired in the existential dimension of delusion. Thus

Buddha nature can be present now, in its fullness and purity, even though it is not an entity of any kind and even though one is enmired in the condition of delusion insofar as it is manifest in acts of practice, or in other words, insofar as, and no farther than, one's actions bring that Buddha nature into the world of experiential reality.

CHAPTER EIGHT

Retrospective and Prospective

As a retrospective, I will first present the *BNT*'s self-summary, which serves as a conclusion to the text and brings closure to a number of its major themes. As a prospective (from the time of the appearance in Chinese of the *BNT*, that is) I wish to offer two things: first, my observations on the teachings of the *BNT* in relation to subsequent developments in Chinese Buddhist thought; and, second, a few brief remarks on the *BNT* in relation to current developments in Western Buddhism.

A. Retrospective: Summary of the Text

The author gives us a summary of his teaching in the tidy form of four meanings of Buddha nature, which serve as the bases for four names for Buddha nature, which in turn serve as correctives or teachings appropriate to four classes of persons.

The first meaning of the Buddha nature is its "inseparability from all Buddha *dharmas* both before and after [realization]" (811c). The Buddha *dharmas* are numberless meritorious qualities of the Buddha nature or *dharmakāya*. The text states that because of the Buddha *dharmas*, the *tathāgatagarbha* is "not empty," (*bu kong*) and being "not empty" indicates the inherent presence of the Buddha *dharmas*. The second meaning of Buddha nature is, "[this nature], under all conditions, is Thus" (812a). This is "because all phenomena lack own-nature." That is, the emptiness of all things is their Thusness and vice versa. Buddha nature is found in this condition, which is universal. Third, Buddha nature "has nothing to do with false thoughts or inverted teachings," and fourth, "the original nature [Buddha nature] is still" (812a). *Still* here is explained as meaning neither produced nor destroyed.

On the basis of these meanings, or qualities, are established four names for the Buddha nature. (1) By virtue of its inseparability from the Buddha *dharmas*, it is called the *dharmakāya.* (2) Because under all conditions the nature is Thus, it is called *Tathāgata* (Thus Come). (3) It is called the *supreme truth* because it is neither false nor inverted. (4) Because it is aboriginally still, it is called *parinirvāṇa*" (812a). Buddha nature then, is, the supreme truth, the nature of things as they are (Thus), the freedom from all error (*parinirvāṇa*), and the embodiment of all the excellent qualities attendant on realization (*dharmakāya*).

Next is taken up the progressive realization of the Buddha nature by four classes of persons. First, the *dharmakāya* (*fa shen*) name of Buddha nature is explained to be the correction for ordinary persons' views of self (*shen jian*). The term *shen* has two common meanings in Buddhism: "body," and "person" or "self." This first conjunction of a type of person (the ordinary person) with a name of the Buddha nature (*dharmakāya*) is a restatement of a point that has been made earlier. If ordinary people can rid themselves of their perverted views of the "me" and the "mine," they will penetrate the realm of Dharma (*dharmadhātu*). Upon perceiving this realm they will have found something indestructible. Being eternal, it deserves the name *true self* (*zhen shen*) or, equivalently, *dharmakāya* (*fa shen*). Thus, what ordinary people grasp as self is not real and as a corrective the term *dharmakāya* is used.[1]

The second name, *Tathāgata,* is a corrective to the inverted views of the Hīnayāna. The Hīnayāna, says the author, do not recognize that the Tathāgata is eternal, blissful, self, and pure. They think only of the negation of these qualities on the phenomenal level. Hence their views and practice are inverted and they do not attain the fruit of the Tathāgata path. They think only in terms of the causal stage, in which the wrong views of ordinary persons (like seeing self where there is no self) have to be corrected. However, the *bodhisattva* knows that this causal stage is not to be separated from the fruition stage, in which the virtues of self, eternity, and so on are realized. Hence, the Hīnayāna think only of leaving this world; that is, leaving (*qu*) and not returning (*lai*). The *bodhisattva,* on the other hand, knows that leaving and returning are inseparable. Hence the *bodhisattva* speaks of the Thus Gone (*ru qu, tathā + gata;* i.e., Tathāgata), and the Thus Come (*ru lai, tathā + āgata;* i.e., Tathāgata), but the term *Thus Come* stands especially as a corrective to the Hīnayāna.

The *supreme Truth* is the corrective name for those with "scattered and turbulent minds"; that is, the early stage *bodhisattva.* Two types of confusion are exhibited by these fledgling *bodhisattvas.* One thinks that emptiness is nothingness, that things only exist by virtue of discrimination, and that when the latter ceases, all things will be "empty"; that is, nonexistent. The other thinks that emptiness is something that really exists, something that should be cultivated and attained. As a corrective to these views, the supreme truth is enunciated. This truth is here given in verse:[2]

> There is not a single thing to be removed
> And not a single thing to be added.
> What is should be perceived as it is;
> Seeing the real, liberation is attained.
>
> Because adventitious defilements are empty,
> They have no connection with the *dharmadhātu.*
> The Supreme *dharmas,* not being empty,
> Are inseparable from the *dharmadhātu.* (812b)

Thus the Buddha nature, or Dharma realm, is empty of defilements but not empty of the supreme *dharmas* (the Buddha's innumerable meritorious qualities): "Because there is not one thing that can be removed, it is empty, and because there is not one thing that can be added, it is not empty" (812c). Thus this emptiness is a fullness and this is what the *bodhisattva* must learn.

Nirvāṇa is the name directed to *bodhisattvas* in the tenth or final stage of their training. By definition, only a Buddha attains *nirvāṇa.* This, therefore, is the one name, or level of realization, that stands beyond the reach of the advanced *bodhisattva. Nirvāṇa* is spoken of here in distinctly positive terms as possessing all merit, infinite merit, inconceivable merit, and ultimate, pure merit. It clearly is far from the mere cessation of suffering!

B. The *Buddha Nature Treatise* and Chinese Buddhist Thought

Buddha nature ideas are found in all the four major indigenous schools of Chinese Buddhism: Tian-tai, Hua-yan, Chan, and Pure Land. The concerns of the Pure Land school, however, diverged considerably from those of the former three schools, and consequently there is much less direct attention given to Buddha nature thought (as well as other important philosophical principles) in this school. In Tian-tai, Hua-yan, and Chan, though, Buddha nature thought plays a major role.

The first of these schools to develop as a school, the Tian-tai of the Sui dynasty, affirmed Buddha nature as one of its focal tenets. Both the school's founder, Zhi-yi (Chih-i), and his teacher, Hui-si (Hui-ssu), were very well versed in the *tathāgatagarbha* and Buddha nature literature, though the fortunes of Buddha nature thought varied over the life of the school. Hui-si spoke directly and extensively of Buddha nature as such; it clearly was a major component of his world-view. Zhi-yi was less an advocate of traditional Buddha nature language, preferring to speak of an all-embracing Mind in which subject and object arise together nondualistically, an idea that nonetheless clearly is rooted in the family of ideas found in Yogācāra and Buddha nature thought. Zhan-ran (Chan-jan), the sixth Tian-tai patriarch, revived the Tian-tai school in the eighth-century, again emphasizing the idea of Buddha nature. His work was prized in Tian-tai lineages throughout East Asia.

The Hua-yan school is very closely tied to *tathāgatagarbha*–Buddha nature thought. It incorporated several streams of thought, one of which was the She-lun school, which itself had developed on the basis of Paramārtha's translation of the *Mahāyānasaṃgraha.* Moreover, its major thinker, Fa-zang (Fa-tsang), was an expert on *tathāgatagarbha* and Buddha nature literature, and wrote what is regarded as the most important commentary on the syncretic *Awakening of Faith in the Mahāyāna.* He frequently cited this text, along with others of the *tathāgatagarbha* tradition, as authorities for his own ideas. In his commentary he hierarchically ranked what he considered to be four schools of thought in Indian Buddhism according to his assessment of their profundity and completeness. The lowest rank was held by the Hīnayāna, which was succeeded in turn by the Mādhyamika and the Yogācāran Fa-xiang (Fa-hsiang) school of Xuan-zang (Hsüan-tsang), whereas the highest level was occupied by the *tathāgatagarbha* "school."[3] The rationale for this hierarchy seems to be a desire to affirm the value of the phenomenal world. It also may reflect the understanding articulated in the *Ratnagotravibhāga* and the *BNT* to the effect that *prajñā* thought, with its emphasis on emptiness, is incomplete, because it only negates error, whereas *tathāgatagarbha*–Buddha nature thought is complete, insofar as it both negates error (with its incorporation of the negations of emptiness) and manifests reality (with its affirmation of Thusness and *tathāgatagarbha*–Buddha nature).[4]

Fa-zang created a mind-boggling, systematic philosophy based on *tathāgatagarbha* ideas, but going beyond them. The *Awakening of Faith* instructs the reader in the One Mind in which pure and impure, *saṃsāra* and Thusness intersect. Fa-zang accepts this, interpreting it as a doctrine of the intersection of the phenomenal and the supreme principle. In his system, however, this is only a step toward the ultimate vision of a universe of *dharmadhātu* in which all particulars within the universe not only are mutually interpenetrating, but each also contains the whole *dharmadhātu,* also known as the One Mind.[5]

The influence of Buddha nature thought was most significant of all in the development of the Chan school. The Yogācāra-*tathāgatagarbha* text, the *Laṅkāvatāra Sūtra,* is prominently associated with the early history of Chan: Bodhidharma is supposed to have handed a copy of the text to the second patriarch, Hui-ke (Hui-k'o), commending it to him as a uniquely trustworthy guide. Thereafter, many of the early Chan monks lectured on the basis of the text and wrote comments on it.

Buddha nature thought was more important in some individuals and subsects of Chan than others. It was especially prominent in the East Mountain tradition of Dao-xin (Tao-hsin) and Hong-ren (Hung-jen), Chan's fourth and fifth patriarch, respectively.[6] For example, we have the following. "Hung-jen said to the Great Master [Tao-hsin]: 'What is one-practice samādhi? It is realizing that the Dharmakāya of the Buddhas and the nature of sentient beings are identical.' The Great Master [Tao-]hsin . . . understood then that Hung-jen had entered directly into the one-practice samādhi and had perfectly reached the deep Dharmadhātu."[7]

The connection of these words with the *tathāgatagarbha*

treatise, the *No Increase, No Decrease Sūtra* (*Anūnatvāpūrṇatvanirdeśa*), is apparent; the preceding message also was transmitted by the *BNT*. Such ideas as these in early Chan were passed on to later generations in the important meditation manual, *Zuo-chan yi,* which contains passages like the following: "to seek the pearl, we should still the waves; if we disturb the water, it will be hard to get. When the water of meditation is clear, the pearl of the mind will appear of itself. Therefore, the *Perfect Enlightenment Sutra* says, 'unimpeded, immaculate wisdom always arises dependent on meditation.' "[8]

The "pearl of the mind" made inaccessible by the waves is an obvious metaphor for the concealed Buddha nature. This image combines the use of waves to represent delusion in the *Awakening of Faith in the Mahāyāna* and the *Tathāgatagarbha Sūtra*'s representation of the *tathāgatagarbha* as a precious jewel. The method of practicing meditation follows from this theory. For the *Zuo-chan yi,* the "essential art" of meditation is as follows: "Do not think of any good or evil whatsoever. Whenever a thought occurs, be aware of it . . .; as soon as you are aware of it, it will vanish. If you remain for a long period forgetful of objects . . ., you will naturally become unified."[9] Here, enlightenment is inherent; one need only attain freedom from thought, that is, delusion, and it will become apparent.

The *Platform Sūtra* attributed to the Sixth Patriarch, Hui-neng, usually is said to represent a major turn in Chan thought, with the earlier preference for the *Laṅkāvatāra Sūtra* replaced in him by a preference for the *Diamond Sūtra* and the *prajñā* teachings. This is confirmed by the emphasis on negation in the *Platform Sūtra* in passages such as that in which Hui-neng asserts: "Good friends, in this teaching of mine, . . . all have set up no-thought as the main doctrine, non-form as the substance, and non-abiding as the basis."[10]

But this *prajñā*-like series of sweeping negations does not prevent Hui-neng from affirming, in the following passage, some most traditional teachings from mainstream *tathāgatagarbha*–Buddha nature thought. Hui-neng by no means negates the Buddha nature teachings that were so important in the thought of the patriarchs who preceded him. "If someone speaks of 'viewing purity,' [then I would say] that man's nature is of itself pure, but because of false thoughts True Reality is obscured. If you exclude delusions then the original nature reveals its purity."[11] On the basis of this kind of idea, to *see the [Buddha] nature* (Chinese *jian xing,* Japanese *kenshō*) became a synonym for enlightenment in the Chan and Zen tradition to the present day.

I hope it has been apparent throughout this book that Buddha nature thought is not just a matter of asserting the existence of a Buddha nature but, especially in the syncretic form in which it appears in the *BNT*, is a full philosophical system, inclusive of ontology, epistemology, and soteriology. In the Introduction to this book, I mentioned a number of themes found in the *Buddha Nature Treatise* that came to have widespread significance in the indigenous schools of Chinese Buddhism. I have discussed all of these themes in the course of this book, but it will be useful to return to them here to summarize those ideas found in the *BNT* that subsequently became important on so widespread a scale in the Chinese (and ultimately, the East Asian) Buddhist world. I do not mean to imply that these ideas became widespread as a consequence of their occurrence in the *BNT*; the *BNT* represents here many texts bearing these important ideas. Furthermore, though Buddha nature ideas were one major stream on which later Chinese Buddhist thought drew, the following themes were not derived exclusively from Indian Buddhist sources. Chinese Buddhism is a synthesis of Indian Buddhism and native Chinese traditions; a number of the following themes have their counterparts within the indigenous traditions. I limit myself in the following discussion to merely pointing out parallels between the *BNT*'s major themes and similar themes in the indigenous Chinese Buddhist schools, in the hope that this study can highlight the importance of these themes for Chinese Buddhism as a whole and shed some light upon them.

1. The Positive Nature of Realization

The first theme in importance for the *BNT* and for Chinese Buddhism is the emphasis upon the positive nature of realization, the view of enlightenment as an experiential reality that goes beyond emptiness. In India, Nāgārjuna was one of the greatest ever followers of the apophatic path, the path of the *via negativa* in religious language use. With his commitment to helping humanity to become free of the bondage produced by thoughts, he directed Buddhists away from any tendency to conceive of reality or liberation in any terms whatsoever, much less in terms that carried a positive value connotation. Although Nāgārjuna was careful to create a system in which, technically, reality and liberation were beyond either positive or negative conception, the form of his discourse was sufficiently negative to provoke a critical reaction by Indian Yogācāra and *tathāgatagarbha* authors. These were convinced of the need to clarify the status of liberation such that it would be clear that it was a goal worth striving for.

This view entered China in the texts transmitted by Paramārtha, among others. We have seen that it permeates the *BNT* from beginning to end. On the opening page of the treatise, the author states his primary theme: "Buddha nature is the Thusness revealed by the twin emptiness of person and things. . . . If one does not speak of Buddha nature, then one does not understand emptiness" (787b). At the end of the text, the author succinctly summarizes what his intentions were in writing the *BNT* and what he hopes he has conveyed. He wanted, he writes, "(1) To manifest the inconceivable, aboriginally existent realm; (2) to show what can be attained by the cultivation and practice of the Way; and (3) to reveal that the attainment of the Way results in infinite merits and ultimate perfection" (812c–813a).

Chinese Buddhists, for their part, universally agreed in their conceptions of the ultimate human attainment that "freedom from" suffering was not enough; all the indigenous schools articulated and/or artistically expressed visions of liberation in positive terms as "freedom to" see reality As It Is, or "freedom to" enter the Happy Land. This was not a negation of Nāgārjuna; *śūnya* views were quite important in the foundations of Tian-tai, Hua-yan, and Chan. All of these schools, though, went beyond *śūnya* language to express their supreme vision in various positive constructions, such as "three thousand worlds immanent in a moment of thought" (Tian-tai); or as the *dharmadhātu* in which all phenomena freely interpenetrate (Hua-yan); or as Chan's "this mind is Buddha mind." These three schools, then, all agreed with the *BNT* that the value of *śūnyatā* was to take one beyond *śūnyatā* to the disclosure of reality itself, seen aright.

2. *The Optimistic Conception of Human Nature*

The second important theme of the *BNT* is its optimistic conception of human nature based on the idea of a universal, active

Buddha nature. In Buddha nature theory no person, no matter how depraved in behavior, is to be dismissed as morally, spiritually, or humanly worthless. Each person is a Buddha, not only potentially, but actually.

Against the Buddha nature tradition, Xuan-zang's Fa-xiang school endorsed a plurality of ineluctable spiritual destinies, including future Buddhahood for some, but pratyekabuddhahood, arhathood, and a hopeless destiny of endless wandering in *saṃsāra* for the rest. In this view, human nature is varied, and consequently the ability of education and discipline to mold a person's future attainments is limited.

Just as the Chinese carefully weighed the arguments of Xun-zi (Hsün-tzu) and Mencius on the inherently bad or good moral nature of humanity, so they also carefully weighed the Fa-xiang school's theory of multiple destinies against the Buddha nature tradition's contrary endorsement of universal Buddhahood. As they found, as a people, in favor of Mencius' optimistic view of inherent human goodness, so they found in favor of Buddha nature. The acceptance of the universality of Buddha nature by the Chinese Buddhist community as a whole contributed to a loss of status for Xuan-zang's Fa-xiang school. Due to the latter's adherence to the theory of multiple spiritual destinies and its rejection of universal Buddha nature, this school was relegated to the status of "quasi-Mahāyāna" by a thinker such as Fa-zang when he constructed his hierarchy of Buddhist teachings.

I hasten to add that neither the Confucian nor the Buddhist tradition is as naive as it might sound from this account. Although each claims, respectively, that we are born morally good or spiritually Buddhas, the importance of this position for both traditions is the resulting imperative to bring into tangible manifestation what is present in our concealed "nature"; hence, the importance in each of spiritual self-cultivation or education.

3. *Nondualism and Thusness*

Third, the *BNT* presents us with an ontology based upon nondualism, as opposed to monism, and expressed in the language of Thusness. Monism is an appropriate designation for Indian Brahmanism. It is completely inappropriate to apply it to the views of the *BNT* and likewise has no place in any of the four major indigenous Chinese Buddhist schools. The perspective of nondualism avoids both monism and dualism. Philosophically, Thusness and nondualism begin from the assumption of the emptiness critique, and as a consequence they reject the dualism of ordinary belief in separate entities. However, as the supreme linguistic tool of Mādhyamika discourse, emptiness itself stands in danger of receiving the label *monistic*. Because emptiness is a single principle capable of explaining all of reality, some scholars see in it a weak form of monism.[12] I believe that such a reading of emptiness is wrong insofar as emptiness self-destructs upon use. But in either case, by moving away from emptiness as an even apparently ultimate philosophical principle to embrace that which emptiness frees us to see—reality As It Is—nondualism and Thusness reject any tendency toward even this conjectured weak form of monism. Nondualism, then, explicitly rejects both dualism and monism. It is the ontological term that correlates with the experience of Thusness. This experience, as expressed in the *BNT*, is based on the realization that emptiness merely clears the way for a correct apprehension of reality As It Is. Thusness, then, designates the way things are seen by those who are capable of seeing clearly, the reality As It Is into which one enters when free of delusion.

Tian-tai, Hua-yan, and Chan are all explicit about their nondualism. The classic Tian-tai position is its famous formula of the Threefold Truth: (1) all things are empty; (2) they do, however, have a real temporary or phenomenal existence; (3) being both empty and temporary is the nature of all things and is the Mean. Moreover, each of the three truths interpenetrates the other two, such that each embraces all and all are implicit in each.

The Hua-yan version of nondualism is expressed in its vision of the *dharmadhātu,* the total universe seen aright, as *shi-shi-wu-ai,* the mutual nonobstruction of all phenomena. One reaches this vision as the culmination of a process of progressively deepening insight: One begins from the commonsensical perspective; this beginning view is quickly negated at the second level, at which one gains insight into emptiness; one next realizes the interpenetration of emptiness and phenomena; and finally one leaves emptiness as such behind to speak only of phenomena seen aright; that is, free of dualism.

The genius of Hua-yan is its avowal that in the phenomena revealed in this concluding insight resides absolute value. Hua-yan cosmology is based upon an appreciation of the idea that emptiness, or the interrelatedness of things, implies an interdependent universe. Because the universe is the sum total of each and every one of those interdependent parts, a change in any one of them would constitute a change in the universe as a whole. In this sense, the value of the universe as a whole resides in each individual component, or in other words, each component inherently possesses supreme value. As a result of this cosmology, Hua-yan thinkers are in a position to glorify the most mundane particular.

Chan and Zen masters adopt virtually all forms of expression without accepting any of them as final, emphasizing sometimes one aspect, sometimes another, as useful for teaching purposes. Sometimes, it must be admitted, language of oneness appears. This reflects the fact that one crucial aspect of enlightenment is overcoming the sense we have of being selves separate from all that is not-self. So the contemporary Japanese Sōtō Zen master Shunryu Suzuki writes: "When you are you, you see things as they are, and you become one with your surroundings."[13] Much more common is language in which oneness, emptiness, Thusness, and the like are forgotten (as in Hua-yen) and ordinary phenomena are given as exemplars of ultimate reality without further ado, as we shall see in the fifth theme. Still, the very willingness to embrace all these forms of discourse is evidence of the acceptance of a nondualistic perspective. Shunryu Suzuki has given a relatively direct statement of this perspective, which should be understood as qualifying his above quoted remark:

> Each existence depends on something else. Strictly speaking, there are no separate individual existences. There are just many names for one existence. Sometimes people put stress on oneness, but this is not our understanding. We do not emphasize any point in particular, even oneness. Oneness is valuable, but variety is also wonderful. Ignoring variety, people emphasize the one absolute existence, but this is a one-sided understanding. In this understanding there is a gap between variety and oneness. But oneness and variety are the same thing, so oneness should be appreciated in each existence. That is why we emphasize everyday life rather than some particular state of mind. We should find the reality in each moment, and in each phenomenon.[14]

The influence of Hua-yan can be seen here in Suzuki's statement that "oneness should be appreciated in each existence," followed by his emphasis upon the value of everyday life and of each phenomenon.

The free play with the concepts of plurality and oneness evident in this quotation is a quite characteristic Chan/Zen trait. Though I said earlier that nondualism rejects both dualism (i.e., plurality) and monism (oneness) and that is the case, here Suzuki affirms both plurality and oneness. We already have seen in the *BNT*, though, that one achieves the same result by affirming both plurality and oneness as one achieves by denying both. As contradictory terms, their sense depends upon their mutual negation. With either double affirmation or double negation, the two are emptied. Here Suzuki implies that variety and oneness are two aspects of nondual Thusness seen, as it were, from two different perspectives, neither of which should be construed as absolute. Finally, though, Suzuki negates the concept of either variety or oneness by identifying the two.

4. *Subject-Object Nondualism*

Western understanding of Chinese Buddhism has been too long plagued by our misguided attempts to interpret it in terms of the philosophy of idealism, as we know it in the Western tradition. It is important for a correct understanding of Tian-tai, Hua-yan, and Chan thought that we read it not in terms of idealism, but in terms of subject-object nondualism, the view that mind and world arise together in mutual creation, whether in a deluded or an enlightened manner. This view is transmitted by the *BNT*.

The *BNT* adopts the Yogācāra view, according to which correct understanding of experience is that it is always "experience-of"; that is, the ("subjective") awareness of ("objective") content of some specific kind. In delusion, we look back on the moment of experience that has just occurred and reflectively analyze it into two components, the subjective and the objective. In fact, however, these two, as separate categories, come into existence only with this act of analytic bifurcation. In experience as such, that is, in the moment when present experience occurs, experience is the inseparable, "primitive" unity "experience-of." One important goal of practice is to cease living in the act of analysis of past experience, to cease the consequent identification with the "subjective" half of our experience, and to live instead in the present moment of prereflective experience in which "self" and "world" are not yet separated. This done, "self" and "world" are no longer experienced as separate nor as entities; in fact, the terms are rendered useless. Instead, one "is" this moment of prereflective experience, which is experienced as a moment of action, of process. The content of the present moment of experience is one's identity in the present moment.

This perspective is prominent in Chan; indeed, much of Chan language is incomprehensible without an appreciation of this concern for a return to prereflective experience. The famous Chan master Lin-ji (Lin-chi) developed a system for instruction in Chan called the *four processes of liberation from subjectivity and objectivity.* These are: take away the person but not the objective situation, take away the objective situation but not the person, take away both the person and the objective situation, and take away neither the person nor the objective situation.[15] In each of these, and indeed in this very approach, we see the same kind of playfulness we saw in Suzuki's treatment of variety and oneness; by playing so freely with the categories "person" and "objective situation" in this manner, we see the nonabsoluteness of each and the incorrectness of each as conceived from the perspective of subject-object nondualism.

Some illustrations of these four positions might be as follows. First, the "objective situation only" approach can be seen in "when a frog becomes a frog, Zen becomes Zen."[16] In the absoluteness of a frog As It Is one finds Zen, or enlightenment, or Thusness. Second, teaching with reference to person only is well-illustrated by Lin-ji's famous challenge, "Show me the true man without rank!" Third, the use of blows and shouts to jolt the mind illustrates teaching with reference neither to person nor objective situation. Finally, the fourth approach, speaking of both person and objective situation, is demonstrated in a poem by Dōgen:

> Being-in-the-world:
> To what might it be compared?
> Dwelling in the dewdrop
> Fallen from a waterfowl's beak,
> The image of the moon.[17]

Here human being is portrayed with the image of the moon of enlightenment present in the phenomenal dewdrop. This fourth example conveys the mutuality of subject and object, of person and objective situation. We may say, however, that all four of these approaches are means of pointing at, and transcending, the error of the ordinary dualistic conception of subjectivity and objectivity.

Another illustration of the nonduality of subject and object in Zen is found in Zen master Dōgen's *Shōbōgenzō genjōkōan:*

> Conveying the self to the myriad beings to authenticate them is delusion;
> The myriad things advancing to authenticate the self is enlightenment.
> To study the Buddha Way is to study the self;
> To study the self is to forget the self;
> To forget the self is to be authenticated by the myriad things.[18]

Upon realization of the Buddha Way, the delusory belief in a self separate from others and separate from world is lost. One no longer experiences as a being cut off from everything else, but as an awareness in which "self" and "world" arises simultaneously and in inseparable mutuality.

5. A Positive View of Phenomenal Reality

The *BNT* expresses a positive view of phenomenal reality, as is evident in the perspectives of the first theme (a positive view of realization) and, especially, the third theme (an ontology of nondualism and Thusness). The *BNT* itself does not reach the culmination of this line of thought in which a concrete particular from everyday life is given as a manifestation of the ultimate; that form of expression remains for the indigenous schools of Chinese Buddhism to develop. What the *BNT* does do is to give a consistent and powerful philosophical account of the more abstract point that ultimate reality is to be found in the Thusness of phenomenal reality. This positive apprehension of phenomenal reality will make possible in China Buddhist forms of expression in which ultimate reality/enlightenment is given as manifest in an everyday aspect of phenomenal reality.

Chinese Buddhist's readiness to create a this-worldly Buddhism was no doubt influenced by the this-worldliness of the indigenous Chinese philosophico-religious systems, Confucianism and Daoism. It would have been difficult to create such a Buddhism, however, had there not already been qualities in Buddhism that pointed strongly in this direction. It remained to the Chinese to draw on these elements and creatively envision their implications.

We already have seen some philosophical examples of Chinese Buddhist affirmation of phenomenal reality in the Hua-yan vision of the *dharmadhātu* as *shi-shi-wu-ai* and the Tian-tai threefold Truth in which any one of the three, temporariness for example, can represent all. We need not repeat these examples here. A nonphilosophical example expressive of absolute value realized in the phenomenal is the development in China and other East Asian countries of this-worldly Buddhist or Buddhist-inspired art in which artistic representations of phenomenal reality (as opposed to Buddhas, for example)[19] are given as expressions of enlightenment. Very famous are the Chan or Zen (and Daoist) inspired landscape and still-life paintings, poetry, gardens, tea ceremony, and so on. Two other examples in which phenomenal reality represents enlightenment/ ultimate reality are seen in a Chan saying and a Chan anecdote. Layman Pang Yun says, "Spirit-like understanding and divine functioning lie in carrying water and chopping wood."[20] In a well-known anecdote, the Buddha gives a lecture that consists entirely in holding up a flower. Mahākāśyapa's smile in response to this act becomes the paradigmatic example of transmission of the Dharma for the Chan sect.

The contemporary Vietnamese Zen master Thich Nhat Hanh continues this latter theme very simply in the course of discussing how to set up a home meditation room: "If you want to have a statue or a painting of a Buddha, please be choosy. . . . A Buddha should be smiling, happy, beautiful, for the sake of our children. . . . If you don't find a beautiful Buddha, wait, and have a flower instead. A flower is a Buddha. A flower has Buddha nature."[21]

6. Enlightenment as a Pivotal Conversion

The *BNT* conceives of enlightenment in terms of a pivotal conversion experience from delusion to enlightenment, or from impurity to purity. This is shown in the text's use of the Yogācāra *trisvabhāva* and *āśrayaparāvṛtti* teachings. The author presents *trisvabhāva* as two modes in which persons perceive the world and the world presents itself to persons, the so-called pure and impure aspects of the relative nature (the impure relative nature being delusion and the pure relative nature being enlightenment). *Āśrayaparāvṛtti* he sees as the pivot on which the practicing Buddhist overturns the most deeply established existential habits and attains the ability to see reality aright.

Seng-zhao (Seng-chao) spoke of "sudden" enlightenment before the *BNT* appeared in China. The *BNT,* for its part, never speaks in terms of a "sudden" enlightenment. Nonetheless, it still seems fair to say that the ideas found in the *BNT* (as expressed in the *BNT* and elsewhere) contributed to the ongoing development of this concept and to its importance in later Chinese Buddhist schools. In this text, first, we have the teaching that we are all inherently Buddhas, that perfection in its complete and mature state is present in us all. Second, we have the *āśrayaparāvṛtti* concept of a pivotal conversion experience; and, third, the reading of *trisvabhāva* as indicative of two human existential modes of delusion and enlightenment linked by the pivotal *āśrayaparāvṛtti.* Here are three of the critical raw ingredients of the sudden enlightenment idea in the form it would take in the Chan school.

7. Buddha Nature Is Buddhist Practice

The establishment of the equation of Buddha nature and Buddhist practice is one of the great achievements of the *BNT*. The importance of this achievement is (minimally) twofold. First, it undercuts any possibility of conceiving of Buddha nature as an entity of any kind, as a Hindu-like *Ātman* or even as a purely mental process. Thus it renders invalid charges that the Buddha nature teaching violates Buddhist *anātman* teachings, that it reifies process, that it serves as the foundation of a monistic system, or even that it supports mental-physical dualistic thinking. Second, it provides a solid philosophical defense against those later Chan polemicists who would destroy Chan by rejecting practice on the grounds that they already were Buddha, and so had no need of practice. Of course, it was this very question—Why is there a need to practice Buddhism if we are all inherently Buddhas?—which vexed Dōgen sufficiently to cause him for years to scour Japan and China, as well as his own mind, in search of an answer. The answer he ultimately found takes off from the point at which the *BNT* leaves us: the identity of Buddha nature and practice.

C. Buddha Nature Thought and Western Buddhism

When one considers the encounter of Buddhism with the West, especially in the context of the development of this encounter in Japan and in America, two ongoing events stand out as especially important: Buddhist-Christian dialogue, as it is found in the Kyoto School of philosophy, the Society for Buddhist-Christian Studies, and elsewhere; and Western Buddhism. I believe that, in different ways, theoreticians and practitioners in both of these contexts face in the question of human being (including the question of its transformability) the probable key to the meeting of the two mutually alien worlds and to the success of their respective enterprises. In the question of human being we have a matter of deep, shared concern matched with radically disparate assumptions, concepts, and values. We also have the very foundation of Buddhist philosophy itself, hence, the key to the difference between the two world-views. This subject, although theoretically thorny, is at the heart of what must be resolved to bring the two worlds into mutual comprehension. This no doubt will be a long process; indeed, though the Kyoto School to a certain extent has begun to grapple philosophically with this question, it is evident that it will be some time before adequate answers can be developed.[22] As Buddha nature forms the core of the East Asian Buddhist concept of human being, the role of Buddha nature thought in this investigation must be large. In this is a first point of contemporary significance for the study of the Buddha nature concept.

Hard on the heels of the question of human being and, moreover, conceptually dependent upon it, comes dialogue on ethics, theoretical and applied, another area of shared existential concern coupled with mutual incommensurability. One readily can see that outstanding among the features of the West to which representatives of Buddhism, both Asian and Western, will have to respond is the individualistic humanism that permeates Western philosophy and social institutions. Buddha nature thought has important resources for meeting this challenge, and in this lies a second point of contemporary significance of Buddha nature thought.

I will not speculate as to what Asian Buddhists will make of the challenge of Western humanism, but the conjunction of Western humanism with the teaching of Buddha nature marks a point on which Buddhists in the West almost certainly will build. In the second theme, we saw that one of the implications of the Buddha nature teaching is that "each person is a Buddha, not only potentially, but actually." An American cannot help but note that this "actually" has not yet been realized for its humanistic potential by the Buddhist world. Coming from a tradition of individualistic humanism, we read a Mahāyāna text with references to Buddha nature and the *bodhisattva* ideal and see in it an imperative to social action. Asians may not have seen such an imperative, but with our traditions we can do no other.

Why East Asian Buddhists have been moved to act as little as they have in the social arena is a vast and complex issue that cannot be treated here.[23] I will mention only the single point that the texts prized in the East Asian Buddhist traditions have tended to emphasize such things as nondiscrimination and nonconceptual wisdom, which are difficult to reconcile with the complexities of resolving competing claims, for example, or balancing needs against resources, which require that one be very precise in distinguishing particulars, that one make informed judgments, and that one regard such activities as important and valuable. As we have seen in the *BNT*, however, the old texts do occasionally refer with approval to forms of awareness that fit quite harmoniously with such practical demands. In our text, discriminating, worldly wisdom is the form of *prajñā* identified as the essence of *mahākaruṇā* and *mahākaruṇā* itself is prized as superior to *karuṇā* precisely because of its practical efficacy. Such statements as these no doubt will be mined in the future, at least by Western Buddhists, as the latter strive to create a theoretical basis for the social actions in which they already are engaged and that they conceive in the light of Buddhist teachings of compassion.

There is no doubt that the very existence of such a thing as Western Buddhism will result in the further investigation of such teachings as Buddha nature and the *bodhisattva* ideal, considerable reflection on the implications of these teachings for the modern world, and the practice of these teachings in the realm of social action. Indeed, there already exists "Engaged Buddhism," the active engagement in society and its problems by Buddhist practitioners both as an essential element of their practice and as one of its fruits.[24] It is no risk to predict that this tendency in Western Buddhism will continue to grow.[25]

One of the primary aims of interreligious dialogue is for each partner to critically assess itself in light of the challenge posed by the other; to become clearer about itself, its strengths, and its lacunae; and then to move ahead, in the inspiration of its own past and the challenge of the encounter with the other, as well as the demands of the modern world. The world is shrinking and we are all forced, more than ever, to take serious account of each other. The encounter of Buddhism with the West is one form of this encounter in which the taking seriously of each other is happening. In taking each other seriously, precious new fruits are brought into being as individuals within each culture slowly are transformed by the process of seeing more clearly that which another culture brings to one's attention and expressing in a new form the genius of one's own culture.

NOTES

Chapter 1. Introduction

1. As discussed later, the concept of Buddha nature is very closely related to that of the *tathāgatagarbha,* with which it is almost synonymous.

2. Takasaki Jikidō, "Structure of the Anuttarāśrayasūtra (Wu-shang-i-ching)," *Indogaku Bukkyōgaku Kenkyū* [hereafter, *IBK*] 8 (March 1960): 34.

3. For a discussion of this point, see Alfred Bloom, *Shinran's Gospel of Pure Grace,* Association for Asian Studies: Monographs and Papers No. 20 (Tucson: University of Arizona Press, 1965), Chapter 4, "Faith: Its Definition."

4. *Fo Xing Lun,* attributed to Vasubandhu and translated by Paramārtha, *Taishō Shinshū Daizōkyō* 31, no. 1610: 787–813.

5. Formerly it was believed that the equivalent Sanskrit term for *fo xing* must be *buddhatā* or *buddhatva;* that is, Buddhahood or Buddhaness. However, upon comparison of the Chinese versions of texts containing the term *fo xing* with their Sanskrit and Tibetan equivalents, it became apparent that the term *fo xing* did not correspond to the Sanskrit *buddhatā, buddhatva,* or their Tibetan equivalents. Rather, what emerged was more complex.

   Ogawa Ichijō [" 'Busshō' to buddhatva," *IBK* 11 (March 1963): 544–545] and Shinoda Masashige ["Busshō to sono gengo," *IBK* 11 (1963): 223–226], for example, compare the Chinese text of the *Ratnagotravibhāga* with its Sanskrit counterpart and find that *fo xing* was used to translate compounds of the term *dhātu* (nature, element, realm, principle; e.g., Buddha-*dhātu,* Tathāgata-*dhātu,* etc.), *gotra* (family, lineage), or *garbha.* Ogawa sees these three as of equal status and synonymous meaning and so holds that we can safely take *Buddha nature* to have one meaning rather than several; namely, the term *tathāgatagarbha* and its equivalents. Shinoda, on the other hand, sees the *dhātu* and *gotra* groups as the standard bases for the "Buddha nature" translation, with *garbha* and the remaining terms as exceptions to these standards. Moreover, he explains the basic meaning of both *dhātu* and *gotra* as cause, as in "the *dhātu* is the cause of the arising of the three jewels—Buddha, Dharma and Sangha" and "all merits are born of this *gotra*" (quoted form the *Ratnagotravibhāga*). However, *fo xing* means not only the cause of the Buddha, but also the "essential nature" of the Buddha, enlightenment, and this the term *gotra* cannot convey. Shinoda concludes that *dhātu,* as equivalent to *dharmakāya, dharmatā* and *tathatā,* includes the "fruition" sense of the Buddha, as well as the "causal" sense, and can be taken as the most appropriate equivalent for Buddha nature. Thus *fo xing* would most exactly translate *buddhadhātu.*

Takasaki Jikidō, ["Dharmatā, Dharmadhātu, Dharmakāya and Buddhadhātu—Structure of the Ultimate Value in Mahāyāna Buddhism," *IBK* 14 (March 1966): 78–94] agrees with Shinoda's view and clarifies it. He explains *dhātu* as meaning originally "that which places or sustains something," and hence, like *dharma,* it can stand for rule, principle or truth (ibid., p. 81). In the Abhidharma literature it was taken to mean element, essence, or essential nature. Subsequently, the term *dharmadhātu* came to be interpreted as (1) the nature (*dhātu*) of things (*dharma*), or the truth concerning things, and (2) the totality of phenomena or things. It is also given as meaning (3) the origin or cause of the Buddha's teachings, the Dharma. Thus, with (1) and (2) as the fruition meaning, and (3) as cause, he finds the term *dhātu* to have the bivalence attributed to it by Shinoda.

6. Takasaki, "Structure of the Ultimate Value," pp. 91–92.

7. Whalen Wai-lun Lai, "The Awakening of Faith in Mahāyāna (Ta ch'eng ch'i-hsin lun): A Study of the Unfolding of Sinitic Mahāyāna Motifs" (Ph.D. dissertation, Harvard University, 1975), pp. 107–115.

8. The debate concerning Maitreya is succinctly summarized by Janice Dean Willis in her *On Knowing Reality: The Tattvārtha Chapter of Asaṅga's Bodhisattvabhūmi* (New York: Columbia University Press, 1969), pp. 52–53 (note 42).

9. Stefan Anacker, *Seven Works of Vasubandhu: The Buddhist Psychological Doctor,* Religions of Asia Series Number 4 (Delhi: Motilal Banarsidass, 1984), p. 19.

10. I have emphasized *śāstra* literature in my exposition of Yogācāra roots, but of course *sūtra* literature also played an important role. In addition to the previously mentioned *Mahāparinirvāṇa-sūtra* and *Daśabhūmikā-sūtra,* other *sūtras* associated with the Yogācāra school include the *Saṃdhinirmocana-sūtra,* the *Avataṁsaka-sūtra* (including the *Daśabhūmikā-sūtra* and the *Gaṇḍavyūha-sūtra*), and the *Laṅkāvatāra-sūtra.* As discussed later, the *prajñāparamitā sūtra* literature group also plays a

critical role in the development of Yogācāra thought and should not be associated solely with the Mādhyamika school.

11. Gadjin M. Nagao, "From Mādhyamika to Yogācāra: An Analysis of MMK, XXIV.18 and MV, I.1–2," *Journal of the International Association of Buddhist Studies*, 2 no. 1 (1979): 29.

12. Yoshifumi Ueda, "Two Main Streams of Thought in Yogācāra Philosophy," *Philosophy East and West* 17 (1967): 162–163.

13. Willis, *On Knowing Reality*, pp. 34–35.

14. Ibid., p. 132.

15. For this historical outline, in addition to my own reading of the *tathāgatagarbha* texts, I have drawn mostly from Takasaki Jikidō, *Nyoraizō Shisō no Keisei* (Tokyo: Shunjusha, 1974); Takasaki Jikidō, *A Study on the Ratnagotravibhāga (Uttaratantra) Being a Treatise on the Tathāgatagarbha Theory of Mahāyāna Buddhism,* Serie Orientale Roma No. 33 (Rome: Istituto Italiano per il Medio ed Estremo Oriente, 1966); and William Henry Grosnick, "Dōgen's View of the Buddha-Nature" (Ph.D. dissertation, University of Wisconsin—Madison, 1979).

16. The *Anūnatvāpūrṇatvanirdeśa* is extant only in the sixth century Chinese translation of Bodhiruci; neither a Sanskrit nor a Tibetan text survives. However, fragments of the text in Sanskrit survive as quotations in the *Ratnagotravibhāga* and other texts, so most scholars agree that the text formerly existed in Sanskrit. The Sanskrit title is a reconstruction from the Chinese.

17. *Fo Shuo Bu Zeng Bu Jian Jing, Taishō* 16, no. 668: 467b.

18. This text is extant only in Chinese and Tibetan but Sanskrit fragments have been recovered.

19. The question of universal Buddhahood and the status of the *icchantika* in the *Mahāparinirvāṇa-sūtra* is still, for modern scholars, a moot point. It may be debated whether the *sūtra* attains a consistent position on this issue.

20. See Grosnick, "Dōgen's View," p. 32 f.

21. Ibid., pp. 128 ff.

22. See Takasaki Jikidō, "The *Tathāgatagarbha* Theory in the *Mahāparinirvāṇa-sūtra.*" *IBK* 19, no. 2 (March 1971): 1015–1024.

23. Yevgenii Y. Obermiller, *The Sublime Science of the Great Vehicle to Salvation, Being a Manual of Buddhist Monism* (Shanghai: 1940); and Takasaki, *A Study on the Ratnagotravibhāga.*

24. Takasaki, *A Study on the Ratnagotravibhāga,* pp. 9 and 62.

25. Ibid., pp. 61–62.

26. Ibid., p. 5.

27. Ibid., p. 33. For my summary of the *Ratnagotra,* I rely most heavily on Takasaki's study in ibid.

28. They also appear in altered form in the *Dharmadhātvaviśeṣa-śāstra* and the *Wu Shang Yi Jing* (*Anuttarāśraya-sūtra*). Ibid., pp. 45–53.

29. See ibid., pp. 199 and 200–267.

30. Yamaguchi Susumu, *Hannya Shisōshi* (Tokyo: Hōzōkan, 1951), Chapter 6, "Nyoraizō Shisō."

31. See Takasaki, *A Study on the Ratnagotravibhāga,* pp. 296 ff.

32. Yamaguchi, *Hannya Shisōshi,* p. 88.

33. This is the view of John P. Keenan, Introduction to *The Realm of Awakening: A Translation and Study of The Tenth Chapter of Asaṅga's* MAHĀYĀNASAṄGRAHA, trans. Paul J. Griffiths, Noriaki Hakamaya, John P. Keenan, and Paul L. Swanson; texts by Paul J. Griffiths and Noriaki Hakamaya (New York and Oxford: Oxford University Press, 1989), pp. 30–45.

34. This is the view of Grosnick, "Dōgen's View," pp. 26 ff and 76 ff. Grosnick, however, recognizes the plausibility of the competing view. He notes that the *Mahāyānasūtrālaṅkāra* contains both Yogācāra and *tathāgatagarbha* teachings and goes on to state, "it is just possible that the group of practitioners who promulgated the *tathāgatagarbha* was actually a part of a larger group known loosely as the 'Yogācārins.' For prior to the systematic treatises of Asaṅga and Vasubandhu, the history of the school (if it can be called a school at that time), is difficult to trace." Ibid., p. 79.

35. The date of the *Laṅkāvatāra-sūtra* is uncertain. Consequently, it may have been composed either before or after the prose portion of the *Ratnagotravibhāga.* See Grosnick, ibid., p. 27, note 43.

36. Ibid., p. 81, note 21.

37. Ibid., p. 83.

38. Ibid., p. 77.

39. Ibid., pp. 84 ff. I follow Grosnick in listing the three themes he isolates; however, my interpretation differs from his.

40. *Da Sheng Qi Xin Lun, Taishō* 32, no. 1666: 576b.

41. Ibid., p. 579a.

42. As translated by Daisetz Teitaro Suzuki, *The Laṅkāvatāra Sūtra* (London: Routledge and Kegan Paul, 1932; reprinted Boulder, CO: Prajñā Press, 1978), pp. 190–192.

43. It should be noted that the *Śrīmālādevī-sūtra* also speaks of the *tathāgatagarbha* as the source of both *saṃsāra* and *nirvāṇa*, though it stresses the idea of the innately pure *tathāgatagarbha.*

44. Suzuki, *Laṅkāvatāra Sūtra,* p. 21. My addition in brackets.

45. For the following sketch of Paramārtha's life, I relied heavily on the account in Diana Y. Paul, *Philosophy of Mind in Sixth-Century China: Paramārtha's 'Evolution of Consciousness'* (Stanford: Stanford University Press, 1984), Chapter 1. The reader will find there a much longer and more detailed account of Paramārtha's life.

46. Kōgen Mizuno, *Buddhist Sutras: Origin, Development, Transmission* (Tokyo: Kōsei, 1982), p. 99.

47. Ibid., p. 33.

48. Paul lists thirty-two works attributed to Paramārtha, together with textual information, *Philosophy of Mind,* pp. 175–178.

49. *Fo Xing Lun, Taishō* 31, no. 1610: 787–813.

50. Takasaki Jikidō, "Structure of the Ultimate Value," p. 35. His citation of Hattori.

51. Takemura Shōhō, *Busshōron Kenkyū* (Tokyo: Hyakkaenkan, 1978), p. 37.

52. Ui Hakuju, *Hōshōron Kenkyū* (Tokyo: Iwanamishoten, 1960), p. 366.

53. Takemura, *Busshōron Kenkyū,* p. 6.

54. Takasaki Jikidō, "Busshōron," in Mizuno Kōgen, Nakamura Hajíme, Hirakawa Akira, and Tamaki Kōshirō, eds., *Buttenkaidaijiten,* 2d ed. (Tokyo: Shunjūsha, 1977), pp. 145–146.

55. Grosnick, "Dōgen's View," p. 78. Takasaki, *A Study on the Ratnagotravibhāga,* p. 52.

56. William H. Grosnick, "The Categories of *T'i, Hsiang,* and *Yung:* Evidence that Paramārtha Composed the *Awakening of Faith,*" *Journal of the International Association of Buddhist Studies* 12, no. 1 (1989): 65–92.

57. Grosnick, "Dōgen's View," p. 120.

58. Takasaki, "Busshōron," p. 144. Extant is "Busshōron Setsugi" by Kenshū.

59. Takemura, *Busshōron Kenkyū,* pp. 3–4.

60. William Grosnick gives three main themes of Buddha nature theory in China: subject-object nonduality; the idea that the world of phenomena is present within enlightenment; and the coextensiveness of Buddha nature and practice. He sees these expressed most clearly in Tian-tai and Chan. Grosnick, "Dōgen's View," pp. 181–182.

Chapter 2. The Concept of Buddha Nature

1. The shift from talk of things to talk of words, recognized as freeing a discussion from certain ontological presuppositions. See Willard Van Orman Quine, *Word and Object* (Cambridge, MA: M.I.T. Press, 1960), pp. 270 ff.

2. A. C. Graham, " 'Being' in Western Philosophy Compared with *Shih/Fei* and *Yu/Wu* in Chinese Philosophy," *Asia Major* 7 (December 1959): 99.

3. Ibid., p. 100.
4. Ibid.
5. Ibid., pp. 100–101.
6. The *Tathāgatagarbha sūtra,* for example, states whether or not a Buddha comes into the world, all beings dwell in the *tathāgatagarbha. Da Fang Deng Ru Lai Zang Jing, Taishō* 16, no. 666: 457c.
7. Arthur E. Link, "The Taoist Antecedents of Tao-an's Prajna Ontology," *History of Religions* 9 (1969–70): 187–188.
8. Gilbert Ryle, *The Concept of Mind* (New York: Barnes and Noble, 1949), pp. 22–23.
9. Selected and condensed from the list of meanings in Mervyn Sprung, ed., *The Problem of Two Truths in Buddhism and Vedanta* (Dordrecht, Holland: D. Reidel, 1973), pp. 43–44.
10. The four subjects of contemplation, the four kinds of right effort, the four steps to super powers, the five spiritual faculties and their five associated powers, the seven levels of *bodhi* (wisdom), and the eight constituents of the Eightfold Noble Path.
11. Any supplementary aid to Buddhist practice, as opposed to a necessary aspect of that practice.
12. Note the positive value assigned to conditioned action here. This point will be discussed in Chapter 6.
13. This use of the term *primitive* was suggested by P. F. Strawson in *Individuals: An Essay in Descriptive Metaphysics* (London: Methuen, 1959), pp. 101 ff., where he describes "person" as a "primitive concept" to which both states of consciousness and bodily characteristics are ascribed.
14. For this analysis I draw from Alan Sponberg (who applies it to the same problem in Kui-ji's writings), "The *Trisvabhāva* Doctrine in India and China: A Study of Three Exegetical Models," *Bukkyō Bunka Kenkyūjo Kiyō* 21 (1982): 97–119.
15. Clearly, Dōgen was not the first to state that sentient beings "are" rather than "possess" the Buddha nature.
16. This is typical of the author's use of the term *separation* to indicate dissimilarity, throughout the section from which the passage is taken.

Chapter 3. Soteriology: Buddha Nature as the Practice of Buddhism

1. Soteriology is conceived in this way by Frederick J. Streng in *Emptiness: A Study in Religious Meaning* (Nashville: Abingdon Press, 1967), passim.
2. The four attachments are desire, false views, false morals, and ideas of self.

3. The six destinies are hell, and the worlds of the hungry ghosts, animals, *asura* (demons), humans, and *deva* (heavenly spirits).

4. Each of the five senses has its own consciousness, plus one for the consciousness with thoughts as its objects.

5. Meritorious activities of body, mouth, and mind; i.e., Buddhist practice.

6. I have not been able to locate the source of this quotation.

7. *Dhāranī* embraces the practices of *smṛti* (recollection), meditation, and wisdom.

8. Referred to as *Bao Ding Jing* but meaning *Bao Ji Jing*. Takemura, *Busshōron Kenkyū*, p. 157.

9. Compare this to the title and theme of the *Anūnatvāpūrṇatvanirdeśa* (*No Increase, No Decrease Sūtra*) (*Fo Shuo Bu Zeng Bu Jian Jing*), *Taishō* 16, no. 668, pp. 466–468).

10. The *sambhogakāya* is the "enjoyment" or "communal" body manifest in the pure Buddha lands and visible to advanced *bodhisattvas*. *Nirmāṇakāya* is the "transformation" body in which the Buddha appears among ordinary persons.

11. Or unconditioned wisdom, meditation, and compassion.

12. The abilities to see everything, hear everything, know the thoughts of others, know the previous lives of oneself and others, perform various wonders and know that the defilements are extinct. See Har Dayal, *The Bodhisattva Doctrine in Buddhist Sanskrit Literature* (Delhi: Motilal Banarsidass, 1932), pp. 106 ff.

13. The hells and the worlds of the hungry ghosts and animals.

14. To save all of the innumerable sentient beings, to eradicate all delusions and passions, to penetrate the infinite Dharma, and to fulfill the Buddha Way.

15. As spoken by Samantabhadra in the *Hua-yan-sūtra,* they are (1) to worship all Buddhas, (2) to praise the Tathāgatas, (3) to perform *pūja* worship, (4) to repent and remove karmic hindrances, (5) to make all one's talents accord with the joyful and meritorious, (6) to turn the wheel of the Dharma, (7) to purify all Buddha lands, (8) to always follow Buddhism, (9) to always make sentient beings prosper, and (10) to return one's merits for the good of all. Ding Fu-Bao, *Fo Xue Da Ci Dian* (Taipei: 1946), p. 2091. Also see Dayal, *Bodhisattva Doctrine*, p. 66.

16. These are four bases of super powers, developed by uniting intense concentration and effort with (1) desire, (2) energy, (3) thought, and (4) investigation. See ibid., pp. 104 ff.

17. Namely, "instruction, doctrine, knowledge or wisdom attained, cutting away of delusion, practice of the religious life, progressive status, [and] producing the fruit of saintliness." William Soothill and Lewis Hodous, *A Dictionary of Chinese Buddhist Terms* (Taipei: Ch'eng Wen Publishing Co., 1970), p. 38a.

18. The three periods are past, present, and future.

19. Attributed in the *BNT* to the *(Fo Shuo) Wu Shang Yi Jing* (*Taishō,* no. 669: 468–477) but in fact closely paralleling a passage in the *Fo Shuo Bu Zeng Bu Jian Jing* (*Taishō,* no. 668: 466–468).

20. The tradition also maintains other identifiers, such as the physical marks and the super powers.

Chapter 4. Dereification of Self and Mind

1. In Chapter Three.

2. The text in this section on suffering is corrupt and I take some small liberties in the translation.

3. Cf. D. Seyfort Ruegg, *La Théorie du Tathāgatagarbha et du Gotra* (Paris: École Française d'extrême orient, 1969), p. 368, for a Sanskrit version of this chart based on the *Ratnagotravibhāga.*

4. The five are *rūpa,* form; *vedanā,* sensation; *saṃjñā,* perception; *saṃskārā,* impulses (volition, dispositions, etc.); and *vijñāna,* consciousness.

5. Similar verses are found in the *Ratnagotravibhāga* and the *Mahāyānasūtrālaṅkāra.*

6. In Chapter Three.

7. As cited in Walpola Rahula, *What the Buddha Taught,* rev. ed. (New York: Grove Press [1959], 1974), p. 101.

8. In Chapter Three.

9. In Chapter Three.

10. See Chapter Two.

11. See Chapter Three.

Chapter 5. Ontology: Monism vs. Nondualism

1. Yevgenii Y. Obermiller, *The Sublime Science,* p. 82.

2. Gadjin M. Nagao, " 'What Remains' in Śūnyatā: A Yogācāra Interpretation of Emptiness," in Minoru Kiyota, ed., *Mahāyāna Buddhist Meditation: Theory and Practice* (Honolulu: University Press of Hawaii, 1978), p. 81.

3. Takasaki, *A Study on the Ratnagotravibhāga*, p. 28.

4. Ogawa Ichijō, *Nyoraizō Busshō no Kenkyū* (Kyoto: Nakayamashobō, 1976), pp. 3–41, passim.

5. Yamaguchi Susumu, *Hannya Shisōshi* (Tokyo: Hōzōkan, 1951), Chapter 6.

6. Ruegg, *Théorie,* pp. 291 and 361.

7. The following is derived from Roland Hall, "Monism and Pluralism," in Paul Edwards, ed., *The Encyclopedia of Philsophy,* Vol. 5, pp. 363–5.

8. Obermiller, *The Sublime Science,* p. 81.

9. In this I agree with Ruegg, whose work contributed to my view.

10. Graham, "Being in Western Philosophy," p. 102.

11. *Da Sheng Qi Xin Lun, Taishō* 32, no. 1666; 576a. Cf. Yoshito S. Hakeda, trans., *The Awakening of Faith* (New York: Columbia University Press, 1967), p. 33.

12. Discussed in Chapter Four.

13. Ruegg, *Théorie,* pp. 291 and 361.

14. Cf. ibid., pp. 379 f. Ruegg's analysis contributed to my understanding here.

15. See Peter Gregory, "The Problem of Theodicy in the *Awakening of Faith,*" *Religious Studies* 22: 63–78.

16. Nagao Gadjin, "Amarerumono," *Indogakubukkyōgakukenkyū* 41 (1968): 23–27. An English version of this article is available as Nagao, "'What Remains' in Śūnyatā," pp. 66–82.

17. "Amarerumono," ibid., p. 26b.

18. Ibid., p. 27b.

Chapter 6. Engaging in Spiritual Cultivation

1. One who can bear the Dharma vessel is one who is fit to practice Buddhism.

2. The idea of these four foundations to practice is an old Buddhist tradition, stemming back to the *Aṅguttara-Nikāya* and other texts. Takemura, *Busshōron Kenkyū, p. 307.*

3. The ten knowledges are an outline of the Hīnayāna path and are given in the *Abhidharmakośa* of Vasubandhu. The list begins with (1) the worldly knowledge of the ordinary person who has not yet begun the practice of Buddhism and progress up to (9) "exhaustive" knowledge, in which all *kleśa* have been extinguished and the Four Noble Truths have been realized, and (10) no-birth knowledge, in which one realizes that one has concluded the process of knowing the Four Truths, cutting off karma and *kleśa,* realizing *nirvāṇa,* and cultivating the Path, and that there is nothing further to be done. With the tenth knowledge, one has completed the Hīnayāna path. *Fo Xue Da Ci Dian,* pp. 2197–2198.

   Paramārtha renders the first knowledge as "worldly Right Views" (*shi zheng jian*), but in this context I believe he is referring to the first of the ten knowledges.

4. On *bhāvanā,* see Alan Sponberg, "Meditation in Fa-hsiang Buddhism," in Peter N. Gregory, ed., *Traditions of Meditation in Chinese Buddhism,* Kuroda Institute Studies in East Asian Buddhism No. 4 (Honolulu: University of Hawaii Press, 1986), p. 19.

5. The quotation is similar to one in the *Da Bao Ji Jing* (*Mahāratnakūṭasūtra*). See Takasaki, *A Study on the Ratnagotravibhāga,* p. 204; and Takemura, *Busshōron Kenkyū,* pp. 129 and 265.

6. I take the idea of "fruitful tension" from oral comments made by Robert Gimello at a meeting of the American Academy of Religion.

7. Fred Streng has pointed out a passage in the *prajñāpāramitā* literature with similar implications: "Without losing himself in his concentration, he [the *bodhisattva*] ties his thought to an objective support (for his compassion) and he determines that he will take hold of perfect wisdom [which is essentially skill-in-means], and he will not realize [emptiness, because its realization is not the final goal]. Meanwhile, however, the Bodhisattva does not lose the dharmas which act as the wings to enlightenment." *Perfection of Wisdom in Eight Thousand Lines and Its Verse Summary (Aṣṭasāhasrikā-prajñāpāramitā-ratna-guṇa-saṃcaya-gātha),* trans. Edward Conze (Berkeley: Four Seasons Foundation, 1973), p. 222. Cited in Frederick J. Streng, "Selfhood without Selfishness: Buddhist and Christian Approaches to Authentic Living," in Paul D. Ingram and Frederick J. Streng, eds., *Buddhist-Christian Dialogue: Mutual Renewal and Transformation* (Honolulu:University of Hawaii Press, 1986), p. 191.

8. The three kinds of *duhkha* are *duhkha-duhkhatā* (*ku-ku*) the suffering inherent in *duhkha; huai-ku,* suffering in response to the passing of pleasure; *xing-ku,* suffering in response to impermance. The desire realm has all three kinds of *duhkha,* the form realm has the latter two, and the nonform realm, the last. *Fo Xue Da Ci Dian,* p. 320.

9. The three realms of desire, form, and nonform.

10. The fourth *dhyāna* stage is characterized by mindfulness and equanimity and is free of all emotion. See Edward Conze, *Buddhist Meditation* (London: Allen and Unwin, 1956; New York: Harper and Row, 1969), p. 118.

11. Several scholars have made this point. See, for example, Peter N. Gregory, "Introduction" and Alan Sponberg, "Mediation in Fa-hsiang Buddhism," both in Gregory, *Traditions of Meditation.*

Chapter 7. Buddha Nature and the Concept of Person

1. For the idea of these two dimensions I am indebted to Joaquín Pérez-Remón, *Self and Non-Self in Early Buddhism,* Reason and Religion, No. 22 (The Hague: Mouton, 1980).

2. The author refers to the text as *Bao Ding Jing* but it should be *Bao Ji Jing.* Takemura, *Busshōron Kenkyū,* p. 356.

3. *Manovijñāna* is given here as the consciousness responsible for discriminating between "self" and "not-self."

4. The realms of desire, form, and the formless.

5. Āryadeva, *Guang Bai Lun Ben.* Takemura, *Busshōron Kenkyū,* p. 359.

6. I take this translation from Aramaki Noritoshi's paper presented at the

U.S.-Japan Conference on Japanese Buddhism, 1985. I do not intend by it any Christian connotations.

7. This division of humanity into two camps may seem to fit poorly with the *BNT*'s own division of humanity, as mentioned, into three camps; ordinary persons, sages, and Buddhas. Even these three, however, really break down into the same two camps, "those who do not perceive and realize the Buddha nature" (ordinary persons) and "those who do" (sages and Buddhas). Buddhas and sages fit in a general way into the same category of beings who do perceive and realize the Buddha nature, the only difference between them being that, in the case of Buddhas, their "realization reaches the ultimate purity" (805c–806a). In short, the same line of demarcation fits this set of three: purity and impurity, delusion and enlightenment.

8. Juan Mascaró, trans. *The Upanishads* (Middlesex, England: Penguin Books, 1965), the Praśna Upaniṣad, p. 74.

9. Sung Bae Park, *Buddhist Faith and Sudden Enlightenment* (Albany, NY: SUNY Press, 1983), p. 19.

Chapter 8. Retrospective and Prospective

1. This and the following sections on classes of persons are summarized from *BNT*, p. 812a–c.

2. The following verse is found in nine Mahāyāna texts. See Takasaki, *A Study on the Ratnagotravibhāga*, p. 300.

3. Takasaki, *Nyoraizō Shisō no Keisei*, p. 3. In other listings, Fa-zang continues to list the *tathāgatagarbha* tradition as superior to Hīnayāna, Mādhyamika, and Yogācāra, but is itself superceded by two categories: the "Sudden Teaching" exemplified by the silence of Vimalakīrti in the *Vimalakīrti-sūtra* and associated with the Chan school, and the "Complete" or "Perfect Teaching" of the *Hua-yan-sūtra* (*Avataṃsaka*), with which the Hua-yan school especially is associated. Few scholars today would agree with Fa-zang's characterization of the *tathāgatagarbha* tradition as a school comparable to Mādhyamika and Yogācāra.

4. See Peter Gregory, "Chinese Buddhist Hermeneutics: The Case of Hua-yen," *Journal of the American Academy of Religion* 51, no. 2 (June 1983): 231–249.

5. See Francis H. Cook, *Hua-yen Buddhism: The Jewel Net of Indra* (University Park and London: Pennsylvania State University Press, 1977), especially Chapter 3, "The Indian Background of Hua-yen."

6. This point is discussed in two articles in Gregory, *Traditions of Meditation:* Bernard Fauré, "The Concept of One-Practice Samadhi in Early Ch'an," pp. 99–128; and Carl Bielefeldt, "Ch'ang-lu Tsung-tse's *Tso-ch'an I* and the 'Secret' of Zen Meditation," pp. 129–161.

7. Translated by and cited in Fauré, "Concept of One-Practice Samadhi," p. 105. His brackets and ellipsis.

8. Translated and cited by Bielefeldt, "Ch'ang-lu Tsung-tse's *Tso-ch'an I,*" p. 138.
9. Ibid., pp. 136–137.
10. Philip Yampolsky, *The Platform Sutra of the Sixth Patriarch* (New York: Columbia University Press, 1967), pp. 137–138.
11. Ibid., p. 139.
12. See Obermiller, *The Sublime Science,* p. 81.
13. Shunryu Suzuki, *Zen Mind, Beginner's Mind* (New York: Weatherhill, 1970; paperback, 1973), p. 83.
14. Ibid., p. 119.
15. See Chang Chung-Yuan, *Original Teachings of Ch'an Buddhism* (New York: Vintage Books, 1969), pp. 97–101.
16. Shunryu Suzuki, *Zen Mind,* p. 83.
17. As translated by T. P. Kasulis, *Zen Action Zen Person* (Honolulu: University of Hawaii Press, 1981), p. 103.
18. As translated by Francis H. Cook, "Dōgen's View of Authentic Selfhood and Its Socio-ethical Implications" in William R. LaFleur, ed., *Dōgen Studies,* Kuroda Institute: Studies in East Asian Buddhism No. 2. (Honolulu: University of Hawaii Press, 1985), p. 133.
19. This is not to say, of course, that artistic representations of various Buddhas, *bodhisattvas,* scenes of the Pure Land, and so on did not also proliferate in China.
20. From the *Transmission of the Lamp* (8.263), as cited in Fung Yu-lan, *A History of Chinese Philosophy,* vol. 2, trans. Derk Bodde (Princeton: Princeton University Press, 1953; paperback edition, 1983), p. 403.
21. Thich Nhat Hanh, *Being Peace* (Berkeley: Parallax Press, 1987), p. 114.
22. See Hans Waldenfels, *Absolute Nothingness: Foundations for a Buddhist-Christian Dialogue,* trans. J. W. Heisig (New York: Paulist Press, 1980; German edition, Breisgau: Verlag Herder Freiburg, 1976), Chapter 7, "Emptiness and the Appreciation of World, History and Man."
23. There are prominent exceptions to this generalization, of course, such as those seen in the Japanese Sōka Gakkai today.
24. For more information on Engaged Buddhism, see Fred Eppsteiner, ed., *The Path of Compassion: Writings on Socially Engaged Buddhism,* 2d ed., (Berkeley, CA: Parallax Press, 1988).
25. It is not only the encounter with Western expectations that causes Buddhism to develop in this direction. The leaders of the Engaged Buddhism movement include two Vietnamese, Thich Nhat Hanh and Cao Ngoc Phuong, and a Tibetan, the Dalai Lama. Their concerns for an Engaged Buddhism obviously do not stem from the same source as an American's, but from their experiences of the plights faced by their countries in the modern world.

GLOSSARY

ba	拔
ba chu	拔除
Bao Ding Jing	寶頂經
Bao Ji Jing	寶積經
ben	本
ben wu	本無

ben xing	本性
ben you	本有
bu	不
bu kong	不空
bu kong guo	不空過
bu shi	不實
Busshōron Setsugi	佛性論節義
Chan (Zen)	禪
chan ding	禪定
chang	常
chang zhu	常住
chen	沈
chen mo	沈没

Cheng Wei Shi Lun	成唯識論
chu 1	出
chu 2	除
Da Bao Ji Jing	大 寶積經
Da Fang Deng Ru-lai Zang Jing	大方等如來藏經
da gong yong	大功用
Da Sheng Qi Xin Lun	大乘起信論
Dao	道
Dao li	道理
Dao-sheng	道生
Dao sheng yi	道生依
Dao-xin	道信
de cheng	得成

Di-lun	地論
ding	定
ding hui	定慧
Dōgen	道元
du	度
duan	斷
en	恩
fa	法
fa shen	法身
Fa-xian	法顯
Fa-xiang	法相
Fa-zang	法藏
fan fu	凡夫

fan fu xing	凡夫性
fei fei se	非非色
fei san shi fa	非三世法
fei shi you	非實有
fei you fei wu	非有非無
fen-bie-xing	分別性
fo	佛
Fo Shuo Bu Zeng Bu Jian Jing	佛說不增不減經
Fo Shuo Wu Shang Yi Jing	佛說無上依經
fo xing	佛性
Fo Xue Da Ci Dian	佛學大辭典
guan	觀

Guang Bai Lun Ben	廣百論本
guo	過
guo du	過度
Hong-ren	弘忍
Hua-yan	華嚴
huai ku	壞苦
Hui-ke	慧可
Hui-neng	惠(慧)能
Hui-si	慧思
ji 1	寂
ji 2	濟
ji jing	寂靜

jia	加
jia xing	加行
jian xing	見性
jie	解
jie tuo Dao	解脫道
jing 1	靜
jing 2	境
Jue Ding Zang Lun	決定藏論
Kenshū	賢洲
kong	空
kong you bu you	空有不有
ku ku	苦苦
Kui-ji	窺基

lai	來
Lao-zi	老子
li you li wu	離有離無
Lin-ji	臨濟
Ling-run	靈潤
miao	妙
miao ji	妙極
mie yi	滅依
mo 1	没
mo 2	末
nei	内
neng	能

neng she	能攝
neng she zang	能攝藏
neng zang	能藏
Pang Yun	龐蘊
ping deng zhi Dao	平等之道
pu sa	菩薩
qi	棄
qi she	棄捨
qu	去
ru	如
ru-lai	如來

ru-lai xing 如來性

ru-lai-zang 如來藏

ru qu 如去

ru-ru 如如

ru-ru jing 如如境

ru-ru zhi 如如智

san xing 三性

san wu xing 三無性

se 色

Seng-zhao 僧肇

shang xin fan-nao 上心煩惱

she 捨

She-lun 攝論

shen	身
shen jian	身見
sheng ren	聖人
sheng yi	生依
shi 1	實
shi 2	是
shi 3	事
shi-shi-wu-ai	事事無礙
shi you	實有
shi zheng jian	世正見
Shōbōgenzō Genjōkōan	正法眼藏現成公案
su ru	俗如
suo she chi	所攝持
suo she zang	所攝藏

suo sheng	所生
suo zang	所藏
Tian-tai	天台
tong	通
wei	爲
wei shi zhi	唯識智
wo	我
wo bo le mi	我波羅蜜
wu	無
wu mie	無滅
Wu Shang Yi Jing	無上依經

wu sheng	無生
wu suo you	無所有
wu wei	無爲
wu yin	無因
wu zuo	無作
wu zuo yi	無作意
xian	顯
xin	心
xin le	信樂
xing 1	性
xing 2	行
xing ku	行苦
xiu-xi	修習

Xuan-zang	玄奘
Xun-zi	荀子
yi	依
yi shi	意識
yi-ta	依他
yi-ta-xing	依他性
yi-zhi	依止
yin chu xing	引出性
you	有
you bu zhen shi	有不真實
you zuo	有作
zai ru-lai zhi nei	在如來智内
zang	藏

Zhan-ran	湛然
zhen	真
Zhen-di	真諦
zhen-ru	真如
zhen-ru li	真如理
zhen shen	真身
zhen shi	真實
zhen-shi-xing	真實性
zhen shi you	真實有
zhen ti xing	真體性
zhen you	真有
zheng jing	正境
zheng xing	正行
zhi	智

zhi hui	智慧
Zhi-yi	智顗
zhong sheng	衆生
zhu zi xing ru-ru	住自性如如
zhu zi xing xing	住自性性
zhuan	轉
zhuan-yi	轉依
Zhuang-zi	莊子
zi xing	自性
zi xing qing jing xin	自性清淨心
zuo	作
Zuo-chan yi	坐禪儀

INDEX

mode, 150–152; and devotionalism, 3; essence and functions, 55–56; existence and nonexistence, 30–32; and faithful joy, 127–128; five meanings of, 55–56; as found in ordinary persons, *bodhisattvas*, and Buddhas, 80–82; and human transformation, 31–32, 57; and monism, 99–115; and nonduality, 50; and own-nature (*svabhāva*), 34–35, 39; purity and impurity, 50; three kinds of, 41–42; and Thusness, 102; universality of, 1–2
Buddha nature thought, 27–28, 156–168; and Western Buddhism, 169–171
Buddha Nature Treatise: author of, 24; and Buddha nature controversy, 26; and Chinese Buddhist thought, 27–28; textual problems in, 23–24; and Yogācāra, 21
Buddhist practice: and *āśrayaparāvṛtti*, 58–60; and Buddha nature, 151–152, 168; conditioned, 127–128; and four classes of people, 121–122; and wisdom, 51

Cakras (wheels), four, 118–121
Category mistake, 34
Chan (Ch'an): historical relation to Buddha nature thought, 157–159; and need for Buddhist practice, 127, 168; nondualism of, 163–164; positive view of phenomenal reality in, 167; subject-object nondualism in, 165–166
Consciousness-only, 9–10; and subject-object nondualism, 142–144
Cultivation (*xiu-xi*), 122–123

Dao-sheng (Tao-sheng), 13
Dao-xin (Tao-hsin), 157
Deluded existential mode of human being, 145–147
Devotionalism, 3, 13, 15
Dhāranī, 66–67
Dharmakāya: as active, 69; and *āśrayaparāvṛtti*, 61–64; as Buddha nature that dwells in itself, 72; and Buddhist practice, 65–72; and freedom from views of self, 95; as Middle Path, 68–69; as name of Buddha nature, 154; and *nirvāṇa*, 66; and realization, 70–71; and Two Truths, 69–70
Dharmakāyadhātu, 71–72
Dharmapāla, 9
Dialogue, interreligious, 169, 171
Diamond Mind, 96
Discriminating nature (*parikalpita svabhāva*), 43, 46
Dōgen, 149, 165–166, 168

Emptiness (*śūnyatā*): and aboriginal existence, 34; and Buddha nature, 35; erroneous views of, 36–37, 155; and negativity, 16, 34, 36; and Yogācāra, 7–11
Emptiness, fulfillment of: in Buddha nature, 40; in *Ratnagotravibhāga*, 16–17; in Yogācāra, 11; in Yogācāra-*tathāgatagarbha* thought, 19
Empty, not: *See aśūnya*
Engaged Buddhism, 170
Enlightened existential mode of human being, 147–148
Enlightenment: and individuality, 147–148; as pivotal conversion, 167–168; positive nature of, 19, 38–39, 159–160
Eternity of *trikāya*, 75–80
Existence (*you*) and Buddha nature, 30–32, 55–56

Faithful joy, 121, 123–124, 127–128
Fa-xiang (Fa-hsiang), 161
Fa-zang (Fa-tsang), 156–157
Fo xing, 4–5, 14, 173–174, note 5